D1209946

The Lives and Times of Ebenezer Scrooge

PAUL DAVIS

The Lives and Times of Ebenezer SCROOGE

Yale University Press New Haven & London

Published with assistance from the Kingsley Trust Association Publication Fund established by the Scroll and Key Society of Yale College.

Copyright © 1990 by Yale University.
All rights reserved.
This book may not be reproduced, in whole or in part, including illustrations, in any form (beyond that copying permitted by Sections 107 and 108 of the U.S. Copyright Law and except by reviewers for the public press), without written permission from the publishers.

Designed by Richard Hendel
Set in Century Expanded type by G&S Typesetters, Austin, Texas.
Printed in the United States of America by Hamilton Printing Co., Castleton, New York.

Library of Congress Cataloging-in-Publication Data
Davis, Paul B. (Paul Benjamin), 1934–
The lives and times of Ebenezer Scrooge / Paul Davis. p. cm.
ISBN 0-300-04664-2
1. Dickens, Charles, 1812–1870. Christmas carol. 2. Dickens, Charles, 1812–1870—Adaptations. 3. Dickens, Charles, 1812–1870—Characters—Ebenezer Scrooge. 4. Scrooge, Ebenezer (Fictitious character) I. Title.
PR4572.C7D38 1990 89-25105
823′.8—dc20 CIP

The paper in this book meets the guidelines for permanance and durability of the Committee on Production Guidelines for Book Longevity of the Council on Library Resources.

10 9 8 7 6 5 4 3 2 1

FOR MARY

Contents

Acknowledgments

My conscious interest in the adaptability of the *Carol* began when I wrote and directed a stage version in the late sixties. The story easily took dramatic form, assimilating a hippie Marley, music by the Beatles and Simon and Garfunkel, and a love feast at the end. I have been fascinated by the *Carol's* powers of transformation ever since.

Over the years I have incurred many debts to those who have shared their experiences of the story, who have brought me unusual versions, and who have always reminded me of its essential place in our culture. I have yet to meet anyone who does not know the story of Scrooge.

For kindnesses remembered I thank Rudy Bates, Jane Brill, Philip Burton, Eliza Chugg, Benjamin Davis, Joshua Davis, Kate Davis, W. Glen Davis, Bill Dowling, Charles Driscoll, David Dunaway, Sarah Fermi, Enid Howarth, David Jones, Dorothy Klubock, Tom Linehan, David McPherson, Hui Newcombe, Denis Norlander, Gary Scharnhorst, James Thorson. For the many kindnesses forgotten, I ask forgiveness with the hope that I will remember them on some Christmas Yet-to-Come.

I am grateful to several people at Yale University Press who helped in the preparation of this book: to Harry Haskell and Ellen Graham for their editorial suggestions, and to Richard Hendel for his elegant design. Martin Meisel, who read the manuscript for Yale, prompted me to reshape and sharpen several passages.

Many libraries have generously opened their collections to me as I sought the hundreds of editions of the *Carol,* among them libraries at Yale, Harvard, Oberlin, the universities of Iowa, Illinois, Indiana, and California, as well as the New York Public Library, the Library of Congress, and the British Library. I also had access to special collections at the Beinecke Rare Book and Manuscript Library at Yale, the Lilly Library at Bloomington, and the Huntington Library at San Marino. Terry Gesheen of the Museum of Modern Art and Candice Bothwell of the

Wesleyan Cinema Archive aided my search for stills from film versions of the *Carol.* I especially want to thank the librarians at Zimmerman Library at the University of New Mexico, particularly Dorothy Wonsmos and her staff in the interlibrary loan department, who were always patient and helpful in fulfilling my requests for yet another edition of the *Carol.*

For financial aid that enabled me to undertake some of the research for this book, I am grateful to the Research Allocations Committee and to Paul Risser and the Office of Research Administration at the University of New Mexico.

I also thank the *American Scholar,* where a slightly different version of the first chapter appeared as "Retelling *A Christmas Carol*: Text and Culture-Text" in the Winter 1990 issue.

I am especially grateful to Rachel Fermi, Morris Freedman, and Mary Davis, who helped me more than they can know. And finally I thank three mentors, Hannah Matthews, Andrew Bongiorno, and Carl Woodring, who, although they had no direct involvement with this project, by instruction and example made it possible.

Abbreviations

All parenthetical page references to *A Christmas Carol* are to the Oxford Illustrated Edition of the *Christmas Books* (London, 1954). Quotations from other Dickens works are also from the Oxford Illustrated Edition, except for those from *Miscellaneous Papers*, which are taken from the National Edition edited by B. W. Matz (New York: P. F. Collier, [1908]). The following abbreviations are used in the parenthetical citations:

CB Christmas Books
CS Christmas Stories
MC Martin Chuzzlewit
MP Miscellaneous Papers
OMF Our Mutual Friend
PP The Pickwick Papers
SB Sketches by Boz

1

The Carol as Culture-Text

So far from the Christmas Ghost Story *being a colourable imitation of [Dickens'] book, numerous incongruities in the* Carol, *involving the unhinging of the whole plot, have been tastefully remedied by Mr. Hewitt's extended critical experience of dramatic effect and his ready perception of harmonies . . . to . . . a more artistical style of expression and of incident.*

Brief defending Hewitt's piracy of the *Carol,* 1844

Dickens is a terrible writer. In the original, Scrooge was mean and stingy, but you never know why. We're giving him a mother and father, an unhappy childhood, a whole background which will motivate him.

President of Screen Gems, 1968

I cannot remember when I first knew the story of *A Christmas Carol.* I may have heard it read aloud before a Christmas Eve fire, or listened to one of Lionel Barrymore's annual radio performances, or seen a dramatic version at the town hall in Connecticut where I spent my childhood Christmases. I do know that my acquaintance with Scrooge feels preliterate, different from my sense of Dick and Jane, Dr. Dolittle, or Robinson Crusoe. I remember when I first met the Hardy Boys, but I feel as if I've always known Scrooge and Tiny Tim.

I doubt if my experience is unusual. For although the *Carol* began as a written text, it has been passed down orally from one generation to the next. In the thirties and forties, we knew the story through Barrymore, Ronald Colman, and the Roosevelts. Children today see animated television versions or encounter Scrooge McDuck before they learn to read. The *Carol* has inverted the usual folk process. Rather than beginning as an oral story that was later written down, the *Carol* was written to be retold. Dickens was its creator, but it is also the product of its re-creators who have retold, adapted, and revised it over the years.

We remember the *Carol* as a cluster of phrases, images, and ideas. The images of Tim riding on Bob Cratchit's shoulder or of Scrooge huddled behind his desk while Bob shivers on his high stool are etched on our consciousness; "Bah! Humbug!" and "God bless us, every one!" echo in our minds. Yet other parts of Dickens' story have almost disappeared from our folk version. Most of us do not remember, for example, Scrooge's journey to view the celebrations of the miners, mariners, and lighthouse keepers, or his vision in Christmas Future of the debtors whose holiday is lightened by news of his death.

Retellings of the *Carol* often seem to begin with the remembered story rather than with Dickens' words. In the innumerable adaptations almost nothing in Dickens' text has been sacred. Some versions eliminate Scrooge's nephew and his wife. Others turn them into a courting rather than a married couple. In some the Fezziwigs vanish. Others cut out all of the Christmas spirits. Although Scrooge appears in every retelling, he is not always the hero. His occupation changes from money lender to real estate broker to furniture dealer to grain broker to landlord to CEO. His name remains the same, but the names of the characters around him are not so fixed. Scrooge's fiancée – Belle in Dickens' text – becomes Ellen, Mary, and Alice in other versions of the story. His nephew Fred is nearly as often Frank in the retellings, perhaps because the latter name seems more suggestive of his character.

Retellings often add to Dickens' story. Modern adaptors are apt to fill in Scrooge's personal history to explain his character. One elaboration, linking Scrooge's father's dislike of his son to the death of Scrooge's mother while giving birth to him, appears in several recent versions. So does the pilgrimage of the reformed Scrooge to the Cratchit family on Christmas Day. Although this scene does not appear in Dickens' text, it is so lodged in the remembered version that even an eminent critic like Edmund Wilson can write about it as if it did.[1]

A Christmas Carol could be said to have two texts, the one that Dickens wrote in 1843 and the one that we collectively remember. I will distinguish the two by italicizing the title of Dickens' text as *A Christmas Carol* or the *Carol*, and capitalizing references to the remembered version, the "culture-text," and referring to it simply as the Carol. The text of *A Christmas Carol* is fixed in Dickens' words, but the culture-text, the Carol as it has been re-created in the century and a half since it first appeared, changes as the reasons for its retelling change. We are still creating the culture-text of the Carol.

All of Dickens' works have been adapted and altered. Most were on the London stage before they finished their serial careers, and in abridged, modernized, and motion picture versions, they have all been told and retold many times. But none has been redone more than the *Carol*. It has been adapted, revised, condensed, retold, reoriginated and modernized more than any other work of English literature.

For the theater *A Christmas Carol* – just as often titled *Scrooge* – has been adapted by scores of obscure playwrights as well as by such recognized dramatists as George S. Kaufman and Maxwell Anderson. It has been scored for ballet by Ralph Vaughan Williams and others, and Thea Musgrave's opera (1979) is only the most recent on a list of operatic versions. On television and in the movies, the *Carol* has been acted, animated, mimed, marionetted, choreographed, and puppeteered. Its first dramatic reading took place on its first Christmas, and it has been read aloud ever since. Among its many famous readers are Dickens himself, Lionel Barrymore, and Eleanor Roosevelt. The list of dramatic Scrooges reads like a theatrical hall of fame, containing, besides Barrymore, Basil Rathbone, Seymour Hicks, Bransby Williams, Sir Ralph Richardson, Sir Laurence Olivier, Sir Alec Guinness, Ronald Colman, Alastair Sim, Albert Finney, and George C. Scott.

New editions of the *Carol* appear annually. They frequently condense, rewrite, or otherwise, "reoriginate" the story. Even those that keep Dickens' words intact often supplement the text with new illustrations that envision Scrooge in a world that Dickens never made. Since there is an "original" text – the version published in 1843 – one could match later versions against it, distinguish the authentic from the inauthentic, and separate faithful versions that maintain the spirit of Dickens' story from false piracies that pillage the original to serve selfish ends. By doing so we could rescue Dickens from his many self-appointed collaborators.

But making such distinctions would not get us closer to understanding *A Christmas Carol* and its power. For the Carol is the sum of all its versions, of all its revisions, parodies, and piracies. It is as much the Hollywood animation or the Henry Winkler re-creation as it is the fine facsimile complete with copies of the original illustrations by John Leech. Disguised as Lionel Barrymore or Mister Magoo, Scrooge has become common cultural property and is as deeply embedded in our consciousness as George Washington or Dick Whittington, Merlin or Moses. His reoriginations since 1843 have produced a culture-text of remarkable diversity. Reappearing in new guises from page to page and from age to age, Scrooge is a protean figure always in process of reformation.

The story of Scrooge began as a text and became a culture-text. Dickens initiated an ongoing creative process in the Anglo-American imagination. This book describes that process. It is a celebratory history, one that affirms the excesses of our collective imagination and recognizes all the versions of the Carol as manifestations of an ongoing myth in the consciousness of the industrial era.

Charles Dickens both invited and resented the collaboration that would turn *A Christmas Carol* from text into culture-text. He sought public involvement with the story as a way to awaken social concern and to prove to himself that he had not lost his imaginative power. He delighted to hear of good deeds prompted by the *Carol* and of public readings that gathered together the broad audience he envisioned for the story. But he was upset by some of the theatrical adaptations, and when some self-appointed collaborators wanted to share in the financial proceeds from the *Carol,* he angrily asserted his authority over the story. He soon learned, however, that he had begun a process he could not control. Almost from the day it appeared, the *Carol* was literary public property.

Dickens dated the *Carol* from his address to the Manchester Athenaeum on 7 October 1843. He was struck by the goodwill in the faces of the working people in his audience and stirred to write a Christmas story addressed to a similarly broad national audience. For several months he had been looking for an appropriate response to the unsettling parliamen-

Figure 1. Charles Dickens in 1844, from a portrait by Margaret Gillies, engraved by W. J. Linton. From the Dickensian, *July 1905.*

tary report on child labor that had been issued in February.[2] He talked of writing a pamphlet "on behalf of the Poor Man's Child" and of striking a literary "sledge-hammer" by the end of the year.[3] The working-class audience in Manchester may have rekindled this earlier resolve and prompted the sledgehammer blow that Dickens struck when the *Carol* appeared in December.[4]

Dickens (fig. 1) also had more personal motives for writing the *Carol.* In the autumn of 1843 the novel he was publishing in monthly parts, *Martin Chuzzlewit,* seemed to be losing the audience that he had attracted during the first seven years of his writing career. A study of murderous greed and hypocrisy, the novel called forth less of Dickens' idealism than any of the earlier works. He wrote in his letters of the "Chuzzlewit agonies" and complained of the novel's "taking so much out of one."[5] *Chuzzlewit's* Dostoyevskian subject matter inverts the Christian virtues. Its worldly characters have faith only in money and hope only for gain, while Charity Pecksniff, the shrewish daughter of its hypocritical villain, performs a perverse denial of her name. The *Carol,* a story of genuine charity, provided welcome relief for both Dickens and his readers from the depressing world of *Martin Chuzzlewit.*

Chuzzlewit proved so disappointing financially that Dickens' publishers, Chapman and Hall, talked of reducing his monthly payment by fifty pounds.[6] This threat, added to the financial pressures caused by a growing family and mounting household expenses, led Dickens to seek new sources of income. He considered leasing his London house and going abroad where he could live more cheaply. Instead, he invented a new genre, the Christmas book, and devised a new marketing strategy. Rather than turning over the *Carol* completely to Chapman and Hall, he retained control over many of the production decisions so that he could keep more of the earnings. After the book appeared he paid close attention to the balance sheet, and when the bottom line failed to meet his great expectations, he was greatly disappointed.[7]

Dickens' financial and emotional investment in the *Carol* intensified his creative process. The writing was well under way by the end of October, and his sister-in-law said she had never seen him more excited by a project. He worked with such fervor that he "wept, and laughed, and wept again, and excited himself in a most extraordinary manner, in the composition, . . . thinking whereof, he walked about the black streets of London, fifteen or twenty miles, many a night."[8] He completed the manuscript by the end of November, and on 19 December *A Christmas Carol, in Prose, Being a Ghost Story of Christmas* was on the stands. The title was lettered in gold on the cover, the pages had gold edges, and the text

Figure 2.
The first page of the Carol *piracy. From the* Dickensian, *1938.*

AND THE MILKMAID SINGETH BLITHE, AND THE MOWER WHETS HIS SCYTHE,

SCHOOL SCENES REVISITED.

SCROOGE AND THE SECOND SPIRIT AT BOB CRATCHIT'S CHRISTMAS DINNER.

A CHRISTMAS GHOST STORY.

RE-ORIGINATED FROM THE ORIGINAL BY CHARLES DICKENS, ESQ., AND ANALYTICALLY CONDENSED EXPRESSLY FOR THIS WORK

Come, for you know me! I am he who sung
Of ——— the wild and wondrous tale.—SOUTHEY.

There are more things in heaven and earth than are dreamt of in philosophy.—HAMLET.

Rather than want a spirit, bring a corollary.—THE TEMPEST.

How many drink the cup
Of baleful grief, or eat the bitter bread
Of misery, sore pierced by wintry winds!
How many shrink into the sordid hut
Of cheerless poverty! How many shake
With all the fiercer tortures of the mind!—THE SEASONS.

And thereby hangs a tale.—A "WINTER'S TALE."

VERYBODY, as the phrase goes, knew the firm of "Scrooge and Marley," for, though Marley had "long been dead" at the period we have chosen for the commencement of our story, the name of the deceased partner still maintained its place above the warehouse door; somewhat faded, to be sure, but there it was;

AND EVERY SHEPHERD TELLS HIS TALE, UNDER THE HAWTHORN IN THE DALE.

was embellished with eight illustrations by John Leech, four of them hand-colored. It was Dickens' Christmas gift to the nation.

The British people took the gift and made it their own. Nearly all the magazines praised it. Thackeray called it "a national benefit, and to every man and woman who reads it a personal kindness."[9] By February, eight theatrical companies had mounted productions. And on Grub Street the literary hacks were even more expeditious in pirating Dickens' story than he had been in creating it. A magazine that specialized in "reoriginated" versions of popular works, *Peter Parley's Illuminated Library*, immediately appropriated the *Carol*. By the twelfth day of Christmas, 6 January 1844, the first installment of its "A Christmas Ghost Story" appeared, complete with crude new illustrations (fig. 2).[10]

Dickens was incensed. Although all six thousand copies of the first printing of the *Carol* had sold out and two thousand of the second printing were committed before publication, he saw the pirates killing his Christmas goose before it could lay its golden egg. On 8 January, the Monday after the Saturday when the plagiarized version appeared, Dickens filed suit against the pirates, Richard Egan Lee and Henry Hewitt. A temporary injunction forbidding publication of the second installment of the "Ghost Story" was granted on the 10th, and on the 18th Vice Chancellor Knight Bruce continued the injunction, warning the brigands and vagabonds, as Dickens called the pirates, against foolishly pursuing their countersuit.

While the case was being heard, opportunistic playwrights were also busy turning *A Christmas Carol* into post-Christmas gold. Among the eight dramatic productions mounted by early February 1844 were Edward Stirling's adaptation at the Theatre Royal, Adelphi, Charles Webb's *Scrooge, the Miser's Dream* at Sadler's Wells, and C. Z. Barnett's *A Christmas Carol; or, the Miser's Warning!* at the Royal Surrey Theatre.[11] By adding songs and enhancing the melodrama with characters like Barnett's Dark Sam, who tries to ruin Cratchit's Christmas by stealing his wages, these theatrical Carols took London by storm. The *Athenaeum* remarked that their popularity threatened to rival that of *Jack Sheppard*, the *Mousetrap* of the 1840s.[12]

Dickens attended at least one performance of Stirling's *Carol* (fig. 3), advertised as "the only dramatic version sanctioned by C. Dickens, Esqre." He called it "better than usual, . . . but *heart-breaking* to me. Oh Heaven! if any forecast of *this* was ever in my mind! Yet O. Smith [Scrooge] was drearily better than I expected. It is a great comfort to have that kind of meat underdone; and his face is quite perfect."[13] At worst this could be considered a mixed review. And in spite of his misgivings,

Figure 3. The Spirit of Christmas Present revealing the urchins Ignorance and Want to Scrooge in Edward Stirling's theatrical adaptation of the Carol. *From the* Illustrated London News, *1844.*

Dickens made no attempt to close down Stirling's play or any of the other theatrical productions.

The Grub Street pirates seemed to expect similar toleration. They had "re-originated" Dickens' earlier novels and he had made no objection. Legally, they contended, he had given up his right to object because he had not challenged their earlier plagiarisms. They claimed that their activity benefited Dickens by making his work available to an audience that it otherwise would not reach. In effect, they insinuated, they were his artistic collaborators.

These arguments merely increased Dickens' anger. Writing had been his escape from the poverty that dogged his childhood, a way to suppress painful memories of the blacking warehouse where he had worked as a boy while his father was in debtor's prison. His fragmentary autobiography reveals the psychic scars he carried from that experience, particularly the "grief and humiliation" he felt in associating with his common fellow workers, Poll Green and Bob Fagin, as they stood beside him in the window of Warren's Blacking pasting labels on blacking bottles. "No words can express the secret agony of my soul," he later wrote, "as I sunk into this companionship."[14] The pirates recalled these companions of Dickens' secret past. Venal, vulgar, and greedy men, Lee and Hewitt held up an ugly mirror to the profession of authorship, and by bringing themselves forward as his literary collaborators, they suggested to Dickens that writing was not the way to escape the humiliating associations of the blacking factory.

American critics reinforced these disconcerting reflections. When Dickens had spoken out on his tour of America in 1842 for an international copyright agreement to prevent the pirating of British books by American publishers, American newspapers called him greedy and self-serving. *American Notes* (1842) and the American sections of *Martin Chuzzlewit* revived these attacks. His obsession with royalties, the Yankee journalists asserted, exemplified the greed he so roundly satirized in the novel. How could his characterizations of the Americans be believed, they asked? How could his plea for charity be taken seriously? Lee and Hewitt may have reminded Dickens of his mercenary motives for writing the *Carol* and given some troubling substance to these American questions.

These threats to his self-assurance may account for the virulence of Dickens' feelings and the violence of his exultation on 18 January, when he thought his case had been won. "The pirates are beaten flat. They are bruised, bloody, smashed, squelched, and utterly undone," he wrote.[15] But the celebration was premature. Although the pirates lost the legal battle, they were bankrupt and unable to pay damages. They left Dickens with a moral victory and a legal bill for seven hundred pounds. And, to rub salt into the wounds, they regrouped and in a matter of months were again promoting their parasitic versions of Boz.

Dickens' reactions to the pirates and the playwrights reveal contradictory impulses in his aims for the story. On the one hand he wrote to confirm his position as the voice for his established middle-class audience. He wanted to reassure the readers whom *Chuzzlewit* had alienated that he still embodied their belief in entrepreneurial achievement and success. He was still "the inimitable Boz," the literary magician who alone could have created and produced the *Carol*. The book itself represented these bourgeois values. Its hand-tinted illustrations and the gold leaf on the binding attested to the success and authority of its creator. At the same time Dickens also wanted to speak for the urban poor and reach a working-class audience like the one he addressed in Manchester. He tolerated the playwrights because their broad audience included both of the groups to whom his story was addressed. In the theatres the message of the *Carol* was not seriously compromised.

But the workers who attended the plays could not afford to buy the book. The hand-colored illustrations and the gold leaf made the *Carol* too expensive for most working-class readers. At five shillings, a copy of the *Carol* cost one-third of Bob Cratchit's weekly wages. The pirates charged only a penny for their reorigination, and they argued in court that their work enhanced the popularity of the original and enlarged its audience. But as they changed Dickens' words, they also changed the class context for the Carol. In its crude pulp format, "A Christmas Ghost Story" did not speak for the bourgeois achievement of Charles Dickens, and as the "imitable Boz," Dickens no longer symbolized success and achievement. He lost *author*ity over his production. Instead, the "Ghost Story" reflected the world of its semiliterate readers, and in Dickens' eyes the pirates "degraded" the *Carol* to make it "appear a wretched, meagre, miserable thing."[16]

The pirates may have had a better case than even they were aware of. To reach working-class nonreaders who might listen to the tale as they had listened to Dickens' speech in Manchester, the *Carol* needed to be lifted from the pages of the book and lodged in the cultural memory. The pirates and the playwrights were important participants in the beginning of this process. Along with Dickens, they were so successful that in less than two months after the *Carol* appeared, the *Illustrated London News* commented in its review of one of the dramatic productions that "the story on which this piece is founded is too well known to enter into particulars of it."[17]

In spite of his early reservations, Dickens later joined the process and himself became one of his own adaptors. When he turned the story into a public reading, he edited and re-edited the text to suit the many audiences for whom he performed it. Although Carlyle objected to the readings as pandering to readers too lazy to read for themselves, Dickens knew that the story was new in each performance. As he shared the recreation of the *Carol* with his listeners, he joined in celebrating its culture-text.

John Forster, Dickens' friend and first biographer, said of the *Carol:* "Literary criticism here is a second-rate thing."[18] Following Forster's lead, most literary critics have neglected the *Carol*. It is too simple, too popular a work to elicit rigorous explication. Commentators have preferred commendation to close analysis.

Yet from a broader perspective, the *Carol* is one of the most criticized works of English literature. Every new edition, adaptation, parody, or sequel derives from an implicit critical perspective. Each rewriting of the culture-text implies a new reading of Dickens' text.

This body of Carol "criticism" articulates a cultural commentary. Because the Carol is so widely known and its re-creators so diverse in their class and cultural points of view, this criticism broadly encapsulates Anglo-

American culture during the last century and a half. It is not limited to recording the prejudices of the literary elite. It mirrors the mainstream of our culture.

The appeal of the *Carol* has waxed and waned since 1843. Some times are more Dickensian in their celebration of Christmas than others. I have chosen six periods of intense activity to shape this cultural history of the Carol. Each period re-creates the story in response to its own cultural needs. Each contributes to the evolving culture-text of the Carol by re-reading Dickens' words and imagining its own text for the *Carol.* I have described these "texts" and the contexts that produced them. In this dynamic interaction of text and culture-text, we can see a concretization of the process Auden described as "the words of a dead man [being] modified in the guts of the living." For the meaning of the *Carol* is not determined by the words of the author. Its meaning is created anew by each generation of readers.

As the creation of its readers, the Carol is not unusual. The meaning of any literary work emerges from the dynamic interaction of text and culture-text, from the versions of the story created by its readers.[19] Because there are so many public versions of the *Carol* and because these versions represent so broad and diverse an audience, the culture-text of the Carol exaggerates and makes visible the reading process. It provides a case study in literary theory and cultural history.

The Carol story begins in the decade of its creation. For Dickens' contemporaries, the *Carol* was a parable. It told the same popular tale that George Eliot would later relate in *Silas Marner,* that of a miser who learns charity through the agency of a child. But more important in the 1840s, Dickens' story proved that urbanization had not destroyed Christmas. In the British imagination, Christmas was associated with the manor house, peasant revels, and baronial feasts. During the first half of the nineteenth century – particularly in the two decades that preceded the publication of the *Carol* – the growth of industry and cities threatened this rural holiday by threatening its country seat. Dickens' story provided celebratory proof that despite dour Dissenting tradesmen who condemned Christmas revels, the old Christmas could flourish in the new cities. Scrooge's reformation thus became urban Britain's counter-reformation to puritanical excess.

The Victorian Carol connected the city to the traditions of the country. It also revealed a new urban world infused with spirit(s), and so it became a kind of scripture. As Darwinism and doubt undermined the authority of the Bible, secular texts that assumed biblical authority were especially valued. Although we now see the *Carol* as a secular book, Victorians of the 1870s, the decade following Dickens' death, read his Christmas story as a retelling of the biblical Christmas story. Scrooge became a nineteenth-century pilgrim, a modern-day magus seeking the Christ child, while the Cratchits reenacted the Holy Family. For later Victorians, the Carol was secular scripture.

In the decade preceding World War I, the Carol was treated for the first time as a children's story. Remembering Dickens as their childhood reading, the parents in this golden age of children's literature passed the *Carol* on to the next generation as a children's classic in which Scrooge, in the Neverland of fairy tale, is transformed from the baleful ogre into the kindly grandfather. Although some thought of the story as a literary Peter Pan, a text that would not grow up, the carolers of the time, readers like Harry Furniss and G. K. Chesterton, melded the magic of the fairy tale with the darker adult dimensions of the story and turned childish merriment into myth.

Before and after the stock market crash of 1929, some saw the Carol as a denunciation of capitalism, but most read it as a way to escape oppressive economic realities. The British denied the depression by reaffirming a traditional Carol, but in America a revolutionary version of the Carol emerged that made Cratchit the protagonist. It suggested that Americans could escape the depression by freeing themselves from European bankers and celebrating the Christmas of the common man. These distinctly British and American Carols inform the film versions of the thirties.

Restored to his central role in the sixties, Scrooge becomes himself a kind of revolutionary. In the postwar affluent society the "Carol problem" is no longer economic or social. The sixties Scrooge, a Freudian figure tormented by his past, subconsciously conjures up Marley as a way of calling for help. In therapy with the Christmas spirits, he learns to enjoy life in the here and now. After he has turned onto Christmas and tuned into joys he has denied himself, he joins the flower children in the streets to celebrate being human.

If there was joy in the streets of the sixties, in the eighties there is hunger and homelessness. Scrooge is again a social figure placed in the center of unsettling economic realities. The Carol has come full circle, for the economic issues of Dickens' time have been enjoined in the debate over Reaganomics. The contradiction between self-interest and selflessness that inspired the *Carol* in 1843 prompts its contemporary retelling and produces a Carol that makes the unreformed Scrooge its hero.

Dickens wrote his Christmas fantasy "to raise the Ghost of an Idea" (*CB*, 1). In the century and a half since its composition, that ghost has not been exorcised and *A Christmas Carol* continues to give substance to a spirit in the Anglo-American consciousness. This protean fantasy, the culture-text of the Carol, embodies the changing realities of the times as it is re-created by each generation to articulate its cultural identity.

Edward Wagenknecht characterized as a "glaring example of critical irresponsibility" Edmund Wilson's speculation that after Christmas Scrooge reverts to his old self. "We cannot follow Scrooge 'beyond the frame of the story,'" Wagenknecht asserted, "for the simple reason that beyond the frame of the story he does not exist."[20] The history of the Carol since 1843 would suggest otherwise, for Scrooge exists in the Anglo-American consciousness independent of his Dickensian origin. Dickens may have framed our thoughts and established the broad outlines of the story, but the Carol is rewritten each Christmas, and Scrooge, an altered spirit, appears anew with each retelling.

2

Bringing Christmas to the City

The *Carol* in the 1840s

All persons say how differently this season was observed in their fathers' days, and speak of old ceremonies and old festivities as things which are obsolete. The cause is obvious. In large towns the population is continually shifting; a new settler neither continues the customs of his own province in a place where they would be strange, nor adopts those which he finds, because they are strange to him, and thus all local differences are wearing out.

Robert Southey, 1807

There are people who will tell you that Christmas is not what it used to be. . . . Dwell not upon the past. . . . Reflect upon your present blessings. . . . Fill your glass again, with a merry face and a contented heart. Our life on it, but your Christmas shall be merry, and your new year a happy one!

Charles Dickens, 1836

Southey's observation reflected the changes that took place in his lifetime. By 1807 the revolution in industrial technology of the late eighteenth century had spurred the growth of the industrial towns in the north of England, and a new urban consciousness grounded in northern dissent was displacing feudal attitudes derived from the southern landed tradition. Along with many other things, this passage from country to town uprooted country Christmas customs, sometimes replacing them with a Calvinistic puritanism that denounced the celebration of Christmas altogether.

Whether lost on the exodus into the new towns or stifled by the smothering hand of Calvinism, the old English Christmas was largely memory by the beginning of the nineteenth century. The twelve days (or longer) of Christmas festivity, presided over by the Lord of Misrule and celebrated with manorial feasts, yule logs, and feudal games, had disappeared. Sir Walter Scott's loving description of such a Christmas in the introduction to the sixth canto of *Marmion* (1808) is a nostalgic lament in the past tense for the rites of the Christmas feast that enabled one to see "traces of ancient mystery." But by 1808 even those traces have been lost, for all that remains are "some remnants of the good old time" lingering in the Scottish memory. For the "Southern ear," Scott suggests, no echoes remain at all. Washington Irving's benign account of Christmas at Bracebridge Hall (1820), probably the most loving description of a "merrie English" Christmas ever written, repeatedly reminds the reader that Bracebridge is a "bigoted devotee of the old school" and his elaborate manorial festivities are "lingering . . . holiday customs and rural games of former times" no longer continued "in these unceremonious days."[1] Although *The Sketch Book of Geoffrey Crayon, Gent.* purports to describe the narrator's experiences in nineteenth-century England, its nostalgic tone leads the reader to believe that the sketches actually describe an England of memory that has cast "a delightful spell over [Crayon's] imagination."[2] They are remembrances of things past.

Nevertheless, Scott's and Irving's pictures of Christmases past had a strong pull on the Victorian imagination. They contributed to William Sandys' *Selection of Christmas Carols, Ancient and Modern* (1833), the first significant collection of old carols.[3] They informed the pages of *The Book of Christmas* (1837), in which Robert Seymour, Dickens' original illustrator for *The Pickwick Papers*, accompanied Thomas K. Hervey's detailed accounts of the various traditions of Christmas with illustrations (figs. 4, 29) like those that were to decorate the new Christmas cards, the first of which appeared in the same year as *A Christmas Carol*, 1843 (fig.

Figure 4. Robert Seymour, the first illustrator of The Pickwick Papers, *created this Christmas celebrant for* The Book of Christmas *(1837). The figure is a close relative to Pickwick, a character Seymour claimed to have originated.*

Enjoying Christmas

Figure 5. The first known Christmas card, created by John C. Horsley in 1843, suggests that A Christmas Carol *was part of a broader revival of Christmas celebration.*

Figure 6. The panoramic Merry Christmas in the Baron's Hall *(1838), by Dickens' painter friend Daniel Maclise, visualizes the idealized Christmas in Merrie England. Courtesy of the National Gallery of Ireland.*

5). They also shaped the medievalism of the period that found in medieval Christmas merriment a merrier England and a society undivided between the two nations of rich and poor. Dickens' close friend, the artist Daniel Maclise, visually summed up this nostalgic image in his 1838 painting *Merry Christmas in the Baron's Hall* (fig. 6). The crowded panorama shows the baron in the background among his family and influential friends. In the foreground the lower orders play Christmas games before the yule fire while a group of mummers prepare to perform a Christmas masque. Meanwhile, a Christmas procession bringing in the boar's head descends the stairs into the middle of the picture.

By 1843 the medieval Christmas had entered into the political and religious controversy of the period. The traditional Christmas rites became part of a popular "Oxford Movement" that challenged the antiritualistic doctrines of the urban Evangelicals and Calvinists. The feudal festivities also articulated a political ideal, an organic society with natural bonds between rich and poor that represented an alternative to mechanistic industrial England for neoconservatives like Benjamin Disraeli and his Young Englanders. In *Coningsby; or the New Generation,* his polemical novel published just a few months after the *Carol* in May 1844, the future prime minister described a medieval Christmas at the rural seat of Eustace Lyle as a "fresh argument in favour of [the] principle, that a mere mitigation of the material necessities of the humbler classes . . . can never alone avail sufficiently to ameliorate their condition; that their condition is not merely 'a knife and fork question,' to use the coarse and shallow prose of the Utilitarian school; that a simple satisfaction of the grosser necessities of our nature will not make a happy people; that you must cultivate the heart as well as seek to content the belly."[4] For Disraeli and his political sympathizers, the Lord of Misrule could provide the rule for a new social order.

These medieval images influenced the Christmas writings of Dickens, especially *Pickwick,* where the Christmas festivities resemble those at Bracebridge Hall. Wardle is a descendant of the old-fashioned country gentleman, and the physical comedy during the extended celebrations at Dingley Dell evokes the traditional games and practical jokes of Christmases conducted by the Lord of Misrule. The Pickwickians, like Crayon and his friends, also continue the tradition of fireside storytelling solemnizing the dead of winter with tales of ghosts and spirits. But Dickens did not share Disraeli's faith in the wisdom of the past, nor did he sympathesize with ritualistic formalism. Dickens' Christmases do more than recall lost tradition. Even his earliest work, *Sketches by Boz* (1836), which acknowledges its debt to Irving in its title, departs in tone and per-

Figure 7. Mr. Pickwick does a Christmas number as Dickens' genial "Lord of Misrule" at Dingley Dell in this illustration by Hablot K. Browne ("Phiz") for the Christmas installment of The Pickwick Papers, *which appeared in December 1836.*

spective from its model. After advising its reader to "dwell not upon the past; . . . reflect upon your present blessings" (*SB*, 220), the sketch "A Christmas Dinner" describes Christmas among city families like the Cratchits rather than among the country folk of tradition. The sentimentality in this sketch also is closer to that of the *Carol* than to Irving's nostalgia. As the city family sits around the Christmas fire, the reader is reminded of Tiny Tim: "One little seat may be empty; one slight form that gladdened the father's heart, and roused the mother's pride to look upon, may not be there" (*SB*, 220). Even *Pickwick* (fig. 7) does not simply reiterate the traditional country Christmas. Dingley Dell is more the residence of a country smallholder than a manorial estate, and the board is conspicuously spread from a barrel of oysters, an urban – and Dickens-

Figure 8. The arabesques of the contorted tree and the conniving goblin in Phiz's illustration for "The Goblins Who Stole a Sexton" echo the interweaving of dream and reality, interpolated tale and novel, in this Christmas tale from Pickwick.

ian – dish, brought from London by the members of the Pickwick Club. Much of the comedy also depends on the ineptness of the urban Pickwickians in their unfamiliar rural setting.

Wardle's Christmas story, the tale of "the goblins who stole a sexton," links Pickwick's Christmas to the tradition of telling ghost stories before a Christmas Eve fire (*PP*, chap. 29). Passed down to Wardle from his father, the tale describes Gabriel Grub, an "ill-conditioned, cross-grained, surly" sexton, who commemorates Christmas Eve by gravedigging in a dark and lonely churchyard, spelling his labor with breaks for gin (fig. 8).

In the middle of his digging Gabriel is accosted by a goblin who takes him to a cave of goblins. There he shows Gabriel visions of loving families celebrating Christmas, and between the visions he leads an army of goblins who kick the morose gravedigger, a mental and physical regimen intended to counter Gabriel's misanthropy. The next morning when he awakens in the graveyard, an empty liquor bottle by his side, Gabriel knows his nocturnal adventures were real from the soreness of his body where he was kicked by the goblins. An altered man, he leaves the village to return many years later, rheumatic but contented.

Although this tale has been described as the "prototype" for the *Carol*,[5] it contains only the skeleton of the later Christmas story. When, seven years after *Pickwick*, Dickens wrote the *Carol*, he did more than elaborate the tale of Gabriel Grub. The ideas that shape the *Carol* derive from all of his earlier writing about Christmas. The idea of putting the old English Christmas into modern urban dress germinated in *Pickwick*, where the urban Pickwickians clumsily cavort through a country Christmas. In the *Carol* the country house becomes a city warehouse, the lord of the manor a London businessman, and the spirit of misrule spills into the prodigality of the city markets and streets. Dickens transformed the traditional ghost story by moving it from the country churchyard, the hackneyed setting of Gabriel Grub, into the streets of London. There he could write about the middle- and lower-middle-class city people he knew, a familiarity that makes possible the psychological presentation of Scrooge as the therapeutic spirits of the *Carol* replace the ghostly picaros who kick Gabriel into reformation. Among the urban families in the *Sketches* and in Gabriel Grub's vision, Dickens found models for the Cratchits. The *Carol* melded country customs and Christmas lore with a Londoner's vision to create a new Christmas story that was particularly attuned to the emergent urbanity of early Victorian England.

Rapid political and social changes marked the years just prior to the publication of the *Carol*. The passage of the first Reform Bill in 1832 had initiated debate on a whole new agenda of social and political reforms, a debate that divided those who wanted to curb the excesses of the new industrial order from those who wanted to sweep away the impediments to progress inherited from the past. This broad division took particular shape in contests over further electoral reforms, in attempts to change the welfare and educational systems and regulate working conditions in

Figure 9. In George Cruikshank's Table Book *(1845), the artist, a frequent collaborator with Dickens, caricatured the railway as a cannibalistic dragon invading the Englishman's castle and upsetting his Christmas dinner.*

mines and mills, and in an ongoing controversy over agricultural tariffs. Mass demonstrations for the abolition of the Corn Laws and increasingly violent working-class agitation in the anti–Poor Law movement and Chartism gave urgency to these debates.

These social and political issues reflected the material changes in the two decades prior to the publication of the *Carol*. The use of steam to power industry enabled mill owners to move their factories from remote river valleys into new industrial cities. "Steam" became shorthand for industrialization and urbanization, and the symbol for steam was the railway (fig. 9). When the railway boom of the thirties and forties linked London with the factory towns in the north, the trains made the new industrialism visible.

Two aspects of the emerging consciousness were particularly significant. First, an unsettling, quantitative worldview defined industrial England. A self-conscious empiricism, accompanied by the founding of statistical societies to quantify social issues, merged with a sense of economic vulnerability brought on by harsh business cycles and heightened, in particular, by the trade recession of 1842–43. The landmark parliamentary reports on working conditions in factories and mines issued in 1842 and 1843 shocked Victorian readers with revelations about the physical and moral exploitation of women and children, and at the same time made them aware of how little they really knew about the society they lived in. Second, there was also a heightened sense of time. People in the forties believed that they lived in a new age and that there was a sharp break between past and present. They had a clear sense that the past existed in another time, an awareness explicit in Carlyle's prophetic essay *Past and Present*, published in the same year as the *Carol*. Carlyle contrasted anarchic industrial Britain, drifting in the age of "let alone" (his sarcastic translation of *laissez-faire*), with the hierarchical order of medieval England.

Though the past for Carlyle was medieval, the break with that past was more recent. Like the Dickensian orphans who almost remember their parents, the workers in Carlyle's present have a sense that the past has been lost within their lifetime. George Eliot would later date the divide between past and present in 1832, the year of reform, but in 1843 the date was less clearly perceived. There was, nevertheless, a pervasive sense that the present generation of city dwellers were cut off from their rural parents, their connection to a larger collective identity. This lack of family defines their ontological confusion.

The militant empiricism of the period can be seen as an attempt to recover grounds of identity lost in the separation from family and community. The reports of statistical societies and parliamentary commissions, satirized in Carlyle's "statistics" and Gradgrind's blue books, survey an unfamiliar urban present. Monumental and voluminous, the reports were nonetheless paltry in contrast to the losses they were designed to counter. Lacking statistics from the past to define their history and having too few figures to predict the future, the urbanites of the forties were locked in the present, trapped on the cinder pile of fragmentary empirical fact. In

Figure 10. This view of Manchester from the Illustrated London News *(1842) represents a traditional view of the city. A distant prospect from the rural countryside, it shows the city as a single object, centered by the church steeple in mid-picture.*

massive novels like *Dombey and Son* and *Vanity Fair* (both 1847–48), or on the panoramic canvases of Maclise or W. P. Frith, the Victorians tried to develop a gestalt to visualize the whole of their situation and comprehend the radical discontinuity in their history.

Characteristic of the *Carol*'s urban perspective are its "views" of the city. London is not seen from the countryside as an object in the distance, a traditional and "rural" view (fig. 10).[6] It is described only from amid the confusion of its streets. The city has no total presence; it is not objectified. Rather, it is a construct of fragmentary and clouded sense impressions.

A key paragraph in Stave 1 of the *Carol* describes the city disappearing into fog, smoke, and darkness, perceived only in fleeting impressions:

> Meanwhile the fog and darkness thickened so that people ran about with flaring links, proffering their services to go before horses in carriages and conduct them on their way. The ancient tower of a church, whose gruff old bell was always peeping slyly down at Scrooge out of a Gothic window in the wall, became invisible, and struck the hours and quarters with tremulous vibrations afterward, as if its

> teeth were chattering in its frozen head up there. The cold became intense. In the main street, at the corner of the court, some laborers were repairing the gas pipes and had lighted a great fire in a brazier, round which the party of ragged men and boys were gathered, warming their hands and winking their eyes before the blaze, in rapture. The water plug being left in solitude, its overflowings suddenly congealed and turned to misanthropic ice. The brightness of the shops, where holly sprigs and berries crackled in the lamp heat of the windows, made pale faces ruddy as they passed. [*CB*, 11]

The "ancient tower" of the church, symbolizing England past, would have been the focal point for a distant prospect, but it has disappeared into the fog. The urban perspective is from within the city and from street level. It yields only close-up and fragmentary views.

The imagery of fog, fire, and ice in this paragraph concentrates the dominant motifs of the *Carol*. Around the fire, suggesting human warmth and civilization, a temporary community has formed amid the foggy urban confusion. The water plug, linked symbolically to natural rather than civilized man, is plugged, its "overflowings" turned to "misanthropic ice." And Scrooge, like the water plug "left in solitude," is "solitary as an oyster," "ic[ing] his office" and denying himself and his clerk the warmth of civilizing fire (p. 8).

The experience of the city from within is a prospect clouded by fog, smoke, and erratic light (fig. 11). In air that is "palpable brown," even the houses on the opposite side of the street become "mere phantoms" (p. 9). An occasional Dickens character achieves a broader view of the city, as from the rooftop of Todgers in *Chuzzlewit* (chap. 9) or from Riah's roof garden in *Our Mutual Friend* (book 2, chap. 5), but even such panoramic vantage points overlook a smoky "wilderness" and lack the clarity of rural perspectives. Scrooge's narrow perspective is more typical of the characters caught in the labyrinthine confusion of the city streets. Restricted to the fragments of experience available in the city, Scrooge is incapable of a "stadtanschauung" much less a weltanschauung. Sense perception may have been an adequate basis for knowledge in the clear and broad perspectives of the country; in the city, empiricism turns men into solitary oysters protecting fragmentary pearls of objective knowledge from the corrosive ambiguities of the urban fog.

Scrooge's hardness of heart results more from epistemological desperation than from moral choice. The city yields only fragmentary knowledge and empirical Scrooge pretends to no knowledge beyond his immediate experience. Whatever is not his business, it is not his business to know.

Figure 11. Gustav Doré's pictures of the narrow and crowded streets of London in London: A Pilgrimage *(1872), depict the city from within. His urban perspective no longer visualizes the city as a single object viewed from the distance.*

Figure 12. John Leech's original black-and-white vignette for the end of Stave 2 shows Scrooge's attempt to extinguish the Spirit of Christmas Past under his hat. Scrooge could realistically be described here as snuffing a bedside candle. On a more symbolic level he is an angry, anti-Christmas magician, snuffing the truth of his past with his magician's hat.

When the charity solicitors goad him into irritation, he suggests that the poor would be better off dying to decrease the surplus population. But as soon as he states this general social dictum, he realizes that he has overreached his knowledge and gone far beyond his business: "If they would rather die," said Scrooge, "they had better do it and decrease the surplus population. Besides – excuse me – I don't know about that" (*CB*, 12). He retreats to a more limited and empirical position and counters the solicitors with an epistemological, rather than a moral, argument. He simply establishes the "fact" that prisons and workhouses still operate, for in his either/or world, the fact that workhouses exist confirms objectively that poverty does not.

The issues in the confrontation with Marley's ghost are also more epistemological than ethical. By the time Marley arrives, Scrooge's mental security is shaken. He attempts to control the experiential variables, to "secure [himself] against surprise" (p. 16) by bolting doors and checking his house for outsiders, but Marley manages to break down Scrooge's mental fortifications almost as easily as he moves through locked doors. Scrooge rationalizes that such "surprises" as Marley's ghost can be explained away as hallucinations induced by indigestion, but he knows that to deny Marley he must abandon his narrow empiricism and fight "against his senses" (p. 17). When Scrooge finally accepts the ghost, Marley couches his message as one about Scrooge's knowledge rather than his behavior: "Oh! Captive, bound and double ironed, . . . not to *know* that ages of incessant labor, by immortal creatures, for this earth, must pass into eternity before the good of which it is susceptible is all developed! Not to *know* that any Christian spirit working kindly in its little sphere, whatever it may be, will find its mortal life too short for its vast means of usefulness! Not to *know* that no space or request can make amends for one life's opportunities misused!" (p. 20, emphasis added). Scrooge is not charged with immorality for his denial of Christmas. He is accused of willful ignorance (fig. 12).

The confrontation with Marley cracks Scrooge's icy empiricism and turns his attention away from external experience. In the darkness before the arrival of the Spirit of Christmas Past, Scrooge, without sensory input, is still actively conscious: "Scrooge went to bed again, and *thought*, and *thought*, and *thought* it over and over, and could make nothing of it. The more he *thought*, the more perplexed he was; and the more he endeavored to *think*, the more he *thought*" (p. 23, emphasis added). Consciousness of "nothing" is nonetheless preoccupying consciousness. The Spirit of Christmas Past will teach Scrooge how to increase his knowledge by adding the inward truths of memory, thought, and reflection to the fragmentary facts from external experience. Scrooge's misanthropic ice is cracked by Marley and melted by memory. The past within will transform the outer realities of the present.

After recovering his past, a changed Scrooge enters an unfamiliar Christmas Present. When no spirit appears at the chiming of one o'clock,

Figure 13. The brazier in the foggy city street urbanizes the traditional yule fire, shown here in an illustration from Alan Tabor's calligraphic edition of the Carol *(1916).*

its unfamiliarity is apparent. Scrooge is prepared for another spirit, but he is "not by any means prepared for nothing" (p. 38). Years of training in an empiricism of presence are not easily overcome. He has not yet adapted to a world of inner, rather than outer, reality.

The absence of the expected second spirit does not prompt Scrooge to dismiss the whole idea of spirits as humbug, as it would have earlier. Instead he turns his attention inward – he begins to think. Gradually, almost unconsciously, he becomes aware of a light in the room. Representing Scrooge's awakened reliance on inner knowledge and feeling, this light bridges the gulf between past and present and enables Scrooge to see his urban present as a continuation of his rural past. In this light Scrooge can recover the traditions of Christmas that he thought were lost in the move from country to city and reunite the pieces of his life.

The many fires in the *Carol* bring the traditions of the yule log and the Christmas hearth into the city (fig. 13). The light in his rooms, Scrooge discovers, comes from an unaccustomed fire blazing in his fireplace, apparently set by the Ghost of Christmas Present. Scrooge's rooms are warmer than they have ever been, so warm that the spirit goes about half-naked. As he tours with Christmas Present, Scrooge sees the fires in the bakers' ovens warm enough to melt the snow in the streets as they cook the Christmas dinners of the poor; fires in the hearths of the miners and the lighthouse keepers; and the fire where the Cratchit family gathers to salute the day and call down Christmas blessings on all, even on

Figures 14, 15. Randolph Caldicott's illustration for Washington Irving's Old Christmas *(1875, left) shows the squire's toast to the day with the uplifted wassail bowl. The traditional subject is updated in the Cratchit family's toast with their unmatched tumblers, here rendered by E. A. Abbey for the American Household Edition (1876, right).*

Scrooge (figs. 14, 15). The customary images of Christmas, a wintry, snow-covered landscape countered by the beckoning warmth of the yule fire, have been given urban counterparts in the icy temper of Scrooge and the melting fires of the Christmas in the city.

The traditional Christmas celebration was an extended affair. Lasting for the twelve days of Christmas, or even longer, it gathered a family extending vertically through several generations and horizontally to relatives at several removes who gathered in the manor house for the many days of feasting. In the city Christmas is a one-day holiday. Bob works until closing time on Christmas Eve and returns to the office, albeit a bit late, on the morning after Christmas. The city celebrations typically in-

clude only the nuclear family (figs. 16, 17). We know nothing of an older generation of Cratchits, or even of brothers and sisters to Bob and his wife. We know that Fred's mother (Scrooge's sister, Fan) is dead, but his party does not include his father or his wife's parents.

The *Carol* replaces the extended manorial familiy with an urban "family of man." The Spirit of Christmas Past reminds Scrooge of how Fezziwig turned his city warehouse into a kind of manor house and, by inviting all the neighbors to his "office party," transformed his street into an urban fiefdom. Scrooge's nephew Fred makes family of his friends; his Christmas party is an urban, single-generation version of the festivities at Dingley Dell. Cratchit, too poor to extend his family beyond its already too generous proportions, is extended in spirit by being a city dweller. In many versions of the Carol, Bob gives some of his meager wages to a beggar or to the charity solicitors to show that Christmas makes even poor Bob a generous member of a family of givers. In the original version, Bob's membership in the family of man is apparent as he wanders through the city markets to buy his Christmas dinner. The sensuous descriptions of the markets exemplify what Sergei Eisenstein described as the "urbanism" in Dickens' prose, the "head-spinning tempo of changing impressions with which Dickens sketches the city in the form of a dynamic (montage) picture."[7] In Dickens' words, "ruddy, brown-faced, broad-girthed Spanish Onions, shining in the fatness of their growth like Spanish Friars,

Figures 16, 17. Mrs. Cratchit serving the Christmas pudding, depicted by Frederick Simpson Coburn (1901, opposite top), domesticates the tradition of bringing in the boar's head, shown here in Caldicott's version for Irving's Old Christmas *(1875, left).*

and winking from their shelves in wanton shyness at the girls as they went by," (p. 41), or "French plums [that] blushed in modes of tartness from their highly decorated boxes" (p. 42) make Bob, as he shops, part of a celebrating international family (fig. 18). Not linked by relations of blood or property, the new urban family is a microcosm of the human economic community.

The *Carol* is urban in its point of view from within the city, in its emphasis on inner truth rather than external fact, in its use of prose montage, and in its melding of rural tradition with the new urban way of life. It is most urban in its underlying myth. The 1840s made personal the age-old conceptions of the country as the place of simple innocence and the city as the seat of corruption and vanity. The popular mythology claimed that childhood was spent in the country and was lost in the move to the city to take up adult life. For many, especially those in the booming industrial towns in the north, this was "a profound dislocation," leaving the new city-dwellers "cut off, physically and psychologically, from [their] roots and [their] community."[8] Christmas became the festival of "return-

Figure 18.
"The Goose Club" by Hablot K. Browne, Dickens' most frequent illustrator, shows the participants in the club receiving the goose and the bottle of spirits they have purchased by paying a weekly subscription for several weeks before Christmas. The graphic detail in this picture, done for the 1853 Christmas supplement to the Illustrated London News, *recalls the celebratory excess in Dickens' descriptions of the Christmas markets.*

Figures 19, 20. Leech's frontispiece for the first edition of the Carol, *"Mr. Fezziwig's Ball" (left), recalls Phiz's picture of Mr. Pickwick at Dingley Dell (fig. 7). It captures the contemporary relevance of the* Carol *by placing a popular image of the rural Christmas, seen at right in Cruikshank's version of a country Christmas dance (1847), into a Dickensian urban setting.*

ing home" from school or from work in the city to recover briefly the lost childhood in an idealized rural community like that at Dingley Dell "based on mutual affection, trust and boundless generosity."[9] Scrooge's life follows this mythic pattern. Brought up in the country, he moves to the city to become an apprentice in Fezziwig's business. When he leaves the city with the Spirit of Christmas Past, he embarks on a journey to rediscover his lost rural heritage. As the darkness and mists that characterize the urban world vanish, Scrooge finds himself on a "clear, cold winter day" in the place where he was bred. His first melting tears are called forth by the dusty roads of his boyhood home and by his vision of schoolboys returning home for Christmas.

Scrooge's version of the myth, however, is not simplistically idyllic. His rural Christmases past are complicated by a kind of orphanhood. His father, though alive during his childhood, abandoned the boy to lonely schoolrooms. Even when Scrooge's sister Fan came to the school to take him home for Christmas to a "Father [who] is so much kinder than he used to be that home's like Heaven" (p. 29), there is no account in the text of that presumably happy Christmas. It is mentioned merely as a stopover on Scrooge's way to the city to begin his adult life as an apprentice to Fezziwig. Dickens' myth finds its ideal in the memory of Fezziwig's party, not in the country childhood (figs. 19, 20). Though reminiscent of family Christmases in the country, this is a more urban gathering. It extends the community to all the people in the neighborhood and to a few crashers as well. Being part of the urban crowd seems sufficient for entry. Like the uncontrolled energy of the city, the dancing begins as arbitrary and chaotic movement, "always turning up in the wrong place" (p. 32). But gradually it transforms the random collection of individuals into a temporary family, with Mr. and Mrs. Fezziwig as the patriarch and matriarch who bring order to the movement in the traditional dance of Sir Roger de Coverley. The climax of the dance levitates the dancers out of the linearity of temporal life, as Mr. Fezziwig "appear[s] to wink with his legs" (p. 32). At this moment the dancer becomes one with the dance. Then this ideal community—a moment of vision within the memory of Christmas Past—dissipates with the dance, and urban life returns to its ordinary linear confusion.

In the city and in the present, Dickens found the mythic ideals associated with the rural past. If he was looking backward in 1837 when he celebrated Pickwick's Christmas, by 1843 he had committed himself to the urban here and now.[10] While Dickens was writing the *Carol,* Martin Chuzzlewit learned that the ideal he sought could not be found in some frontier American Eden but must be sought in urban Britain. Scrooge discovers Christmas in the streets of London, 1843. He finds it in the survivals of the past as they infuse the urban present, however briefly, with joy and meaning. These survivals and memories become part of a deepened inner awareness that characterizes urban man.

The immediate popularity of the *Carol* with its Victorian readers stemmed in part from its commitment to the present. Victorian reviewers, who devoted much of their reviews to retelling the story and quoting long pas-

Figure 21. Dickens' depictions of common people were often compared in his own time to the genre paintings of Sir David Wilkie, whose 1839 painting Grace before Meat *captures the tone of Dickens' treatment of the Cratchits. Courtesy of the Birmingham Museum and Art Gallery.*

sages from the text, had little to say about Christmas Past. The only passage from Stave 2 that found its way into the reviews was the account of Fezziwig's party. Scrooge's unhappy childhood and lonely schooldays were almost completely ignored. Nearly all the reviews included the description of Scrooge's character from the first stave and substantial passages from Christmas Present. Besides the account of the Cratchit Christmas dinner, several other less likely passages from Stave 3 were reprinted by the reviewers. The descriptions of the streets and markets and of Scrooge's visits to the homes of the miners and the lighthouse keepers, passages which now seem incidental or peripheral to the tale, appeared in many of the reviews. The apocalyptic description of the urchins Ignorance and Want, a section often omitted from modern adaptations of the story, was also frequently quoted. For the Victorians, the heart of the story was in Christmas Present. They read the *Carol* as "a tale of the times."

The reviewers frequently compared Dickens to the painter David Wilkie (fig. 21), whose genre paintings of humble life they linked with the realistic literature of the period. The Cratchit family stood at the center of this "realistic" tale, which had as its object "the claims of the poor on the merciful sympathies of their fellows."[11] Nearly all the reviewers agreed that

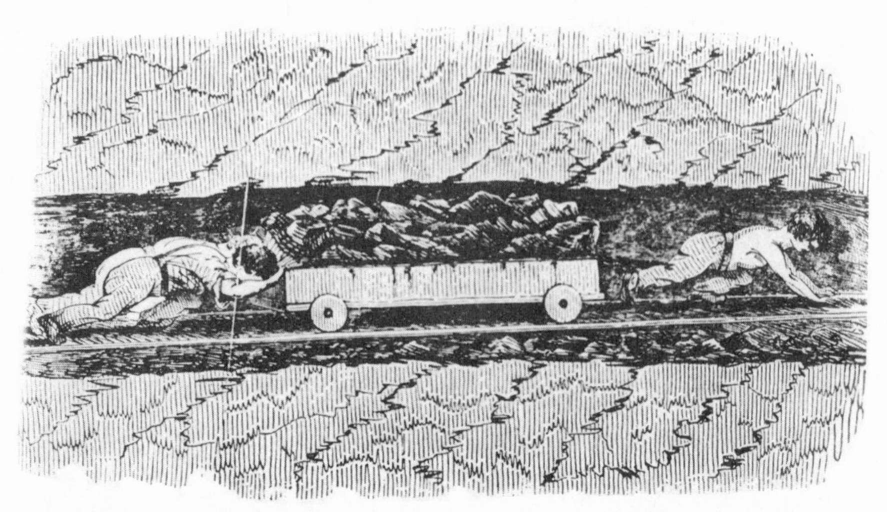

Figure 22. The images of children working in the mines in the 1842 parliamentary report became visual metaphors for the general condition of working children. Stripped of the clothing of civilization, chained to their work, and buried in oppressive ignorance, they were the living counterparts to Dickens' urchins Ignorance and Want.

the most notable thing about the book was its "sympathy for human suffering."[12] A Chartist reviewer named Dickens "the poet of the poor" and compared him to Burns in his "delineation of the children of the people."[13] Even American critics, intensely irritated by Dickens' anti-American sentiments in *American Notes* and *Martin Chuzzlewit*, found "his sympathy for human suffering . . . strong and pure [and] . . . more finely displayed in the work under notice, than in any of his previous productions."[14]

The severe trade recession of the mid-forties, the Chartist agitation, and the continuing debate over social issues in Parliament and the press made the plight of the poor an especially topical issue in 1843. At the center of this heightened consciousness were the reports of the parliamentary commissioners investigating the employment of women and children in mines and factories that appeared in 1842 and 1843. These reports, graphically illustrated with pictures of the oppressive conditions suffered by the workers (fig. 22), shocked their Victorian readers, spurred a movement for factory reform, and prompted a literature of social concern. Elizabeth Barrett's "The Cry of the Children" (*Blackwood's Magazine*, August 1843) and Thomas Hood's "The Song of the Shirt" (*Punch*, December 1843) gave poetic expression to this aroused social conscience. Numerous novels, often subtitled "a tale of the times," made literary use of material from the parliamentary reports. The most notable was probably Disraeli's *Sybil* (1845), the second in his trilogy of political novels that began with *Coningsby*.

Dickens was also moved. After reading the second report of the Children's Employment Commission, published in February 1843, he wrote to one of the commissioners, Dr. Thomas Southwood Smith: "I am so perfectly stricken down by the blue book you have sent me, that I think (as soon as I shall have done my month's work) of writing, and bringing out, a very cheap pamphlet, called 'An appeal to the People of England, on behalf of the Poor Man's Child.'"[15] A few days later he wrote to Smith saying that he had "reasons . . . for deferring the production of that pamphlet until the end of the year. I am not at liberty to explain them further, just now; but *rest assured* that when you know them, and see what I do, and where, and how, you will certainly feel that a Sledge hammer has come down with twenty times the force – twenty thousand times the force – I could exert by following out my first idea."[16] Whether or not Dickens had *A Christmas Carol* specifically in mind in March, it is clear that his response to the parliamentary report was an important factor in making his Christmas story a tale for the times.[17]

The tone in much of the topical writing of the period is one of discovery – the discovery of an unfamiliar urban, industrial nation that no

Figure 23. Punch's *allegorical "Capital and Labour" (1843) visualizes the abstractions of the two nations as two worlds linked by the coal tunnels and the laboring children of the parliamentary reports.*

longer can be characterized as a green and pleasant land. Nevertheless, the Victorians were also learning that they could accommodate themselves to the city of their adult life, even though the terms of accommodation would be different from those of their rural childhood. Instead of the immediate, face-to-face relationships of the country, life in the city was more abstract, more generalized. The debate over political economy in the 1830s, and the work of the new statistical societies and parliamentary investigators, helped define the abstractions by which human relationships in the city could become familiar (fig. 23). The "tales of the time" gave these abstractions particularity.

The countryside that Scrooge discovers in Christmas Present lacks the mythic coloring of the countryside in Christmas Past. The miners, lighthouse keepers, and mariners represent a contemporary rural England, hard working in narrow circumstances. In the city, the Cratchit family's discussion about Peter going out to work and Martha's excuse for arriving late to Christmas dinner – that she had been working on Christmas Eve as a milliner's apprentice – call up the images of the working children of the parliamentary reports. R. D. Grainger, who wrote the section of the report on the dressmaking industry, described the "protracted labour" in the London sweatshops as "quite unparalleled in the history of manufacturing processes. I have looked over a considerable portion of the Report of the Factory Commission, and there is nothing in the accounts of the worst-conducted factories to be compared with the facts elicited in the present inquiry."[18] The young women testifying in the report, typically in their teens and early twenties, worked long and debilitating hours. The account of Emily Pennington, sixteen years old, might well be that of Martha Cratchit:

> Has been an apprentice as a milliner 2 years and three-quarters; is boarded and lodged; paid a premium of 20*l*. for five years. There are two busy seasons; one beginning in October and ending about Christmas; the second begins about April or Easter, and ends at the latter part of July. In the winter season begins to work half-past 7 A.M., and leaves off about 11 P.M., if they are not very busy; occasionally goes on till 12, not later. In the summer begins at half-past 6 A.M., and leaves off about 1 in the morning; "has sat up till 2 or 3." Has never worked all night. Generally the work is finished earlier on Saturdays than on other nights, being about 10 in the busy season. Does not begin earlier on Mondays. Never works on Sunday: goes to church regularly. In the winter busy season has breakfast at 7 A.M., for which a quarter of an hour is allowed; dinner at half-past 12, for which there is no limited time, generally about a quarter of an hour; tea at 6, a quarter of an hour allowed; supper at 10, for which there is a quarter of an hour or 20 minutes. . . . If they sit up till 1 or 2 in the morning a cup of coffee is allowed, but nothing to eat. . . . When she has sat up a long time has pain in the back, and the legs ache; has had swelling of the feet. The work does not try her eyes. Is rather round-shouldered; this is not uncommon. Had very good health before she came here, but since has been several times ill: has a cough every winter. . . . One or two of the young women have fainted when they have gone up to bed or to tea. Two of the dressmakers wear spectacles: they are 18 or 20 years of age. Has as much food as she likes.[19]

The matter-of-factness in this testimony disguises the revelatory impact that the report had at the time, as it revealed "the second nation" and detailed the lives of the poor. Dickens symbolizes the revelatory mood of the reports in Christmas Present's disclosure of the two urchins, Ignorance and Want, lurking beneath his robe. A childless bachelor by choice, Scrooge is reminded that in the economic family of the city, he is father to these children of urban neglect.

Even though these social issues raised by the *Carol* were intensely topical in 1843, the book was not dismissed as partisan propaganda, as many other "tales of the time" were. Dickens may have been disappointed that so little attention was paid to the controversial economic message embedded in his story. In *The Chimes*, his Christmas book for 1844, he treated political and social issues much more explicitly. Reviewing *The Chimes* for the *Edinburgh Review*, John Forster argued that the two Christmas books had the same lesson, but what was treated as "individual lapse" in the *Carol* became "social wrong" in *The Chimes:* "Questions are here [in *The Chimes*] brought into view, which cannot be dismissed when the book is laid aside. Condition of England questions; questions of starving labourer and struggling artizan; duties of the rich and pretenses of the worldly; the cruelty of unequal laws; and the pressure of awful temptations on the unfriended, unassisted poor."[20] The characteristic contemporary reaction to the *Carol* was to praise Dickens' concern for the less fortunate as fellow feeling appropriate to the season. Such readers may naively have ignored the Malthusian proportions of Cratchit's family, the ideological implications of Scrooge's comments on decreasing the surplus population, or the veiled allusions to the parliamentary reports, but their reaction seems truer to the tone and feeling of Dickens' tale.

The gentleness of the *Carol*'s politics is apparent when it is compared to *The Chimes* or, even more so, when compared to Christmas books by other writers who tried to re-create Dickens' success.[21] One such imitation, W. H. Shepstone's *Christmas Shadows* (1850), illustrates by contrast the deftness of the *Carol*. The tale describes how a dream awakens D. Cranch, a hard-hearted clothing manufacturer, to realize how harshly he treats his clerks, cutters, and seamstresses. Their sufferings are told in considerable detail, derived, perhaps, from the parliamentary reports on seamstresses and milliners, so that we know their exact wages and the nature of the work each of them does. Cranch is described wholly in economic terms. We know nothing of his personal history; his greed is entirely a result of seeking his own self-interest in a system that encourages buying cheap and selling dear. He does not dream of his past as Scrooge does. He lives totally in the present and within the ideology of laissez-faire. He is transformed by confronting the future in the form of two allegorical ghosts, Starvation and Conscience, who teach him political truths about the poor people who work for him by showing him a vision of his death and the suffering of his daughters afterwards, when they are forced to work as seamstresses to survive. After one dies and the other attempts suicide to escape her misery, Cranch awakens reformed. He calls a surprise brunch for his workers and triples their wages.

Clearly siding with the reformers in the ongoing controversy about government regulation of industry, *Christmas Shadows* details conditions in the garment business, but it lacks psychological depth. Without personal history or consistency of character, Cranch is contradictorily portrayed. During the day he is a cruel employer driven by self-interest to gratuitious meanness. Yet in the evening at home he is a doting father. The vision of his daughters' suffering that prompts his conversion is neither as disinterested nor as inevitable as Scrooge's vision, and hence his conversion is less convincing as an alternative to the self-interested economics that created him in the first place. The measure of Dickens' control of his politically charged and topical subject matter can be taken in the contrast between the *Carol* and *Christmas Shadows*. If *A Christmas Carol* is Dickens' "sledgehammer" for the poor, it is wielded with the gentleness of Joe Gargery's angelic arm.

While Dickens managed to be topical without becoming partisan, some readers did express vague reservations about the "cockney" tone of the story.[22] Such objections seem to refer to the occasional colloquialisms in the diction or to "Newgate novel" intrusions, like the scene of Old Joe, the fence in Stave 4. Such scenes did not idealize common life as the Cratchit scenes do, and some Victorian readers found these "realistic" touches objectionable in a Christmas story. Dickens' new genre seemed to such readers to call for idealized visions of Christmas in the country.

For modern readers the "vulgarity" of the *Carol* is more apparent in the parodies and stage adaptations of the period than in Dickens' original. Peter Parley's pirates argued in court that their "reoriginated" version would make the story available to a whole class of readers unreached by the original. Although we have no copy of this parody, presumably the pirates vulgarized the language in their retelling to make it more suitable for common readers. C. Z. Barnett's *A Christmas Carol; or, the Miser's Warning!*, which opened in early February 1844, made several changes to fit the story to stage conventions of the period. Cratchit's character, for example, is expanded with cockney wit. In the opening scene, when Scrooge accuses him of using too much coal, Bob replies Wellerishly, "I've been trying to warm myself by the candle for the last half hour, but not being a man of strong imagination, failed."[23] He tells the nephew behind Scrooge's back: "Old covetous! He's worse than rain and snow. They often come down, and handsomely too, but Scrooge never does!"[24] In Dickens' original, such cockney wit belongs to Scrooge or to the narrator. Giving it to Bob allies him to some popular stage figures of the day, but it considerably changes his character.

Barnett also modifies the plot to add "low life" and melodrama. On his way home from work, for example, Bob is mugged for his wages. This misfortune gives Scrooge's nephew, allegorically named Frank Freeheart for the purposes of this "citizen melodrama," an opportunity to aid Bob with a golden sovereign. Bob returns the favor later in the play when he pleads with Scrooge to help Frank after the young man is financially ruined when a trading vessel he has invested in sinks. The thief, Dark Sam, turns up again at Old Joe's after Scrooge's death, expanding that scene into the centerpiece of Christmas Future in the play. The restraint of Dickens' urban Christmas story is apparent in comparison to the cockney stereotypes produced for the stage. Some of the contemporary objections to the vulgarity of the *Carol* may have been based on these stage versions rather than on Dickens' text.

Many elements of the *Carol*, especially the character of Scrooge, neatly fit contemporary stereotypes. Nearly all the Victorian reviews and adaptations characterize Scrooge simply as "the miser." Webb's adaptation, subtitled "The Miser's Dream," probably presented Scrooge in terms of this stereotype, and Stirling's version, the first specifically to identify Scrooge as a moneylender, made his miserliness understood in terms of that traditional connection. Barnett's "The Miser's Warning" dramatized only one segment from Christmas Past, Scrooge's confrontation with his fiancée when she releases him from their engagement because he has placed his love for gold ahead of his love for her—a scene that reinforces the characterization of Scrooge as the conventional miser. While the *Carol* cockneyfied Christmas, finding urban analogues for the traditional elements of the feast, it also told a familiar moral story.

Dickens' mixture of the familiar with the new made the *Carol* a Christmas tale for the times. It addressed the preoccupying social concerns of the period in familiar terms. One did not need to understand the laws of political economy or know the sociology of industrial England to recognize the miser hoarding his gold. While this conventional reading oversimplified Scrooge's character and his role in the story, he was not, to the Victorians, the emotional center of the tale. That place was held by the Cratchit family.[25] Scrooge discovers Christmas not so much for himself as for the good of Tiny Tim – "the poor man's child." Though some Victorian readers thought the *Carol* reduced the meaning of Christmas to food and drink—the most common criticism of the story—most accepted gustatory misrule as excess in the good cause of awakening the social conscience.[26] Again the deft mixture of elements in the tale offered virtues to counter objections, whether the objections came from priggish puritans or partisan political economists.

Though no one claimed in 1843 that Dickens invented Christmas – that hyperbolic suggestion would surface later on – many seemed to feel that he had rediscovered it and freed it from puritan constraints. The book was generally recognized, even on first reading, as a "classic," and the test of its literary quality became its power to move its readers to good works and celebration. Lord Jeffrey, critic and editor of the *Edinburgh Review* from 1803 to 1829, wrote to Dickens on the day after Chritsmas, when the *Carol* had been on the streets for little more than a week, to say that the tale had "prompted more positive acts of beneficence . . . than can be traced to all the pulpits and confessionals in Christendom, since Christmas 1842."[27] Even Thomas Carlyle was moved. After reading the *Carol*, he suppressed his Scotch puritanism, ordered a turkey, and invited some friends for Christmas dinner.

If Dickens' contemporaries needed the *Carol* to rediscover Christmas, Dickens shared their need. Burdened with financial obligations and with what Mrs. Longfellow, wife of the poet, called "the tediousness of Chuzzlewit," he had both financial and psychic reasons for writing the *Carol*.[28] The intensity of his concentration on the tale, written in little more than a month suggests that the little book liberated important areas of his imagination.

"To keep the Chuzzlewit going, and do this little book, the Carol, in the odd times between parts of it, was, as you may suppose, pretty tight work," Dickens wrote to an American friend. But finishing the tale liberated him to celebrate Christmas with the energy of a reformed Scrooge. "When it was done, I broke out like a Madman. . . . Such dinings, such dancings, such conjurings, such blind-man's buffings, such theatre-goings, such kissings-out of old years and kissings-in of new ones never took place in these parts before."[29] In accounts of their childhood Christmases written many years later, Dickens' children recalled this particular Christmas, especially for a spectacular magic show conjured up by their father and John Forster. Jane Welsh Carlyle described the two friends in this performance as exerting "themselves till the perspiration

Figure 24. Dickens as the Christmas magician invokes the Spirit of Christmas in this drawing by Joseph Clayton Clarke. Using the pseudonym "Kyd," Clarke produced several series of watercolor sketches of Dickens characters in the 1880s and 1890s. From the Dickensian, *1905.*

was pouring down and they seemed *drunk* with their efforts. Only think of that excellent Dickens playing the *conjuror* for one whole hour—the *best* conjuror I ever saw."[30] The same might be said for the magical little story he conjured up for his larger audience that same Christmas (fig. 24).

3

Founder of the Feast

A Christmas Carol as Secular Scripture

If we would tremble with a real holy fear, we must come into the light, and see everything as it stands out beautifully and gloriously, not stay in the darkness, where there are nothing but dim shadows and spectres which frighten us, and which we wish to fly from.

F. D. Maurice, 1843

Every man that writes is writing a new Bible; or a new Apocrypha; to last for a week, or for a thousand years; he that convinces a man and sets him working is the doer of a miracle.

Thomas Carlyle, 1832

As he was walking down Drury Lane near Covent Garden market on the day that Dickens died, 9 June 1870, Theodore Watts-Dunton overheard a "barrer gal" exclaim: "Dickens dead? Then will Father Christmas die too?" Many years later, Watts-Dunton remarked of the incident, "It was from her I learnt that there were at the time thousands and thousands of the London populace who never read a line of Dickens – who never, indeed, had had an opportunity of reading a line – but who were, nevertheless, familiar with his name. They looked upon Dickens as the spirit of Christmas incarnate: as being, in a word, Father Christmas himself."[1] Dickens has held this position in the popular mind ever since. His little book has been described as "the greatest book in the world," and he has been characterized as the "voice" (fig. 25), "spirit," and "inventor" of Christmas, indeed, "the Founder of the Feast."

This reputation is based on a relatively small number of Dickens' works. Although Christmas figures in some of his later novels, notably *Great Expectations* (1861) and *The Mystery of Edwin Drood* (1870), these darkened Christmases are not the ones that earned Dickens his popular reputation. The hearty and happy Dickensian Christmas is derived largely from two early works, *The Pickwick Papers* and *A Christmas Carol*. While the *Carol* did not meet Dickens' financial hopes when it appeared in 1843, it was an enormous popular success. It went through ten editions in little more than a year and reached a broader audience than his longer novels. Dickens wrote the *Christmas Books*, the *Carol* and the four that followed, for this broad popular audience, the same audience to which he directed his two general circulation magazines, *Household Words* (1849–1859) and *All the Year 'Round* (1859–1870).[2] The annual Christmas numbers of these magazines, as Katherine Carolan has suggested, also helped to establish Dickens' reputation as the literary Father Christmas.[3]

But nothing did more for Dickens' popular image than his public readings. From the first reading in 1853 to the last shortly before he died (fig. 26), Dickens made the *Carol* the pièce de résistance in his repertoire. Philip Collins lists 127 performances during Dickens' reading career, the most for any of the longer readings, and he describes the *Carol* as "the quintessential Dickens reading . . . the greatest of platform pieces from his works."[4] Carlyle moralized that in public readings Dickens and Thackeray "exhibit[ed] themselves to a lot of inquisitive people who were too lazy to read what they paid their shillings to listen to."[5] But in what Carlyle viewed as an invitation to moral laxity, Dickens saw opportunity – a chance to reach the large nonreading audience. He gave his first

Figure 25. In December 1870, Harper's Monthly Magazine *marked the Christmas following Dickens' death with a memorial border.*

Figure 26. The Illustrated London News *depicted Dickens giving his last public reading of the* Carol *in March 1870.*

public performance in Birmingham just after Christmas 1853 to benefit the Educational Institute there. The audience, described by the *Times* as "2000 people, whose lives are one long round of toil," inspired Dickens with their rapt attention.[6] "They lost nothing, misinterpreted nothing, followed everything closely, laughed and cried," he wrote.[7] At his later commercial readings he always insisted that there be shilling seats so that the less affluent members of this larger audience could attend.

The readings were much more than readings. They were performances, high points in the history of Victorian theatre. Longfellow wrote of Boston being "Dickinized" in 1867 when Dickens made his American tour.[8] Devotees camped out in the streets to gain admission to the theater, and stories abounded of professional scalpers selling tickets at many times their original price. Those who were lucky enough to get a ticket saw a one-man show, a mixture of reading and performance, in which Dickens brought the story to life by portraying the characters in different voices.

Dickens did not read his original text. He created a special reading text and modified it constantly, reducing the original to a three-hour reading for its first performance in Birmingham. Over the years he gradually trimmed that version to a one-and-one-half-hour performance. The cuts he made kept drama at the expense of narrative. In performance, narrative could be supplied by gesture, facial expression, and tone of voice. He also cut social comment and criticism, removing, for example, Scrooge's discussion of sabbath observance with the Spirit of Christmas Present and the revelation of the urchins Ignorance and Want. What remained most intact over the years were the sections describing the Cratchit family, especially their Christmas dinner, the centerpiece of the reading.[9]

Although he marked these changes in his prompt copy, Dickens recited rather than read the story. "I have got to know the Carol so well," he remarked, "that I can't remember it, and occasionally go dodging about in the wildest manner to pick up lost pieces."[10] So the reading varied from night to night. At Sunderland, he did "such a number of new things" that his manager "stood in amazement in the Wing, and roared and stamped as if it were an entirely new book, topping all others."[11] Dickens surprised even himself. After a performance in Paris, he exulted, "I got new things out of the old Carol – effects I mean – so entirely new and so very strong, that I quite amazed myself."[12] For both audience and performer, the readings possessed the immediacy and excitement of good theater.

Kate Field, a journalist who attended many of the American readings, has left a lively account of "twenty-five of the most delightful and most instructive evenings of my life."[13] As the reading of the *Carol* begins, her companion comments that Dickens' voice seems "limited in power, husky, and naturally monotonous," but as Dickens takes on the voices of the characters in the story and adds dramatic gesture, the power of the reading begins to reveal itself. In a husky, grating voice he becomes Scrooge standing before the knocker on his door: "Then there comes the change when Scrooge, upon going home, 'saw in the knocker Marley's face!' Of course Scrooge saw it, because the expression of Dickens's face, as he rubs his eyes and stares makes me see it, 'with a dismal light about it, like a bad lobster in a dark cellar.'" During the Fezziwig ball, he tells the story with his hands: "Dickens's expression . . . is delightfully comic, while his complete rendering of the dance where 'all were top couples at last, and not a bottom one to help them,' is owing to the inimitable action of his hands. They actually perform upon the table, as if it were the floor of Fezziwig's room, and every finger were a leg belonging to one of the Fezziwig family."

The high points of the reading for the Victorian audience came in the Cratchit sequences. In Christmas Present and Christmas Future, Dickens focused the reading version on the Cratchit story, which he left largely uncut. Field recalls Bob's account of Tim at church as "the most delicate and artistic rendering of the whole reading," communicating "a volume of pathos." The high point of the evening for her was the family's Christmas dinner: "What Dickens *does* is frequently infinitely better than anything he says, or the way he says it; yet the doing is as delicate and intangible as the odor of violets, and can be no better indicated. Nothing of its kind can be more touchingly beautiful than the manner in which Bob Cratchit – previous to proposing 'a merry Christmas to us all, my dears, God bless us' – stoops down, with tears in his eyes, and places Tiny Tim's withered little hand in his, 'as if he loved the child, and wished to keep him by his side, and dreaded that he might be taken from him.' It is a pantomime worthy of the finest actor." Dickens dazzled his audience by playing twenty-three different roles during the reading of the *Carol;* he captured their emotional sympathy with his portrayal of the Cratchits. Kate Field's critical friend who found Dickens' voice monotonous at the beginning was, by the end, a convert to the Dickens Christmas.

The reading became a kind of familiar rite, the audience waiting for particular scenes (fig. 27) such as the Cratchit Christmas dinner or the conversation between Scrooge and the boy he sends to fetch the prize turkey. Dickens' manager reported that loud sobs from the audience often interrupted the Tiny Tim scenes.[14] Dickens was also moved. After the first performance in 1853, he was so "animated" that he "felt as if we were all going up into the clouds together."[15]

For those attending the readings, Dickens took on the power of his story. "People may think in perusing Mr. Dickens' books that he must be a man of large humanity," one listener commented; "in hearing him read they *know* that he must be such a man."[16] To hear him read the *Carol* at Christmas, remarked one American reviewer, was like hearing the very sound of the Christmas bells.[17] Philip Collins notes that the *Carol* predisposed Dickens' listeners "to credit him with moral as well as tech-

Figure 27. The audience at Dickens' readings, depicted here by Fred Barnard for the Household Edition of Forster's Life of Dickens *(1879), came expecting to be moved to laughter and tears.*

nical virtues"; in doing so they gave the *Carol* reading, unlike the other readings, "an element of a rite, a religious affirmation."[18] Edwin Mead, who attended all the Boston readings as a young man to sell souvenir copies of the texts, recalled the experience late in his life as "sacramental," with Dickens "radiating his blessed Christmas gospel."[19] By the time of Dickens' death in 1870, the *Carol* had become the first gospel in the Dickensian scripture. It preached the good news of Christmas and Charles Dickens was its prophet.

No prophet is wholly honorable in his own country. When the *Carol* first appeared, "it moved us all . . . as if it had been a new gospel," Mrs. Oliphant reported.[20] But by 1870 it had encouraged such a rash of poor imitations that it no longer seemed to her to have "great elevation of sentiment or spiritual discrimination," and she denigrated it as a tract promoting only "the immense spiritual power of the Christmas turkey."[21] Mrs. Oliphant repeated the most frequent Victorian criticism of the *Carol*, that its Christmas ideal was self-indulgent and vulgar. Some self-denying Calvinists thought it downright sinful. Probably the most famous statement of this point of view was Ruskin's comment to a friend that Dickens' Christmas was nothing more than "mistletoe and pudding – neither resurrection from the dead, nor rising of new stars, nor teaching of wise men, nor shepherds."[22] Although Ruskin celebrated architecture that was religious without being ecclesiastical, he was unable to perceive the same quality in Dickens' story.

In an age preoccupied with religious controversy—with debates between Evangelicals and Tractarians and with spiritual doubts prompted by evolutionary science and the German Higher Criticism – religious issues found their way into much of the literature. J. H. Y. Briggs quantifies the Victorian obsession with religion by noting that in 1860 "more than 50 percent of all monthly periodicals were religious [and] as late as the 1880s half of the new books published in Britain were of a religious nature."[23] Ruskin and readers like the reviewer for the *Christian Remembrancer* who found "not a scrap of religion" in *The Chimes*[24] apparently expected their Christmas stories to be part of this more explicit religious literature, and there were, as Kathleen Tillotson has pointed out, "a mass" of such explicitly religious novels and tales.[25] Had Dickens been writing to meet Ruskin's expectations, he might have produced something closer to Robert Browning's *Christmas-Eve* (1850).

There are notable similarities between Browning's narrative poem and Dickens' ghost story. Both recount a dream-vision in which the protagonist learns the true meaning of Christmas through a three-stage journey of discovery. Browning's narrator, like Scrooge, is distanced from his fellow men. When he attends a Christmas Eve service in a Nonconformist chapel at the beginning of the poem, he cuts himself off from his fellow worshipers by his satiric condescension toward their faults and foibles. When he finds the service unbearable, he leaves, only to be confronted on the common outside by a vision of Christ who has him cling to the hem of his robe as they travel, like Scrooge and the spirits of Christmas, first to the Christmas Eve mass at St. Peter's in Rome and then to a lecture by a German rationalist theologian at the University of Göttingen. In these three visits Browning's narrator observes three versions of the main alternatives in mid-Victorian religious debate: Evangelical Nonconformity, Tractarian Anglo-Catholicism, and rationalist demythologizing doubt. At the end of his vision, he reawakens in Zion Chapel, where the annoyed glances of the other worshipers indicate to him that he has fallen asleep. His visionary experience, however, has changed his attitude toward his fellow worshipers. Instead of discomfort in their ragged presence, he accepts the "oozings muddy" of the chapel service as the water of life:

> – Better to have knelt at the poorest stream
> That trickles in pain from the straitest rift!
> For the less or the more is all God's gift,
> Who blocks up or breaks wide the granite-seam.[26]

The narrator finds in the simple chapel his rock of Horeb. Cleft by God's power and Moses's rod, it spills forth redeeming water to quench his spiritual thirst. He gives up his satiric attitude – his "Attacking the choice of my neighbours round, / With none of my own made" (lines 1339–40) – and he chooses the chapel in spite of its shortcomings, joining the other worshipers in singing a hymn.

At the end of the poem, Browning's narrator makes a Dickensian choice and affirms heart over head, but the process by which he arrives at this choice is much more intellectual than Scrooge's. He tests the arguments for each religious persuasion, finds each flawed in a different way, and finally affirms the existential and spiritual necessity of choosing the most congenial of the three. The satiric voice, present almost to the very end of the poem, expresses the intellectual uneasiness in this debate between self and soul. The Hudibrastic verse form in which the whole poem is cast reminds the reader, perhaps, of the inconclusiveness in the poem's resolution of its natural experience and spiritual message.[27]

To meld a secular story with a spiritual theme was not an easy matter. Religious readers, particularly Tractarians, were apt to think such attempts "vulgar" if they demeaned the spiritual by dressing it in ragged secular clothing.[28] Two mid-Victorian imitations of Dickens' story illustrate the kind of explicit scripturalizing that demythologized the *Carol* for Mrs. Oliphant. *The Anniversary: A Christmas Story* (1856) turns its Christmas dream-vision around the parable of the prodigal son. Living sinfully in London, its hero dreams of living righteously at home in the country. When he awakens, he repents and returns home to marry the girl of his dreams. The sentimental clichés of this tale contrast sharply with Dickens' urban realism and turn this Christmas Eve dream-vision into a trite sermon with the biblical parable as its text.

A later anonymous tale, *Christmas Eve with the Spirits; or, the Canon's Wanderings through Ways Unknown; with some future tidings of the lives of Scrooge and Tiny Tim* (1869), offers a sequel to its Dickensian model. The dream-vision of its clergyman-protagonist reveals that his parishioners have fallen into sin because of his neglect. The melodramatic captions to the book's illustrations – "Passion Enthroned: God Dethroned"; "Wrecked by Man: Saved by God" – suggest its religious enthusiasm, as do the visions the clergyman sees, including one of the crucifixion at the climactic point in the narrative that prompts the clergyman to renew his vocation by reminding him of Christ's sacrifice. The story ends with a vision of the death of Scrooge, many years after the time of the *Carol*. Scrooge has retired from business to do good works. His nephew now manages the firm and employs Cratchit as his foreman. We see Scrooge on his deathbed attended by Tiny Tim (fig. 28), now a young man who calls him "Granny," and his death becomes a beatific vision of the happiness at death of one who, unlike the clerical protagonist, has taken Christ's charity as the model for his life. At Scrooge's funeral, "Tiny Tim laid a wreath of roses upon the coffin, and would have flung himself upon it in his passionate grief, had not they withheld him. – Most truly could it be said of him, 'In sure and certain hope of the resurrection to eternal life,' for nobly had he redeemed his time."[29] Thus Scrooge enters the hagiography of the period, a figure of religious instruction along with Christ himself. Scrooge's canonization tells us something of the *Carol*'s spiritual impact for its later Victorian readers, even though its spiritual message was much more sublimated, more displaced, than the messages in these vulgar imitations.

J. Hillis Miller has described Victorian England as a world in which God has "disappeared," where "everything is changed from its natural state into something useful or meaningful to man. . . . The city is the literal representation of the progressive humanization of the world. . . . Life in the city is the way in which many men have experienced most directly what it means to live without God in the world."[30] Writing for these new urban readers, Dickens sought to express spiritual truth in the humanized language of the self-mirroring secular city. The spiritual ignorance haunting London's Chartist streets was not to be ministered to, he believed, with "the comfortable conviction that a parrot acquaintance with the Church Catechism and the Comandments is enough shoe-leather for poor pilgrims by the Slough of Despond, sufficient armour against

Figure 28. Tiny Tim comforts the dying Saint Ebenezer in this illustration by A. R. Dorrington for Christmas Eve with the Spirits *(1869).*

the Giants Slay-Good and Despair" (*MP,* 1:36). Dickens considered his art "an imitation of the ways of Providence,"[31] and he wanted his Christmas story to transform the life of its reader in the way the spirits transform Scrooge's life. Thomas Hood implied that the *Carol* would do just that when he compared it to Bunyan: "How the miraculous change was effected (it was not exactly by Faith, Hope, and Charity), by what spiritual Trio (not Gin, Rum, and Brandy) the Worldly Wiseman was converted into a Christian, must be unriddled by the book itself."[32]

The *Carol* is Dickens' nativity story for urban man, the first gospel in the "secular scripture" of Victorian fiction. Although it does not retell a biblical parable or simply recast the story of the first Christmas in Victorian dress, the *Carol,* like many novels of the period, as Barry Qualls has shown,[33] is deeply rooted in Bunyan and the Bible. One of the pleasures these novels offered to their Victorian readers derived from attuning oneself to perceive the mundane infused with spiritual truth. Though Ruskin and a few others could not see through the "naturalism" of the *Carol* to its supernatural level, many more Victorians were moved by its spiritual power. The hedonism that offended a few straitlaced Calvinists and the vulgarity that bothered some otherworldly Tractarians prompted many others to exclaim with Edwin Whipple: that Dickens "christianizes eating and drinking, and contrives to make the stomach in some odd way an organ of the soul. . . . The glutton idolizes meat and drink; Dickens idealizes them."[34] Dickens' progress for his urban pilgrims embodied a natural supernaturalism.

Although Dickens did not give his first public reading of the *Carol* until ten years after he wrote it, the story was written to be read aloud. Both folksong and folktale – a "carol" and a "ghost story of Christmas" – it was instantly traditional. An established classic in the nation's literature from the day it first appeared, this ghost story, like the gospels as understood by the new biblical criticism of the period, was basically an oral story, a traditional expression of the mythology of its community.

The orality of the *Carol* is apparent in its narrator. Reminding his listeners that the spirits are as close "as I am to you now, and I am standing in the spirit at your elbow" (*CB*, 24), he confirms by his presence the truth of the story he is telling. In the tradition of the ghost story, he also turns retelling into re-enactment. As Christmas Eve repeats earlier Christmas Eves, so the narrator's telling repeats Scrooge's dream, and as the narrator is transformed in the telling, he becomes the medium who turns the listener into a participant in the transformation rite of the tale.

The narrator articulates a genial and avuncular version of Scrooge's epistemological dilemma. Though apparently the traditional storyteller, he is not blessed with omniscience. His opening paragraphs are as much about the problems of narratorial knowledge as they are about the substance of the tale:

> Marley was dead, to begin with. There is no doubt whatever about that. The register of his burial was signed by the clergyman, the clerk, the undertaker, and the chief mourner. Scrooge signed it. And Scrooge's name was good upon 'Change for anything he chose to put his hand to.
>
> Old Marley was as dead as a doornail.
>
> Mind! I don't mean to say I know, of my own knowledge, what there is particularly dead about a doornail. [*CB*, 7]

All the reader really needs to know is that Marley died seven years before the Christmas Eve of the *Carol*. But the narrator lists the documentary sources for his knowledge, reflects on whether he has any experiential confirmation for the validity of the proverbial simile "dead as a doornail," and elaborates the question of Marley's status for several more paragraphs. He so belabors the issue that he communicates a nervous uncertainty rather than the absolute assurance expressed by his words. Even the opening sentence – "Marley was dead, to begin with" – is unstable. The inverted syntax, the hanging final preposition, and the ambiguity of what beginning is referred to, inject unsettling doubt about the apparent certainties of the tale.

Lack of assurance characterizes the narrator throughout Stave 1. Rather than telling the episode with the knocker, for example, he challenges the reader to explain it to him: "And then let any man explain to me, if he can, how it happened that Scrooge . . ." (p. 15). And his repeated assertion of "it is a fact that . . ." calls attention to the lack of factual basis for much of what he says.

The uncertainty that plays in the narration ironically re-enacts the epistemological contradictions in Scrooge's character. Just as Scrooge, to maintain his urban empiricism, must suppress his memories of the past and his awareness of much that goes on around him, so the narrator must pretend to certainties about Scrooge's story that are not possible in a ghost story. In fact, Marley is not as dead as a doornail. His mysterious presence initiates Scrooge's transformation. And although the text is in the past tense, implying that it is an account of events over and done – and furthermore events that occur only to narrow-minded old misers – the story is being retold on Christmas Eve, a night of mystery and uncertainty for everyone. These circumstances of the retelling make past tense nervously present.

Our assurance that the fog on Christmas Eve will be swept away by the light of Christmas morning depends on our belief in story – either the story of Scrooge's awakening or the story of the Christ child's birth. Time and change cast such stories into question. Nineteenth-century doubters asked whether Christ could be present in the city as he had been in the country, whether in a world haunted by the spectres of Ignorance and Want there was room for a manger, whether imagination could still transform a world in which "business" occupied us entirely. Like the narrator and the nineteenth-century reader, we enter the rite of rereading nervously doubting our belief in story. We begin Scrooge's story caught in a midwinter awareness of the otherness of time that makes us doubt the unchanging truth of the story. Rediscovering Scrooge's enduring power to transform winter into Christmas, we affirm more than the lasting viability of Dickens' tale. In reaffirming Scrooge, we implicitly reaffirm the biblical Christmas story. The authority of the text lies in its capacity to restore our belief in story itself.

Robert Patten has described the dynamic of the *Carol* as one in which the narrator's voice is for the reader comparable to the voices of the spirits to Scrooge: "In insisting on the analogy between the narrator's voice and the Christmas Ghosts, Dickens provides one way of taking their eruption into the fictional world: our senses respond to his voice as Scrooge does to the Ghosts, and we respond to the story he tells as Scrooge does to the times which the Ghosts present. The *Carol* becomes the analogue to Scrooge's experience."[35] Sharing the oral tradition that articulates the conversion process of the tale, the reader enters Scrooge's community.

The oral devices in the *Carol* also turn the tale into ceremony. The association of Scrooge with ice and cold in the opening stave and the similes used to establish his character – "solitary as an oyster," "hard and sharp as flint" – make him larger than life, a mythic "Old Man Winter" in his annual recurrence. His repetition of "Bah! Humbug!" becomes a kind of chorus to his character. So oral is the prose that it occasionally falls into blank verse, as in the lines spoken by Marley's ghost that set the biblical pattern of the story: "Why did I walk through crowds of fellow beings with my eyes turned down,

> And never raise them to that blessed Star
> Which led the Wise Men to a poor abode? [*CB*, 21]

Rhythm and repetition undermine the naturalism of the prose and heighten its supernaturalism. Discussing the word *home* in the scene where Scrooge's sister rescues him from the lonely schoolroom, Pearl Solomon suggests that such repetitions can become "estatically incantory."[36]

> "I have come to bring you home, dear brother! . . . To bring you home, home, home!"
>
> "Home, little Fan?" returned the boy.
>
> "Yes! . . . Home, for good and all. Home, for ever and ever. Father is so much kinder than he used to be that home's like Heaven! He spoke so gently to me one dear night when I was going to bed that I was not afraid to ask him once more if you might come home; and he said Yes, you should. [*CB*, 29]

This scene conjures up in words the popular Victorian images of "Christmas home," pictures of schoolboys returning to their country homes for the holiday (fig. 29).

Stephen Leacock has suggested that the ghost story flourished in the mid-nineteenth century because people no longer believed in ghosts, "at least as a serious, everyday part of their creed."[37] But the *Carol* is more ambivalent. If the ghosts are merely part of an exemplary fantasy, the repetition and incantation in the story nonetheless recall traditional ways

Figure 29. Robert Seymour's version of schoolboys returning home for The Book of Christmas *(1837) portrays a joy denied to the young Scrooge, who was left alone at school for the holiday.*

of knowing and believing that undermine Scrooge's Victorian empiricism. Dickens plays with this ambivalence between truth and fiction when Scrooge jests with Marley, suggesting that he is not real but just the result of indigestion. As he repeats the cycle of his life, Scrooge learns that forgotten truths of repetition and ceremony better explain his upset than the physical state of his stomach. The ghost *story* contains more truth than present empirical reality.

As a ritual of cyclic retelling, the *Carol* is, as Leacock points out, "better known in scenes, . . . than at its full length."[38] We recognize Scrooge in his office with Cratchit in his cell, without being told that it is a scene from Dickens' story (fig. 30), and the image of Bob Cratchit holding Tiny Tim on his shoulder has become so indelibly fixed in our imagination that we can identify it in silhouette. The iconographic method pictorializes the story, turning it from continuous narrative into a chain of remembered scenes, a series of visual stations along its narrative journey. This visual version of the *Carol* represents Dickens' sense of Christmas. In "A Christmas Tree" (1850), he describes his own remembrances of Christmas as just such a series of iconographic images:

> What images do I associate with the Christmas music as I see them set forth on the Christmas Tree? Known before all the others,

Figure 30. A recent advertisement casts Fred as a calculator salesman offering to modernize his uncle's office, but the allusion to Dickens' story is never made explicit in the text. See fig. 87 for another example of a similarly embedded allusion. © 1983 Hewlett-Packard Co. Reproduced with permission.

keeping far apart from all the others, they gather round my little bed. An angel, speaking to a group of shepherds in a field; some travellers, with eyes uplifted, following a star; a baby in a manger; a child in a spacious temple, talking with grave men; a solemn figure, with a mild and beautiful face, raising a dead girl by the hand; again, near a city gate, calling back the son of a widow, on his bier, to life; a crowd of people looking through the opened roof of a chamber where he sits, and letting down a sick person on a bed, with ropes; the same, in a tempest, walking on the water to a ship; again, on a sea-shore, teaching a great multitude; again, with a child upon his knee, and other children round; again, restoring sight to the sick, strength to the lame, knowledge to the ignorant; again, dying upon a Cross, watched by armed soldiers, a thick darkness coming on, the earth

Figure 31. The illustrator who best captures Dickens' "magic-lantern" technique is Harry Furniss. This 1910 montage for his edition of Dickens' works visualizes some of the superimposed images in the opening stave.

> beginning to shake, and only one voice heard, "Forgive them, for they know not what they do." [*CS*, 11]

For Dickens, Christmas called up not just the Christmas story; it evoked the whole life of Christ, articulated in iconographic images.

We know Scrooge's life as a similar set of images: bent over his desk in the cold office, denying coal to his clerk; standing in amazement before his door knocker; kneeling in fright before Marley's ghost. We see him as a child reading in a lonely schoolroom; as a young man preparing the warehouse for Fezziwig's party; as an old man cowering before his gravestone; as a reformed man leaning out his window on Christmas morning and asking the boy in the street what day it is. This magic-lantern technique piles all the Christmases in Scrooge's life one on top of the other and allows for rapid transitions in the narrative (fig. 31), creating a visual shorthand to tell the essentials of Scrooge's life. It also connects our consciousness with those of the narrator and Scrooge, for we understand Scrooge's life as he does, as spots of time in his consciousness of his own personal history. The rapid transitions from one of these moments to the next embody in microcosm the principle of conversion at the core of the story.

Some of these iconographic scenes simply recount conventional images of Christmas. The description of Belle's Christmas with her family recreates the familiar pictures of family Christmases, and the nephew's Christmas party, particularly the game of blindman's buff (fig. 32), also represents a well-established popular illustration. The iconography is more powerful when conventional imagery is adapted to the particulars of Scrooge's story. Such is the case in the descriptions of Scrooge in Stave 1, which turn him into a latter-day emblem of Avarice. Although Scrooge is often portrayed as a miser counting his stacks of gold, the text describes him in less traditional terms. He is preoccupied with his business, not with counting money, and his business is limited to the narrow self-interest defined by laissez-faire economics. Instead of being associated with a purse, as in the traditional iconography of Avarice (fig. 33), Scrooge is tied to his desk, a workaholic whose riches are represented by wastepaper in a world where money has become paper transactions (fig. 34). Rather than Avarice, he might better be described as an emblem of Business.

In the description of Fezziwig's ball, Dickens similarly modernizes the traditional Christmas celebration, moving it from manor house into city warehouse. Leech's rendering of this image (fig. 35) has the solidity and earthiness of the caricature tradition, showing the Fezziwigs as substantially reminiscent of their predecessors in the well-fed gentry. Dressed in

Figure 32. Arthur Rackham's 1915 edition celebrates the conventional iconography of the Carol *in illustrations like this rendering of the game of blindman's buff.*

the clothes of an earlier period and dancing the traditional Sir Roger de Coverley, they represent the persistence of tradition in the plain and humble setting of the urban warehouse. By the time of Sol Eytinge's 1869 representation of the scene (fig. 36), the picture has lost much of its "natural" grounding to take on a more spiritualized iconography. Eytinge seems to have worked with Leech's illustration in mind; the door and the fiddler in the background remain, but their positions in the picture are reversed, and one of the children in the foreground of Leech's picture

Figure 33. Dickens was familiar with this traditional emblem of the miser from Holbein's Dance of Death *(1538), a book that fascinated him as a child.*

seems to have stood up to dance with Fezziwig. The cockney energy in Leech's illustration is also blunted. The couple kissing under the mistletoe have been replaced by the couple demurely holding hands. Significantly, in Eytinge's picture Mrs. Fezziwig disappears and melts into the crowd. Fezziwig alone becomes the vision of Christmas Past; caught in the moment of his "cut" in the dance, he seems almost to be levitating, floating weightlessly above the floor in a moment of spiritual ecstasy.[39]

Similarly, the scene of the Cratchits' Christmas dinner accrues spiri-

Figure 34. Sol Eytinge's illustration of Scrooge confronting the charity solicitors (1869) captures Dickens' alteration of the traditional emblem from the miser surrounded by his gold to the businessman engulfed in wastepaper.

tual significance. By transporting the traditional Christmas feast from the spacious manor house to the cramped quarters of the urban underclass, Dickens translated scenes of crowded country feasts into the now-familiar image of the Cratchits crowding around their Christmas goose or awaiting Mrs. Cratchit's triumphal entry with the steaming pudding. Their dinner scene that epitomized Victorian versions of the story, mixed,

Figure 35. The rustic frame for Leech's frontispiece as it was reset for the Cheap Edition of the Works of Charles Dickens in 1852 emphasizes the earthiness in Leech's picture.

in Alfred Harbage's words, "a detailed genre picture and a master plan – of Saturnalia Christian-style."[40]

The iconographic method relates the *Carol* to the popular visual progresses of William Hogarth. Scrooge's story is reduced to a series of discrete scenes, linked moments telling the whole of his life, from unhappy childhood, to rejecting love for money, to lonely old age. It could be rendered iconographically as "The Miser's Progress." But the frame of the story in which Scrooge is redeemed from the inevitability of his past inverts the Hogarth pattern.

Figure 36. The finer engraving and shading in Sol Eytinge's 1869 illustration of the dance reinforce its later, more "spiritual" perspective.

The story's redemptive frame makes Scrooge's progress more like Bunyan's *The Pilgrim's Progress* than one of Hogarth's moral tales. Like Bunyan, Dickens characterizes life as a spiritual journey; Fred tells Scrooge that Christmas is "the only time . . . when men and women . . . think of people below them as if they really were fellow-passengers to the grave, and not another race of creatures bound on other journeys" (p. 10). Scrooge also seems to be re-enacting Bunyan's Christian in scenes like those with the charity solicitors. Their second meeting, after his conversion, could have come from the pages of *The Pilgrim's Progress:*

> He had not gone far, when coming on towards him he beheld the portly gentleman, who walked into his counting-house the day before, and said, "Scrooge and Marley's, I believe?" It sent a pang across his heart to think how this old gentleman would look upon him when they met, but he knew what path lay straight before him, and he took it.
>
> "My dear sir," said Scrooge, quickening his pace, and taking the old gentleman by both hands. "How do you do?" I hope you succeeded yesterday. It was very kind of you. A merry Christmas to you, sir!"
>
> "Mr. Scrooge?"
>
> "Yes," said Scrooge. "That is my name, and I fear it may not be pleasant to you. Allow me to ask your pardon. And will you have the goodness" – here Scrooge whispered in his ear. [*CB*, 73–74]

After the revelations of the spirits, Scrooge is on the straight and narrow path to the Celestial City. He has learned to practice his charity inconspicuously and not to pray on street corners like a Pharisee.

Both the *Carol* and *The Pilgrim's Progress* recount "dream visions," though Bunyan insists that his story is divine revelation and Dickens suggests that Scrooge's dream may be only a device of literary fantasy. These two literary dreams are memorable, however, not because of their spiritual revelations and allegory, but rather for their everyday realism. We remember Bunyan's book not as dream but as an account of a journey filled with common people speaking everyday language and telling of ordinary experiences. The cold office of Scrooge and Marley, with its dying fire and atmosphere of preoccupation with business, is much more memorable in the *Carol* than the "vague allegorical force" of the three spirits.[41] Dickens' story succeeded while most of the imitations failed because Dickens did not, like his imitators, stress the allegory in his story.

Both the *Carol* and *The Pilgrim's Progress* are explorations of the relationship between the eternal and the temporal. In the seventeenth century, when earthly life was seen as an episode in an eternal existence, Bunyan could characterize that episode as a linear journey, enabling his readers to perceive the spiritual dimension of their everyday experiences on the road. Dickens, writing at a time when for many God was dead, put more emphasis on the eternal. Enacting the timelessness of eternity, Scrooge's life is not linear but simultaneous. He lives the whole of it in a single night.

From his experience Scrooge gains an eternal perspective, learning to live simultaneously "in the Past, the Present, and the Future." Many adaptations have "straightened out" the impossible conflicts in the time scheme of the story – making the ghosts appear at progressively later hours or as parts of a single dream – to give more "linear" sense to Dickens' narrative. The temporal confusion, however, expresses the miraculous, Dickens' way of embodying spiritual truth in his nineteenth-century story. From the eternal perspective, Scrooge's life is seen in toto in a Christmas Eve meditation, just as Dickens' meditation on the Christmas tree recalled not merely the nativity story but the whole of Christ's life in simultaneous images.

Attempting to visualize this insubstantial truth at the heart of the story, some Victorian illustrators produced emblematic pictures representing no single moment in the text, but synthesizing the vision of the story as a whole, as in Eytinge's 1869 frontispiece (fig. 37) showing Scrooge sitting up in bed looking at the three ghosts in the air above him. But most Victorians did not find the spiritual truth of the *Carol* in the ghosts. They agreed with Kate Field in considering them the weakest part of the story, "too monotonous, – a way ghosts have when they return to earth."[42] Like most of her contemporaries, she found the spiritual message in the story of the Cratchits rather than in the allegorical spirits. George M. Baker's 1874 dramatic adaptation of the story tries to represent emblematically the spiritual importance of the Cratchits by placing them in the center of a concluding iconographic *tableau vivant:*

> *Music: curtains at back are drawn, disclosing 'A Christmas Picture.' In the centre, the* GHOST OF CHRISTMAS PRESENT, *seated as before with his torch raised, red fire blazing in it. At his L., the blindfolded gentleman, in the same position as before, with the lady getting away from him; on his L., the lady with the fan; R. of* CHRISTMAS PRESENT, MRS. CRATCHIT, *with a pudding in her hands;* MARTHA *at her R., with* TINY TIM *in her arms. Two of the children opposite to them, looking at the pudding.* TINY TIM *speaks, when curtain is fairly drawn, 'God bless us every one!' 'The Christmas Carol' is then sung by an invisible chorus; and the front curtain falls upon the whole picture.*[43]

Baker's earthly tableau is more representative of the later Victorian understanding of the *Carol* than is Eytinge's more "eternalized" picture.

For the Victorians the Cratchits were the center of the story. Dramatic adaptations of the period often made Bob Cratchit rather than Ebenezer Scrooge the lead role. In an 1859 production of Stirling's Carol, for ex-

Figure 37. Eytinge's emblematic frontispiece for the Carol *(1869) summarizes the allegory of the tale.*

ample, the premier actor of the company, J. L. Toole, took the part of the clerk. The *Times* review made no mention of Scrooge or the actor who played him, concentrating its entire commentary on the Cratchits: "Mr. Toole's rendering of the part of Bob Cratchit, and Mrs. Mellon's Mrs. Cratchit were in the correctest taste and singularly effective. The scene in which the family are represented at their Christmas dinner was a perfect histrionic triumph, and the 'gods' could not well have been thrown into greater pleasurable excitement if they had been actually permitted to partake of the humble family's festive treat, instead of merely witnessing it."[44]

The dinner scene, apparently the high point of the evening, was staged with the same kind of realistic thoroughness that led John Everett Millais to secure a real carpenter as the model for Joseph in his painting *Christ in the House of his Parents*. A Christmas dinner, complete with a fully cooked goose and plum pudding, was prepared for each evening of the forty-night run. Toole filled the plate of the girl who played Tiny Tim, and she would retire to the chimney corner and quickly put away all that he gave her. Each evening he served her a bit more and each evening she just as quickly cleared her plate. Finally he put half the goose and extra large servings of applesauce and potatoes on the plate. As she sat in the corner he watched her pass food from her plate into the darkness behind the stove. There he found her little sister sharing the meal. When Dickens heard the story, he remarked, "Ah, you ought to have given her the whole goose."[45]

Victorian readers were struck by the reality of the Cratchit family. The *Gentleman's Magazine*, in its original review of the book, for example, praised the "truth" of Bob and Tim: "Tiny Tim is quite perfection, and will serve as an illustration of the great affection shewn by the poorer classes to a diseased or deformed child. Indeed it is impossible to visit the gardens of Hampton Court on a Monday in summer without seeing numerous proofs of this. Often have we watched a mechanic carrying in his arms, a little cripple, eying it with affection, and occasionally pointing out some object of interest to it. Sometimes, he will gently seat it on the grass, watching it while it plucks a daisy, or crawls over the verdant turf. Nor is this to be wondered at. The children of the poor are partakers with their parents of the same dish, the same room, and frequently the same bed. They are the sharers of their poverty as well as of their more smiling hours, and are their constant companions, the objects of their love, whether in weal or woe; and to the credit of the poor, it may be added, that when sickness or old age arrive, the tie of affection is unbroken, and they continue to share in the hard earnings of their offspring."[46] But by the 1870s the portrayal of the Cratchits was much more than simply accurate and sympathetic reportage. In Dickens' latter-day Christmas story, the Cratchits became the Holy Family and Scrooge a nineteenth-century worldly wiseman making his pilgrimage to the humble house of the "poor man's child."

This later Victorian reading of the *Carol* might be described as typological. As an account of the Cratchit family, the story was both contemporary and a re-enactment of the original Christmas story. Although it embodies eternal truths, it does not articulate them as theological abstractions. It is not allegory and it cannot be read as a one-for-one translation of its biblical model. Rather, it embodies the crucial elements of its original. The relation of Scrooge to Tiny Tim in this latter-day scripture is that of type and antitype in traditional typology. As the solitary child abandoned by his father, the psychologically crippled Scrooge is a type to the literally crippled Tiny Tim, his antitype. Carrying his crutch, Tim re-enacts the Christ child, born to carry his cross. To gain an eternal perspective on his life, Scrooge must recognize, however subliminally, the links between himself and Tiny Tim, that he is both "father" and "double" to the child and that they both re-enact their biblical ancestry.

Underpinning this typological structure is a division into Old and New Testament worlds, into type and antitype. Linked by the sign on his office to "dead-as-a-doornail" *Jacob* Marley, *Ebenezer* Scrooge inhabits an Old Testament consciousness. He worships golden idols – the specific reason for which his fiancée leaves him – and he grounds his beliefs in the law, in the efficacy of "prisons and workhouses." Just as the biblical Jacob learned God's truths in a dream, so this latter-day Jacob announces a dream to Scrooge that will transform him from a man who legalistically confines his business "to the narrow limits of [his] money-changing hole" (*CB* 20) to a man who does his "Father's business" (Luke 2:49). The good tidings that Marley's dream brings to Scrooge teach him that "Mankind [is his] business," and "raise [his eyes] to that blessed star which led the Wise Men to a poor abode" (pp. 20, 21), leading him to the humble hearth of the Victorian Christ child.

In the Cratchit home, the names – Peter, Martha, Timothy – tend to be drawn from the New rather than the Old Testament. Tim even links himself with the Christ child when he hopes "that the people who saw him in the church, because he was a cripple, . . . might . . . remember, upon Christmas day, who made lame beggars walk and blind men see" (p. 45). His family name and the crutch (cross) he carries emblemize his role as the antitype "mankind" announced in Jacob's dream.

Two key biblical allusions support the underlying typological structure of the story. In the opening stave, as Scrooge sits in front of his fireplace before the arrival of Marley, he sees the biblical figures decorating the tiles on the fireplace displaced by the "face of Marley, seven years dead, [that] came like the ancient Prophet's rod and swallowed up the whole"

(p. 20). The allusion is to Aaron's rod in Exodus 7:12, which represented divine power in the hands of Moses and Aaron. The force of this allusion is not merely to suggest that Scrooge is either an unbelieving pharaoh or a latter-day Israelite who has forgotten his ties to the Lord. The allusion is typological. Its fulfilling antitype appears in the fourth stave. When Scrooge, directed by the ominous figure of Christmas Future, cowers before a corpse stretched out on a bier before him and is unable to pull back the veil that covers the body, the narrator comments: "Oh cold, cold, rigid, dreadful Death, set up thine altar here, and dress it with such terrors as thou hast at thy command: for this is thy dominion! But of the loved, revered, and honored head, thou canst not turn one hair to thy dread purposes, or make one feature odious. It is not that the hand is heavy and will fall down when released; it is not that the heart and pulse are still; but that the hand was open, generous, and true; the heart brave, warm, and tender; and the pulse a man's. Strike, Shadow, strike! And see his good deeds springing from the wound, to sow the world with life immortal!" (pp. 64–65).

The allusion is again to Exodus, now to the rod of Moses striking the rock of Horeb to produce a spring for the thirsting Israelites (Exod. 17:6). This episode, a very common Victorian type, interpreted the "rock of ages" as Christ and the "cleft" as Christ's wounds flowing with healing blood.[47] In the typology of the *Carol*, Jacob's dream swallows up the whole of Scrooge's life and heralds the healing power of the poor man's crippled child. Dead Marley as type prepares the way for Tim as antitype, and Tim's wound prompts the converson of Scrooge to good deeds. Scrooge is linked with both type and antitype, with both Marley and Tiny Tim. He is converted when he gives up being "dead as a doornail" with Marley and becomes as a little child with Tim. In the vision of Christmas Future, Peter Cratchit's apt funeral text for his brother is Mark 9:36, "And he took a child, and set him in the midst of them." And through this vision Scrooge becomes "as a child" again. Imitating Marley and Tim, Scrooge becomes an imitation of Christ. He is the body beneath the veil, whose wounds will flow as good deeds and "sow the world with life immortal."

Dickens' typological Christmas story links Old and New Testaments in the transformation of Scrooge. It also links the nativity with the crucifixion and resurrection. Dickens often associated Christmas and Easter. He described Christmas as a ceremony of remembering those who had died in the preceding year and celebrated Christ's birth as the annunciation of His redeeming death and resurrection. The cycle of the three spirits imitates the cycle of the three days from Christ's death to His resurrection.

As in "A Christmas Tree," the holiday in the *Carol* calls up not just the story of Christ's birth, but the story of his whole life.

For Ruskin and Mrs. Oliphant, and for many later readers who consider Scrooge's conversion merely an economic or humanitarian change, the "theological" underpinning of the *Carol* has not been apparent. The story's retelling of the original Christmas story is too displaced, its supernaturalism too natural, to make it seem more than a gospel of food and drink. But as typology the *Carol* does not distinguish spiritual truth from its historical embodiment; it also does not separate the spiritual from the secular. It is not allegorical, abstract, or otherworldly. Unlike the "Scrooge" of the etherialized *Christmas Eve with the Spirits,* whose death is the beatific vision of his spirituality, Scrooge's saintliness is worldly. The wound of his redemption will flow with good deeds, with active concern for Bob and his family, and he will achieve a kind of immortal life within this life, an immortality of charity.

As Scrooge leaves his house on Christmas morning and goes into the streets of the city, London is transformed into the Celestial City, his kingdom of God on earth. Scrooge does not have to wade through the river of death like Bunyan's Christian to reach the heavenly city. He brings that city to earth. From his wounds flow the good deeds that transform this world and turn the cold and icy streets of London into the golden sunshine of Christmas morning. "He dressed himself 'all in his best,' and at last got out into the streets. The people were by this time pouring forth, as he had seen them with the Ghost of Christmas Present; and walking with his hands behind him, Scrooge regarded every one with a delighted smile. He looked so irresistibly pleasant, in a word, that three or four good-humoured fellows said, 'Good morning, sir! A merry Christmas to you!' And Scrooge said often afterward that, of all the blithe sounds he had ever heard, those were the blithest in his ears" (p. 73).

Theologically, *A Christmas Carol* is an early version of what came to be known later in the century as "the social gospel." Centering its doctrine on the belief that the kingdom of God would be realized on earth, the social gospel movement saw history as an evolution toward this emerging Christian society. The family, led by a dominant and loving father, was its model in small of the Christian kingdom. The experience of conversion revealed itself in commitment to this earthly kingdom and in the performance of good works.[48] This doctrine, particularly prevalent in the

United States from about 1880 on, had its roots in Evangelical social concern, in the social theology of F. D. Maurice developed during the thirties and forties, and in Unitarianism, with which Dickens was involved in the mid-1840s. Dickens may have arrived at his social gospel from these influences that were at work at the time he was writing. Its presence in the *Carol* made his tale particularly apropos in the decades after his death when the social gospel movement was ascendant.

As "social gospel" *A Christmas Carol* is the story of the Cratchit family. In evolutionary terms they represent a stage in human development beyond Scrooge, for they have transcended the competitive ethic of laissez-faire capitalism to create a family/community based on love, self-sacrifice, and sympathy. The *Carol* is less explicit in presenting this evolutionary motif than *Dombey and Son*, published four years later, where the Tootle family, linked to the emerging world of the railroad, represent a similar advance in human relations. At the center of the Cratchit Christmas story is the family's love feast, their Christmas dinner emblematic of the Christian tradition of agape.[49] This scene centered later Victorian versions of the *Carol*. One popular abridgement reprinted only the account of the Cratchit dinner as presenting the essence of the story.[50]

The father of this model community, Bob Cratchit represents its values to his family when he encourages his children in Christian behavior and chides Mrs. Cratchit for refusing to toast Scrooge as "the Founder of the Feast" (*CB*, 48). When Peter puts on his father's "monstrous shirt collar (Bob's private property, conferred upon his son and heir in honor of the day)," he represents the priority this Christian community places on sharing and its rejection of the preeminence of private property (p. 44). He also becomes a smaller version of Bob, and the family's conversation about his imminent entry into the workplace calls up visions of him as the Cratchit man of the next generation, breadwinner and loving father to his own family.

Bob's importance as father places him and his family in sharp contrast to Scrooge. Scrooge's father is absent from his son's life. As a child Scrooge is abandoned by his father to lonely schoolrooms. As a young man, Scrooge seeks opportunity in the city and, like many other uprooted economic migrants of his generation, he is cut off from family and home. Guided by what Ruskin called "the gospel of getting on," Scrooge rejects family and withdraws into lonely bachelorhood. He is not a father himself and is essentially fatherless.

The social gospel in America emerged, in part, as a theology for a new generation in the industrial cities, a generation no longer preoccupied with running to the economic frontier for new opportunity. Its familial ideal, an image of human interdependence and sharing, replaced the earlier ideal of the economic individualist seeking fulfillment on his own. A settled urbanite, Cratchit represents the father of the new social gospel generation. As he guides his children to a life in the city similar to his own, his example enables the reformed and "fatherless" Scrooge to become a second father to Tim and adopt a role he has not known earlier in his life.[51]

In the late-Victorian Holy Family, the father takes precedence over the mother, for it is his vital presence in this miniature Christian community that marks its difference from the dislocated families of the early industrial period, when economic necessity often separated the father from his wife and children. In the late-Victorian Carol as displaced Christmas story, Bob and Tim replace the Madonna and child. The image of Bob holding Tiny Tim emerges as the central icon of the tale, a symbolic representation of the patriarchal Victorian ideal.

Illustrating Dickens' story for an early-Victorian audience, John Leech had not cast Bob and Tim in central roles. His illustrations focused on Scrooge and the spirits. He did not even depict the Cratchit Christmas feast. Bob Cratchit appears in only one of his pictures (fig. 38), a black-and-white tailpiece showing him sharing the bowl of smoking bishop with Scrooge. But later Victorian illustrators devoted themselves to the Cratchits. Three of the six illustrations E. A. Abbey produced for the American Household edition in 1876, for example, depicted the Cratchits, including a picture of the family circle dominated by Bob and his two sons as they toast "the Founder of the Feast" (see fig. 17). Sol Eytinge included six illustrations of the Cratchits in his 1869 edition, one of them a second version of his 1867 picture of Tim riding on Bob's shoulder (fig. 39), probably the first version of this most familiar icon from the story. Frederick Barnard repeated the Bob-Tim illustration in his pictures for the English Household edition in 1877, giving the subject a more emblematic rendering (fig. 40). Tim, holding his crutch, rides on his "blood horse" while the church tower in the background suggests the source of their strength. The well-dressed little girl on the right of the picture responds to the power of Tim's example as she secretly slips a coin into the hands of a beggar. If Joseph is often conspicuously absent from images of Christ's nativity, Mrs. Cratchit is notably missing in this patriarchal rendering of the Christmas icon. Lacking a Christian name, she is a shadowy figure at best. As father and son replace mother and child in the later Victorian "Dombeyization" of the *Carol*, Mrs. Cratchit disappears into the shadows altogether.[52]

Perhaps the most crucial moment in Dickens' reading of the *Carol*

Figure 38. Leech's final illustration for the original Carol, *showing Scrooge and Cratchit sharing a bowl of smoking bishop, resolved the story by resolving the differences between master and man.*

came when Bob Cratchit mourned the death of Tiny Tim. The New York *Nation* noted that Dickens made "a 'point' of [this moment] more decidedly than of any other passage in the evening's entertainment."[53] Although Kate Field found it overdone, observing that "here, and only here, Dickens forgets the nature of Bob's voice, and employs all the powers of his own, carried away apparently by the situation," most of his audience were deeply moved by what Charles Kent described as "a long-suppressed but passionate ouburst of grief."[54] The change in Dickens'

Figure 39. Eytinge's illustration of Bob holding Tim on his shoulder for the Ticknor and Fields edition of Dickens' works (Boston 1867) is the first rendering of what has probably become the best-known image from the Carol.

Figure 40. Frederick Barnard's picture of Bob and Tim for the English Household Edition (1877) places the father-son icon in an emblematic context.

voice may have been deliberate, but it was probably a case of the storyteller being drawn into the story and moved by it as if he were a participant. Clearly Dickens hoped that his voice would draw the audience into the story and move them as well, as Kent said it did, so that "Bob's tearful outcry brimmed to the eyes of those present a thousand visible echoes."[55] The conversion experience of the *Carol* could not be Scrooge's alone.

Becoming like Bob a father to Tiny Tim, needed to be the collective experience of all who read or heard the message of this social gospel.

Barry Qualls characterizes Carlyle's idea of the conversion necessary for nineteenth-century man as the "defeating of solipsism by confronting the self's demons and madness and reaching outwards towards others."[56] Scrooge enacts this pattern as he is transformed from the "solitary oyster" seeking only his own self-interest into Tiny Tim's second father. In the process he restores fatherhood to the secular city where God has died and the father has disappeared. His good works will become the healing spring to transform the city into the kingdom of God on earth.

When Dickens brought his social gospel to Boston in 1867, the healing power of his message was felt by many, including Mr. Fairbanks, a manufacturer of scales from St. Johnsbury, Vermont. During the reading Fairbanks's wife noted that her husband's "face bore an expression of unusual seriousness." Afterwards he confided to her that he felt he "should break the custom we have hitherto observed of opening the works on Christmas Day."[57] Not only did he close his factory for Christmas from 1867 onward, but also every Christmas Eve he sent each factory hand home with a turkey for the holiday, becoming, like Scrooge, "the Founder of the Feast."

4

The Children's Hour

A boy ten years of age was seen to enter Westminster Abbey shortly before evening prayers. Going straight up the main aisle, he stopped at the tomb of Charles Dickens. Then, looking to see that he was not observed, he kneeled at the grave and tenderly placed upon it a bunch of violets. The little fellow hovered affectionately near the spot for a few moments and went away with a happy, contented smile on his face. Curiosity led a gentleman present to examine the child's offering, and this is what he found written in half-formed letters on an envelope attached to the violets: "For it is good to be children sometimes and never better than at Christmas, when its Founder was a child himself."

Popular anecdote, reported in 1912

I like to fancy God in Paradise
Lifting a finger o'er the rhythmic swing
Of chiming harp and song, with eager eyes
Turned earthward, listening –

The Anthem stilled – the angels leaning there
Above the golden walls – the morning sun
Of Christmas bursting flower-like with the prayer,
"God bless us Every One."

James Whitcomb Riley, 1885

Dickens was a mythologist rather than a novelist; he was the last of the mythologists, and perhaps the greatest. He did not always manage to make his characters men, but he always managed, at the least, to make them gods. They are creatures like Punch or Father Christmas. They live statically, in a perpetual summer of being themselves.

G. K. Chesterton, 1906

In 1908 the *Dickensian*, journal of the recently formed Dickens Fellowship, exulted that the *Carol* was recited "every year in hundreds of chapels, church halls, and schoolrooms throughout the country."[1] The Carol had been institutionalized in the last quarter of the nineteenth century, and in the popular imagination it became part of a generalized fiction known as "the Dickens Christmas." This construction blended bits of Scrooge and Cratchit with Pickwick and Dingley Dell, and added some memories of the author and some nostalgia for Victorian customs and childhood. A staple in the December issues of popular magazines, the Dickens Christmas was history in the process of becoming myth. As the friends and relatives who had shared Dickens' dinner table died, their accounts of the "Apostle of Christmas" became legends added to the growing collection of Dickens Christmas lore.

The modernity and urbanity of the *Carol*, so apparent to its original readers, disappeared in the rose-colored nostalgia of the Dickens Christmas, which a newspaper poet located in an undefined past "When life was like a story holding neither sob nor sigh, / In the golden olden glory of the days gone by."[2] Another versifier blended Pickwick and Scrooge and placed them together in a yuletide arcadia:

> Let Fezziwig, with "winking" calves,
>   And his good lady take the floor;
> And let changed Scrooge the turkey send,
>   With lightened heart, to Cratchit's door.
>
> Come, warm the Christmas hearth anew,
>   Ere modern cynic hearts grow cold,
> And sing, as genial Wardle sang,
>   "Give three cheers for this Christmas old."[3]

Characterized by Edward Everett Hale as "a lover of old-time manners and customs," Dickens had become to 1910 what Irving and the medievalists had been to Dickens' own time.[4]

There was a large measure of Pecksniffery in the celebration of the Dickens Christmas. Theodore Watts-Dunton, speculating on what Dickens would find were he to return to earth for Christmas in 1907, suggested sadly that gentility and pretension had become so pervasive that, in spite of widespread sentiment for Christmas old, there would be few of the "old Fezziwig party" to welcome the writer with plum pudding and an old-fashioned Christmas ball.[5] For the new Fezziwig party dissociated the Carol from the markers that made it a sacred text for the Victorians. The familiar pictures by John Leech were displaced by the work of modern illustrators, and the public readings with Dickens re-creating his well-known text were forgotten as the Carol left the reading hall and entered the music hall.

The *Carol* was no longer "owned" by Chapman and Hall, Dickens' original publishers, whose editions had almost always included the original illustrations by Leech. Between 1900 and 1915 a host of new editions appeared, at least twenty-one of them containing new illustrations. The variety in these pictures – from the realism of George Alfred Williams (1905; see figs. 49, 53) to the wistful romanticism of Arthur Rackham (1915; see figs. 32, 47, 51, 73) and the neo-caricature of Harry Furniss (1910; see figs. 31, 41, 42, 54, 55, 56, 57) – suggests the *Carol's* status as a general cultural property. The works of Charles Dickens no longer required the "official" illustrations of Phiz, Leech, and the other original illustrators or even the semi-official pictures by such later Victorian artists as Sol Eytinge and Fred Barnard.

Several new dramatizations of the story also appeared, displacing the standard Victorian adaptation by Edward Stirling. At the same time dramatizations moved from the theater into the music hall and cinema. Seymour Hicks, after a successful run in J. C. Buckstone's adaptation, took *Scrooge,* his one-man simplification of the story, into the music hall. Scrooge was also probably the best-known of Bransby Williams's music hall impersonations of Dickens characters. Williams first recorded Scrooge on cylinder in 1905; he and others rerecorded the tale almost annually during the following decade. Film versions appeared in 1908, 1910, 1912, 1913, and 1914, making the *Carol* a standard of the silent cinema.

By the opening years of the twentieth century, the *Carol* was common cultural currency, spent each Christmas for whatever cause its readers chose. In this free-trading cultural climate, Edwin Charles's objection to Seymour Hicks's music hall Scrooge seems an antiquated survival of high Victorianism: "I have no objection to music-halls, but I do not think they are fitted either by the necessities of their programme or by their environment, for the exploitation of sacred subjects. I regard *A Christmas Carol* as a sacred subject, and I believe there are thousands of other Dickens worshippers who think with me in that respect. It is a sermon, amplifying and exemplifying Holy Writ itself, telling all in a practical and material manner of the newer and holier duties of man to man which Christ came down on earth to teach. It is a work to be read over quietly and pondered over seriously, so that its glorious lesson of Charity to all men may sink into the heart."[6] In becoming a modern cultural institution, the Victorian *Carol* had been desacralized.

By 1910 few readers personally remembered the charismatic author performing his text in the public readings. He was remembered instead as the author who created the characters that had inhabited their childhood. Henry James, for example, describing his childhood as "practically contemporary . . . [with] the fluttering monthly numbers" of Dickens' novels, recalled hiding under a table as a small boy to listen to the account of the Murdstones' cruelty to David Copperfield being read aloud. When he broke into "sobs of sympathy" with the child hero, he was discovered and sent to bed.[7] The Dickens stories were so embedded in Virginia Woolf's childhood that they became frames for her experience. Writing in later life (1925) of *David Copperfield*, she commented: "There is perhaps no person living who can remember reading *David Copperfield* for the first time. Like *Robinson Crusoe* and *Grimm's Fairy Tales* and the Waverley Novels, *Pickwick* and *David Copperfield* are not books, but stories communicated by word of mouth in those tender years when fact and fiction merge, and thus belong to the memories and myths of life, and not to its aesthetic experience."[8] What was true for *David Copperfield* was doubly true for *A Christmas Carol*. By the turn of the century it had become a children's classic.

As a children's book, the *Carol*'s status with adults was problematic. If it remained "a book which no one can bear to criticize," as it did for George Gissing,[9] it was also a book that many adults found hard to read. Like Elizabeth Bowen, whose childhood experience with Dickens had left her unable to enjoy his work in later life, many moderns thought of the *Carol* as a literary Peter Pan, a text that "would not grow up." They celebrated its childish sentiments in numerous children's editions, but they were unable to respond to it as serious adult literature. This arrested point of view was transcended by readers like G. K. Chesterton and Harry Furniss, who connected memories of childhood with their adult experience and saw the story whole.

As one of childhood's forms of thought, the Carol was available in the cultural memory as a framework for adults playing children's games. Once the Carol lost its status as a sacred text, modern adaptors were much readier to take liberties with it than their Victorian predecessors had been. The latter, even though they imitated and pirated the *Carol*, had an implicit reverence for the story, if only for its commercial success. "Irreverent" parodies, imitations using the *Carol* as a framework for political or social commentary, seem to have begun in 1885 in *Punch*. In the

Figure 41. Bendizzy's ghost visits Scroogestone in Harry Furniss's parody of Leech's original illustration, for Punch *(1885).*

following two decades parodies of the *Carol* appeared regularly in the Christmas issues of *Punch* and other popular magazines.

Punch's original pastiche, an account of the visit of the ghost of Bendizzy (Disraeli) to Scroogestone (Gladstone), was accompanied by four Furniss caricatures imitating Leech's original illustrations (figs. 41, 42).[10] In the text, which verbally echoes the original, Scroogestone confronts visions of past and present political troubles, particularly Irish troubles, and then awakens on Christmas to share a bowl of Christmas punch with Mr. Punch. Just a few months before Gladstone left office for the last time at age eighty-five in 1893, the magazine again punched the Liberal prime minister. Sir John Tenniel's modernization of Leech's picture of Scrooge standing before the Spirit of Christmas Present (fig. 43) shows the Spirit of Christmas 1893 surrounded by the political troubles beset-

Figure 42. Mr. Punch replaces Bob Cratchit in Furniss's celebratory "A Merry Christmas to You!"

ting Sadstone's fragmented Liberal party in place of the food and drink garnered at the feet of Leech's spirit.[11]

A 1901 parody, also in *Punch*, took on the Tory politics of the day.[12] The Ghost of "Old Morality" (W. H. Smith, first lord of the Treasury and leader of the House of Commons during Lord Salisbury's first administration from 1887 to 1891) visits the Tory heir apparent, "Prince Arthur" (Arthur Balfour, who would become prime minister in July 1902, succeeding his uncle, the marquis of Salisbury). The ghost counsels the prince that the time is ripe for decisive action to liberate the majority from the tyranny of the Irish minority. While *Punch* took on the Tories, the *Pall Mall Gazette* (1901) used the Carol to satirize the Liberals.[13] Reversing the Scrooge and Marley roles, their parody recounted the visit of the ghost Krooge (President Kruger of the Transvaal) to Morley (John

Figure 43. Sadstone meets the troubling Spirit of Christmas Present in Sir John Tenniel's cartoon for Punch *(1893).*

Morley, Liberal politician and Gladstone's biographer, who continued his mentor's moderate liberalism). The jingoism of the Boer War period, which condemned Morley and some of his Liberal colleagues as pro-Boer "traitors," informs the piece. Morley is a "boer-headed man" who assures Krooge that he has "no sympathy with England – none." Krooge foretells the visits of the spirits from the three wings of Morley's party, but only the extreme Right and Left actually appear. The Spirit of "old and trusted Liberalism," the party's center, remains asleep and is discovered by Morley at the end to be "the ghost of his former self."

Americans, too, found in the *Carol* a useful vehicle for political games. Directing his satire to the cause of trust busting, an anonymous writer for the New York *Critic* (1905) described an "Old Scrooge on the Day After" who is not permanently converted by his Christmas dream.[14] By Boxing Day he has reverted to a cynical, small-time robber baron. "A rich man has no business wasting his estate on miscellaneous charity at Christmas or at any other time," he cautions. "He should save it to endow colleges and build public libraries, with his name over the door, and erect magnificent mausoleums after he's dead." This J. P. Morgan of a Scrooge particularly objects to the government interfering with the Christmas plans of large trusts: "There was the Sugar Trust, now. The Sugar Trust, following its regular custom, was preparing to skimp a mere little 20 or 30 per cent. out of the Christmas candies. And a government prosecutor jumps up and starts a suit to dissolve the Sugar Trust, thereby spoiling the whole day for the Havemeyer family, not to mention Mr. Spreckels and all the little Spreckelses." After lamenting in similar fashion the mistreatment of the oil, wool, beef, and baking trusts, the satirist provides a Bumblean explanation of the public outcry which has prompted the government to action: "It's plain to me that somebody has been giving the people too much meat to eat and it has made them cocky. I'll say this much though – It wasn't Mr. Swift and Mr. Armour. They did their best to prevent gorging."

In its monthly Dickens bibliography during these years, the *Dickensian* listed an increasing number of such modernizations, sequels, and parodies of the *Carol* with titles like "The New Christmas Carol," "Scrooge Up to Date," or "A Modern Scrooge." While Dickensians liked the attention such articles gave to Dickens, they were sometimes divided about the kind of attention the articles brought. A dramatic parody by Mrs. Alfred Mond, *A Message from the Forties; being a Story of Protection adapted from* A Christmas Carol *by Charles Dickens* (1909),[15] prompted them to formal debate. The play turned the story into a polemic for free trade in which the ghost of Richard Cobden converts from a protectionist into a tariff reformer a modern Scrooge who opposes free trade because he can see no benefits to his business. Two members of the Dickens Fellowship squared off in the *Dickensian*. One approved the play because it attempted to alleviate the sufferings of the poor as the original story had done; his opponent attacked it because it promoted laissez-faire economics which Dickens had consistently opposed.[16]

But the debate was beside the point, at least from a Dickensian point of view. For none of these parodies attempted to say anything new about Dickens or about the *Carol*. They began with an arrested memory of the story, a simplified framework inherited from childhood, on which they hung their adult concerns. William Dean Howells argued that the same childish version of the *Carol* was the model for the many Christmas stories published in popular magazines. Their unreality derived, he suggested, from imitating the "imperfect art of [Dickens'] time."[17]

From his adult perspective in 1891, Howells claimed the Dickens *Christmas Books* had lost "the preternatural virtue they once had" and appeared as a mere "child's-play, in which the wholesome allegiance to life was lost." By the realistic standards that held sway at the turn of the century, Dickens' stories had become "monstrosities." Howells argued that the whole system of belief that gave them credence in an earlier time had disappeared. "People always knew that character is not changed by a dream in a series of tableaux; that a ghost cannot do much towards reforming an inordinately selfish person; that a life cannot be turned white, like a head of hair, in a single night, by the most allegorical apparition; . . . and gradually they ceased to believe that there was virtue in these devices and appliances." For a modernist generation who found the crucifixion, in Shaw's caricaturization, too dramatic to be true, Scrooge's fantastic conversion was beyond belief.

James Joyce also associated Dickens with childishness in "Clay," a story in *Dubliners* (1914) in which he parodied the style of *A Christmas Carol* to reveal the gulf between simplitic Victorian optimism and the pain of modern life. Maria, the story's spinster protagonist, leaves the laundry where she works to celebrate All Hallows' Eve with her family. Although she loses the plum cake she buys for the children, has practical jokes played on her at the party, is laughed at by her drunken brother, and gets the prayer book rather than the ring in the games (symbolizing that she will go into a convent rather than marry), Maria does not become consciously aware that the whole evening should undermine her unspoken belief that "every one was so fond of Maria."[18] Angus Easson has shown how the discontinuity between the Dickensian style and the substance of the story reveals "the double vision of the writer, who gives a surface reality and then points, by implication, beneath that surface to a view of the true nature of Maria's character."[19] Joyce's double vision mirrors that of his time. It celebrates the childish simplicity of Maria's worldview and at the same time recognizes its impossibility in the present – even for Maria. By the end of the story the adult Maria is at least subconsciously aware that her childish Dickensian optimism is a fairy tale.

Maria is, in a sense, a Victorian child who has lived beyond her time. The children of the new generation tease to the edges of her consciousness the painful awareness that the optimistic myths by which she lives no longer hold meaning for her life. And her brother's tears at the end of the story express his pain in seeing her loss of innocence and knowing the taint of his own modernity. "Clay" is a tough-minded *Peter Pan*, an adult version of a children's story repeated in various guises in the golden age of children's literature at the turn of the century. As a tale of childhood memory in the minds of the adults of the period, the Carol became one of these stories, retold to celebrate the golden years of childhood and to mark their passing.

When the *Strand Magazine* in 1911 proposed celebrating Christmas with a Dickens children's party, they suppressed the connection between Christmas and Easter, between Christmas Present and Christmas Yet-to-Come, so central in Dickens' understanding of the holiday. "This is the season of parties," the magazine announced, "the season of happiness, of good cheer, of merriment – of Dickens. It is the season, *par excellence*, of good children, of happy children, of merry children – why not of Dickens children?"[20] After proposing costumes for childish versions of Marley, Tiny Tim, and Scrooge, as well as other Dickens characters, they quoted the passage describing blindman's buff and the other games at Fred's party as the model for the children festivities. The game of blindman's buff replaced Fezziwig's ball in the illustrations of the period as the archetypal Christmas celebration in the book. Nearly every illustrator depicted Topper chasing the plump sister as they celebrated the holiday by becoming children again (fig. 44; see also fig. 32).

The narrator's comment as he describes Fred's party became the central text in the *Carol* as children's story. In the midst of the games, he remarks: "It is good to be children sometimes, and never better than at Christmas, when its mighty Founder was a child himself!" (*CB*, 53). Nearly all the articles about the Dickens Christmas quoted this passage; text editions set it for schoolchildren to memorize; and Dickens' daughter Mamie, writing in the *Ladies' Home Journal*, chose it as the central message of the story.[21] Victorian readers would have singled out as the key passage Fred's speech about Christmas as a time when we think of those beneath us "as fellow passengers to the grave." But the social gospel that informed the Victorian Carol had been displaced by the gospel of childish gaiety.

The dimensions of this shift in sensibility can be measured in the changing response to this passage over the years. In 1844 the *Christian Remembrancer* implied that it bordered on blasphemy: "[Dickens] has, how-

Figure 44. Topper's triumph in C. E. Brock's 1905 picture of adults playing children's games.

ever, thought fit to make an attempt at a religious allusion here and there, one at least of which could well have been spared – that occasioned by some of his grown-up characters playing at blind-man's buff, and forfeits, on which he says, 'It is good to be children sometimes, and never better than at Christmas, when its mighty founder was a Child Himself.' We do not believe that Mr. Dickens is aware of the extreme irreverence of this way of speaking; but we are mistaken if numbers of his readers will not be pained by it; and we feel bold to assure him, that his expunging, or altering, the sentence in his next edition, will give general satisfaction."[22] Even early-Victorian readers who did not have religious scruples about the passage might have found it vulgar or socially inappropriate. Thomas Hervey, in 1837, lamented the passing of the childish pranks and games of the old Christmas in his modern time "when all fellows are walking about the world with telescopes in their hands and quadrants in their pockets." The scientific spirit represented by these instruments ran counter to childish celebration and repressed infantile merrymaking. Hervey was philosophical about the change. "The great wisdom of the world is, we presume, one of the natural consequences of its advancing age; and though we are quite conscious that some of its former pranks would be very unbecoming, now that it is getting into years, . . . yet we are by no means sure that we should not have been well content to have cast our lot in the days when it was somewhat younger."[23] By 1907 the religious scruples of the *Remembrancer* had been forgotten and Victorian seemliness had become an archaism. Articles on the Dickens Christmas fondly recalled Dickens' own childish exuberance in celebrating the holiday when even the Founder had become a child. And G. K. Chesterton attributed the power of Dickens' story to its childishness. "Everybody is happy," he claimed, "because nobody is dignified."[24]

Tiny Tim holds a central place in the children's Carol, but he is no longer the Christ child of the Victorians. In the change that came over children's literature during the last quarter of the nineteenth century, Bunyan's *The Pilgrim's Progress,* which had held its position for nearly two hundred years as the most popular story for children, was displaced by *Alice in Wonderland.*[25] Similarly, to go through the looking glass into the modern age, Tiny Tim had to escape the Victorian nursery where he was defined by his relation to the patriarchy – to Bob, Scrooge, and, ultimately, God – and enter the golden world of childhood. There his story would be transformed, much as Huck Finn transformed *The Pilgrim's Progress* into a story "about a man that left his family it didn't say why."[26] Then, with the Darling children from Barrie's *Peter Pan* (1904), Tim could leave his Victorian home without saying why and go to the Neverland to play eternally at children's games.

The crucial question became whether Tiny Tim could survive this transformation from Victorian to modern. Would he, like Peter Pan or Christopher Robin, emerge as the fantasy-master of an imaginary arcadia? Or, like the works of Dickens that had been read so avidly during the Victorian childhood, would he die and be forgotten when it came time to put away childish things? For those in the golden age of childhood who could not join Peter Pan and believe in fairyland, Tiny Tim did indeed die.

George Gissing represents one version of this adult worldview. Writing in 1898 to challenge a critic who described Dickens' characters as types, Gissing declared that they were "not abstractions, but men and women of such loud peculiarities, so aggressively individual in mind and form, in voice and habit, that they for ever proclaim themselves the children of a certain country, of a certain time, of a certain rank. Clothed abstractions do not take hold upon the imagination and the memory as these people of Dickens did from the day of their coming to life."[27] His insistence on the realism of Dickens' characters and their social contexts leads him to contradict Dickens on the question of Tiny Tim's mortality: "Tiny Tim serves his admirable purpose in a book which no one can bear to criticize; we know that he *did* die, but in his little lifetime he has softened many a heart."[28] As a social realist, Gissing knew that Tim and children like him were the inevitable victims of economic oppression. He understood Dickens' social criticism and reformism, but he could not accept the fantastic elements in the story. Denying the Christmas miracle of Scrooge's conversion and Tim's rebirth, he made the story into a social document. But without the power of transformation, the Carol could not enter the Neverland.

Gissing and the realists killed Tim from a lack of sympathy for the miraculous dimension of the story; the sentimentalists killed him out of kindness. James Whitcomb Riley, the "Hoosier Poet" who modeled his career on that of Dickens, provides the instructive example. Riley (1849–1916) began as a journalist and newspaper poet and went on to become one of the most popular public readers in the final decades of the nineteenth century. His books were standard gifts for Christmas giving, a holiday he celebrated in many of his poems and tales. An early Christmas story, "The Boss Girl" (1885), a conscious imitation of Dickens, reveals Riley's idea of his mentor's work.[29] The story describes a boy who cadges money from some businessmen, including the narrator, with the line that he needs just eighty-five cents to buy a shoe-shine kit. When he looks further into the boy's situation, the narrator discovers that he is really getting the money to support an alcoholic father and a dying sister. Visiting the family on Christmas Day, the narrator learns that the boy has saved all his money to buy presents for his sister, but as soon as she opens the presents she dies. The tale's depressing urban setting, its sentimental melodrama, and the heart-rending self-sacrifice of the urchin seemed to Riley Dickensian ingredients for a moving Christmas story. But working in prose and with an unfamiliar urban subject matter, Riley's tale achieves only a distanced and condescending pity. He cannot share Scrooge's transforming joy.

Riley's accustomed medium was verse, his familiar milieux the countryside and the frontier town. In one of his most popular platform pieces, the dialect poem "Dot Leedle Boy" (1876), a German immigrant tells in broken English of the death of his child on Christmas Eve.

> I told you, friends – dot's someding,
> Der last time dot he speak
> Und say, *"Goot-by, Kriss Kringle!"*
> – dot make me feel so veak
> I yoost kneel down and drimble,
> Und bur-sed out a-gryin',
> *"Mein Gott, mein Gott in Himmel! –*
> *Dot leedle boy of mine!"*[30]

The "realism" of the dialect mirrors the speaker's difficulty in verbalizing the rending emotions he feels and engenders condescending pity in reader and writer for this inarticulate spokesman of human feeling. The immigrant, like the child, proves an effective vehicle for a generalized and inchoate sentimental appeal, but he lacks the power to change reality with language or imagination.

In the later years of his life, Riley so identified with Dickens, and particularly with the *Carol,* that he closed his letters with the valediction "God bless us Every One."[31] His poem on Tiny Tim, used as the epigraph for the collection of stories that included "The Boss Girl," reduced the *Carol* to a sentimental myth telling of God stilling the heavenly chorus of angels so that he could hear the child's blessing. Though Riley sought to re-create the feeling of the *Carol,* his simplified version of Dickens imprisoned his characters as victims of a paralyzing pathos. Neither the shoe-shine boy nor the German immigrant has Scrooge's power to change his life and miraculously make Christmas happen. Just under the surface of Riley's sentiment is despair. His poetic myth of Tiny Tim's prayer leaves unstated the recognition he shares with hard-headed realists like Gissing that Tiny Tim has indeed died.

Both Riley and Gissing maintain an adult, and essentially Victorian, perspective on the story. Tim as Christ child was related to the children in Victorian Evangelical novels who, "initially converted by some God-fearing adult, . . . go on to convert other people by a mixture of winsomeness, piety, and pathos."[32] Freed from this Bunyanesque role later in the century, these children go on to become what Humphrey Carpenter has called the type of "the Beautiful Child," a figure like Little Lord Fauntleroy who "is distinguished by his naivete (especially in contact with the adult world), by an almost heavenly innocence (which can

Figures 45, 46. Two versions of Tiny Tim as "the Beautiful Child": left, *by Harold Copping for a volume of* Children's Stories from Dickens *(1911):* right, *by A. C. Michael for an illustrated edition of the* Carol *(1911).*

spill over into sheer idiocy), and, of course, by radiant good looks."[33] Tiny Tim's relatively insignificant and passive role in the original story made him a good candidate for treatment as a Beautiful Child late in the century. In illustrations for the many children's editions produced at the time, Tim is depicted from this sentimentalizing perspective. To the icon of Tim riding home from church on his "blood horse," modern illustrators added another that might be entitled "God Bless Us, Every One" (figs. 45, 46). These illustrations show Tim alone. Sometimes he is making his famous prayer. More often the invocation is simply a caption to an idealized rendering of the Beautiful Child. In a world darkened by Hardyan despair and poised on the brink of World War I, Tim's prayer articulated an adult wish to recover the innocoence of the lost childhood.

But to do that they would have to do more than imagine Tim as the Beautiful Child. They would have to imagine the Carol as a children's story that could change the world. Humphrey Carpenter has commented that "adult fiction sets out to portray and explain the world as it really is; books for children present it as it should be."[34] The Tim of the children's story is no longer the crippled child martyr. In the Neverland of the world as it should be, he is the child who saves himself by saving Scrooge.

Although Dickens did not write the *Carol* for children, its point of view resembles that in many of the children's books of the golden age. U. C. Knoepflmacher has proposed that these children's stories contain a double point of view.[35] They return through memory to the past to recapture the innocence of the child's consciousness, but they also retain the ironic distance of the adult. The tension between the perspectives of innocence and experience gives these stories their characteristic tone, an ambivalence between a celebration of children's games and an awareness of their inevitable end.

E. Nesbit remarked that "there is only one way of understanding children; they cannot be understood by imagination, or observation, nor even by love. They can only be understood by memory. . . . I was a child once myself, and by some fortunate chance I remember exactly how I used to feel and think about things."[36] Memory has an important thematic role in the *Carol,* particularly in Stave 2, but the memories are usually colored by an adult sense of regret. Even Tiny Tim is seen largely from a sentimental adult perspective, approaching the child's point of view, perhaps, only in the idealized picture of the father-son relationship in Stave 3. The child's consciousness described by E. Nesbit appears most notably in the tableaux of Scrooge's schooldays, where he recalls his ecstasy over *Robinson Crusoe* and *The Arabian Nights* or his excitement when Fan came to fetch him from school. The child's point of view is also present in the narrator's insistence on the literal truth of Scrooge's adventures. When he admonishes the reader, "There is no doubt that Marley was dead. This must be distinctly understood, or nothing wonderful can come of the story I am going to relate" (*CB*, 7), he sounds very much like the eight-year-old narrator in Dickens' later children's book, *A Holiday Romance* (1868), who begins by telling his readers: "This beginning-part is not made out of anybody's head, you know. It's real. You must believe this beginning-part more than what comes after, else you won't understand how what comes after came to be written. You must believe it all . . ." (*RP*, 691). The style of the later work, written for American children twenty-five years after the *Carol*, may be closer to that of Thomas Bailey Aldrich in *The Story of a Bad Boy* (1870) or of Mark Twain in *Huckleberry Finn* (1884–85) than to that of the *Carol*. But the substance of the two beginnings is similar. Both promise the truth of the child who accepts the marvelous literally.

The dominant point of view in the *Carol*, however, is that of an adult. When the narrator speculates on the phrase "dead as a doornail" or discusses Hamlet's father, he facetiously addresses an adult reader. His distance from childhood prompts irony or idealizing sentiment more often than empathy with the child's perspective. The adult voice of experience most poignantly enters the story in the narrator's frustrated wish to join Belle's frolicking children as they tease their older sister on Christmas Eve. His longing to share their happiness is coupled with the recognition that only an adult can know that longing. "I should have liked, I do confess," he concludes, "to have had the highest license of a child, and yet to have been man enough to know its value" (*CB*, 36). Loneliness, loss, and pain color many of the Christmases in the *Carol*. It is as often the season of death as the season of innocent joy. Remembering the loss of Belle, the deaths of Marley, Fan, and, perhaps, Dick Wilkins, and foretelling the deaths of Tiny Tim and Scrooge, the narrator most often sees Christmas through darkened adult eyes.[37]

To lighten the dark *Carol* into a children's book, the adaptors of the early twentieth century emphasized the children and the children's games in the story. Scrooge's childhood, the Cratchit scenes, Belle's family, and Scrooge's conversation with the boy who announces Christmas Day at the end – all of the scenes involving children – gained new prominence in the illustrations. Although no earlier artist had attempted any part of

Figure 47. Arthur Rackham's treatment of Belle's children crowding around the porter to get their Christmas presents (1915).

the scene of Belle's Christmas – the final tableau of Christmas Past, for example – several of the illustrators in the first two decades of the twentieth century gave it prominent representation. Arthur Rackham devoted two of his twelve color illustrations to it, one showing Belle's children frolicking around her, the other depicting the arrival of the porter with the children's Christmas presents (fig. 47).

In its focus on present-giving, Belle's Christmas was also a more modern celebration than many others in the book. Dickens had not considered present-giving central to the Christmas festival. His grandson reported that he never gave presents outside the family circle and the family ritual of present-giving involved taking the children on an annual Christmas Eve visit to a toy store and allowing them to choose whatever they wished.[38] His celebration centered instead on the Christmas feast. When he adapted the story for the readings, the one section he left virtually intact – for him the crucial celebration in the tale – was the Cratchits' Christmas dinner. The prominence given by modern illustrators to the passing moment of present-giving in the *Carol* made the Dickens Christmas into something closer to the children's holiday of the early twentieth century.

The idealizing illustrations that augmented the child's point of view also heightened the tension in the explicit narration of the *Carol* between the child's Christmas of celebratory games and the adult awareness of childhood's end. This tension surfaces after Scrooge's conversion, when the narrator interrupts the story to assure the reader that Tim did not die: "To Tiny Tim, who did *not* die, he [Scrooge] was a second father" (p. 76). The same tension prompted James Barrie to break the dramatic illusion in *Peter Pan* (1904). After Tinker Bell takes poison, Peter steps to the front of the stage and addresses the audience directly: "She says – she says she thinks she could get well again if children believed in fairies! . . . Do you believe in fairies? Say quick that you believe! If you do believe, clap your hands! . . . Oh, thank you, thank you, thank you!"[39] Peter's theatrics and the *Carol* narrator's assurances were not sufficient to convince all their adult audience that Tim and Tinker Bell could be saved. Even sympathetic adults like Gissing and Riley were convinced that Tim did die. But if he was to be saved, the child's perspective implicit in the story needed to triumph over adult skepticism embedded in its narration.

On the tree of childhood memory described in Dickens' 1850 essay "A Christmas Tree," fairy tales hold a place as important as the Bible story. Among its transformations, the tree not only recalls the life of Jesus, "the very tree itself changes, and becomes a bean-stalk – the marvellous bean-stalk up which Jack climbed to the Giant's house. And now, those dreadfully interesting, double-headed giants, with their clubs over their shoulders, begin to stride along the boughs in a perfect throng, dragging knights and ladies home for dinner by the hair of their heads. . . . I debate within myself whether there was more than one Jack (which I am loth to believe possible), or only one genuine original admirable Jack, who

Jack brings the Giant prisoner to King Alfred.

achieved all the recorded exploits" (*CS*, 7). Dickens implicitly answers this question in another essay for *Household Words*, "Where We Stopped Growing" (1853), in which he imagines himself as the one original Jack. Along with *Robinson Crusoe*, *Don Quixote*, and *The Arabian Nights*, he includes the tales of Jack as things he never put behind him: "We have never outgrown the putting to ourselves of this supposititious case: whether if we, with a large company of brothers and sisters, had been put in his (by which we mean, of course, in Jack's) trying situation, we should have had the courage and the presence of mind to take the golden crowns (which it seems they always wore as night caps) off the heads of the giant's children as they lay a-bed, and put them on our own family; thus causing our teacherous host to battle his own offspring and spare us" (*MP*, 1:339). The Darling children and Peter Pan have played out this childhood fantasy on the stage nearly every Christmas since 1904. Similarly, Dickens, by applauding a fairyland he never outgrew, affirmed his belief that the Jack of the child's imagination could conquer the giants of adult oppression (fig. 48) just as Peter Pan routs Captain Hook.

Figure 48. George Cruikshank's Jack (opposite) presents the giant he has captured to King Alfred in this illustration from The Cruikshank Fairy-Book *(1853). Although Dickens praised these illustrations by his old friend and collaborator, he objected to Cruikshank's didactic alterations preaching temperance and other causes in the fairy tales that accompanied the illustrations. Dickens vehemently expressed his opinion in "Frauds on the Fairies" in* Household Words *(1853), an essay that contributed to the estrangement of the two old friends.*

The link between Peter Pan, Tiny Tim, Scrooge, and Jack is the children's story. It enters the *Carol* in the account of Scrooge's childhood reading in Stave 2. In a vignette ignored by most Victorian adaptors, Scrooge sees himself as a child left to spend the holiday alone at school:

> At one of these [desks] a lonely boy was reading near a feeble fire; and Scrooge sat down upon a form, and wept to see his poor forgotten self as he had used to be. . . .
>
> The Spirit touched him on the arm, and pointed to his younger self, intent upon his reading. Suddenly a man, in foreign garments: wonderfully real and distinct to look at: stood outside the window, with an ax stuck in his belt, and leading by the bridle an ass laden with wood.
>
> "Why, it's Ali Baba!" Scrooge exclaimed in ecstasy. "It's dear old honest Ali Baba! Yes, yes, I know! One Christmas time, when yonder solitary child was left here all alone, he *did* come, for the first time, just like that. Poor boy! And Valentine," said Scrooge, "and his wild brother Orson; there they go! And what's his name, who was put down in his drawers, asleep, at the Gate of Damascus; don't you see him! And the Sultan's Groom turned upside down by the Genii; there he is upon his head! Serve him right. I'm glad of it. What business had *he* to be married to the Princess!"
>
> To hear Scrooge expending all the earnestness of his nature on such subjects, in a most extraordinary voice between laughing and

crying, and to see his heightened and excited face; would have been a surprise to his business friends in the city, indeed.

"There's the Parrot!" cried Scrooge. "Green body and yellow tail, with a thing like a lettuce growing out of the top of his head; there he is! Poor Robin Crusoe, he called him, when he came home again after sailing around the island. 'Poor Robin Crusoe, where have you been, Robin Crusoe?' The man thought he was dreaming, but he wasn't. It was the Parrot, you know. There goes Friday, running for his life to the little creek! Halloa! Hoop! Halloo!" [*CB*, 27–28]

Clearly Scrooge survived loneliness and neglect through the companionship of children's books and the imaginative life they engendered. Reading provided "ecstasy" in what was otherwise a melancholy childhood. Harry Stone has shown that reading was just as important to Dickens himself, a sickly child who substituted books for children's games: "Dickens was convinced that the literature he read as a child had been crucial to his imagination. He was equally certain that the litrature he read as a youth prevented him from perishing. The literature of childhood was the source of all his 'early imaginations'; the literature of youth 'kept alive my fancy, my hope of something beyond that place and time.' At the center of the latter period was the blacking warehouse, and Dickens literally believed that reading, and the imagination nurtured by that reading, allowed him – but only barely allowed him – to survive."[40] Although Dickens' contemporaries were not attuned to the importance he attached to childhood reading, the readers at the turn of the century were. Nearly every illustrator included a rendering of the child Scrooge surrounded by the heroes of his books (fig. 49). At a time when children's reading had become much more widespread and when children were encouraged to read the tales of adventure and imagination that Dickens loved rather than the instructive tracts he deplored, they knew that even a crippled child could slay giants in the Neverland of the imagination.

It is not surprising that *Robinson Crusoe* (1719) holds so important a place in Scrooge's memories, in Dickens' accounts of his own reading, or in the history of children's literature, for Crusoe alone on his island is like the child alone with his books. Freed from the constraints of society and the adult world, he could live in a child's garden of the imagination, where he could slay giants, defeat pirates, or rule oriental kingdoms. Linking himself as a child reading with Tiny Tim who "gets thoughtful, sitting by himself so much, and thinks the strangest things you ever heard" (p. 45), Scrooge recovers the child's ability to remake the world in imagination. Tim restores to Scrooge the power to kill giants and believe in fairyland.

Figure 49. George Alfred Williams depicts the two Scrooges sharing the ecstasy of childhood reading as they watch Ali Baba pass the window of the lonely schoolroom (1905).

The boy's magical connection with Scrooge comes closest to the surface in the scene following Tim's oft-quoted blessing. The family go on, with some misgivings, to toast Scrooge as the founder of their feast. "Tiny Tim drank it last of all, but he didn't care twopence for it. Scrooge was the Ogre of the family. The mention of his name cast a dark shadow on the party. . . . After it had passed away, they were ten times merrier than before, from the mere relief of Scrooge the Baleful being done with" (p. 48). The narration here is close to the child's point of view, casting Scrooge in his fairy-tale role and playing on the wish of the fairy tale that the Ogre be "done with." We do not know what spells Tiny Tim may be wishing on his antagonist as the family goes on with their Christmas games, but we do know that "Scrooge had his eye upon them, and especially on Tiny Tim, until the last" (p. 49).

Instead of the physical derring-do that Jack and Peter Pan use to defeat their giants, Tiny Tim employs the psychological resources of the imaginative child. He captures the ogre's obsessive attention by mirroring Scrooge's life in his own. In Christmas Present he reminds Scrooge of his own lonely childhood and of the child within that he has repressed and crippled. Tim's one expressed wish, "that he hoped the people saw him . . . because he was a cripple, and it might be pleasant to them to remember upon Christmas Day, who made lame beggars walk, and blind men see" (p. 45), carries for Scrooge a double message. He is reminded not only of Jesus, but also of his own ogreish power either to cripple the child or to enable him to walk again. When Tim dies in Christmas Yet-to-Come, Scrooge also dies. Scrooge's survival is inexorably linked with Tim's, and his ultimate choice to become a second father to the boy saves both of them. In this adult fairy tale, psychology and imagination transform the Baleful Ogre into the Fairy Godfather.

If Tim imagines himself as the Jack of fairy tale, it may be as a figure like the tiny boy in Oscar Wilde's "The Selfish Giant" (1888). This story could be considered a fairy-tale transmutation of the Carol in which "Tim" is both the Victorian Christ child and the Jack of fairyland. When the giant bars his garden to all trespassers to keep out the children who play there, the garden is thrust into perpetual winter. The giant, too, is wintry like his garden, until one day he sees a child there too small to climb into one of the trees, "and the Giant's heart melted as he looked out. 'How selfish I have been!' he said; 'now I know why the Spring will not come here. I will put the poor little boy on the top of the tree, . . . and my garden shall be the children's playground for ever and ever.'"[41] When he does so, the garden blooms again and children play there as before. But the tiny child disappears and the giant longs for his return. After many years, when the giant is "old and feeble," the child comes back and the giant joyfully runs out to greet him:

> And when he came quite close his face grew red with anger, and he said, "Who hath dared to wound thee?" For on the palms of the child's hands were the prints of two nails, and the prints of two nails were on the little feet.

But the child assures the giant that they are "the wounds of Love," and he tells him:

> "You let me play once in your garden, you shall come with me to my garden, which is Paradise!"
>
> And when the children ran in that afternoon, they found the Giant lying dead under the tree, all covered with white blossoms.

Although Wilde was writing for children, his ending, focusing on the giant rather than on the child, expresses an adult perspective on the story. The giant's end, like the deaths of Scrooge and Tiny Tim in Christmas Yet-to-Come, raises adult questions about death and the meaning of life. These deaths are not simply another children's game as death is to Peter Pan, who exclaims, "To die will be an awfully big adventure" (p. 545). Tiny Tim's suffering, death, and rebirth represent more than a child's fantasy of a way to command adult attention. They are the pattern for Scrooge's life. They also become the pattern for Dickens' expressed intent in the *Christmas Books* of taking "old nursery tales" and "giving them a higher form."[42]

This higher form emerges from the dialectic between child and adult perspectives that underlies the structure of the children's books. Like many children's stories, *A Christmas Carol* is a framed tale, in which a "real" or "adult" world encloses a world of fantasy and dreams. The rules of the frame are adult rules, of Scrooge as businessman or of the patriarchal Mr. Darling. But in the enclosed story the rules change. Peter Pan and the Christmas spirits fly off in a dream logic where the constraints of the adult world no longer apply. Dickens signals the transition from frame to tale with the conventional marker, "Once upon a time – of all the good days in the year, on Christmas Eve – old Scrooge sat busy in his counting house" (*CB*, 8). If this transition has the effect of enclosing Scrooge's encounters with the spirits into a "story," it also gives Scrooge an independent reality as the defining figure in the frame outside the story. The closing transition in the *Carol* is not so clearly marked as, for example, the Darling children's return home from the Neverland. Does Scrooge reenter the world when he awakens, or when he opens his window onto the street, or in the narrator's final summary, or not at all? This ambiguity may indicate an important difference between the *Carol* and the children's books of the golden age.

The issue is in part a theological one. Gillian Avery has suggested that the belief in fairyland promoted by *Peter Pan* and the other children's books offered a faith to replace beliefs lost in the later nineteenth century: "There was during these years a yearning in those who wrote for children to present them with some sort of faith to replace the Christian teaching which had been implicit in Victorian books . . . and which had become unfashionable. . . . They also recognized that it is difficult to preach an ethnic convincingly in the absence of a faith, and so fairies became the new guardian angels."[43]

Following Avery's lead, Humphrey Carpenter similarly characterized *Peter Pan* as "an alternative religion."[44] But in the end this new religion failed to liberate its believers. When the Darling children return from the Neverland, Peter is left outside the window. "No one is going to catch me, lady, and make me a man," he asserts to Mrs. Darling, "I want always to be a little boy and to have fun" (p. 574). Then he returns to the land of make-believe while Wendy and the Darling boys grow up and accept adult responsibilities. They have had their fling, but at childhood's end they must leave Peter behind, reducing their visits to one a year when Wendy

Figures 50, 51. In Peter Pan, *flying separates child from adult, for the ability to fly is lost when adult responsibilities replace the belief in fairyland. Above, an adult Wendy watches her infant daughter, tutored by Peter, fly around the bedroom in a 1911 illustration for* Peter and Wendy *by F. D. Bedford, who later illustrated a children's* Carol *(1923). Scrooge must also fly with the spirits to recover the truths of childhood, but the truths he rediscovers are not to be given up at childhood's end. The adult truths that give Dickens' nursery tale its "higher form" are suggested in the contrast between Arthur Rackham's tormented flying phantoms for the* Carol *(1915, below) and the floating innocents from* Peter Pan.

spends her holiday doing Peter's spring cleaning. Their adult world has not been significantly changed by the encounter with fairyland. The window between their bedroom and the Neverland remains closed and locked.

Scrooge, on the other hand, opens the window on Christmas morning to bring together the truths of the inner dream world and the realities of the streets (figs. 50, 51). The transition back to the frame is unneeded because the two worlds have become one. Dickens had no doubt that the transformation of the ogre in fairyland could also be the conversion of the hard-hearted man in reality. As tale and frame merge at the end of the *Carol*, the truths of childhood reform the adult, and the stories of Jack and Jesus come together on Dickens' Christmas tree.

In the children's book, Scrooge as the ogre transformed into benevolent godfather returned to the center of the story. The Cratchits, who had centered the tale for many Victorian readers as representatives of the urban family or as a displaced version of the Holy Family, moved to the periphery. In his 1906 school edition, Edmund Broadus suggested that the Cratchits may be too prominent in the text when he asked students to consider whether "too much attention [is] given to the Cratchits in Stave Three – so much as to detract from the interest in the main story? What intrinsic justification is there for such attention to them?"[45] Even though he seemed to expect a negative answer, he raised a question that would not have been asked thirty years earlier.

Scrooge is also central in the theatrical versions of the period. J. C. Buckstone's *Scrooge* (1901) replaced Stirling's *A Christmas Carol* as the standard dramatic adaptation. The leading actors of the day, especially Bransby Williams and Seymour Hicks, were famous for their portrayals of the miser. F. Dubre-Fawcett has described Hicks's performance as particularly forceful: "Instead of the doddering senility so often portrayed in the first scene of the play, Hicks invested the character with startling aggressiveness, waspish and intolerant to the last degree."[46] So strong were these performances that both Williams and Hicks took their productions from the stage into the music hall, where they played one-man versions of the *Carol* as the story of Scrooge. Edwin Charles, who objected to the desecration of Dickens' story in the music hall, attacked these vaudeville versions for giving too much prominence to Scrooge and neglecting "Tiny Tim, the pivot on which the conversion of Scrooge turns."[47]

As the pivot moved from the Cratchit family to Scrooge, the story emphasized personal, rather than social, change. In the Victorian Carol, Tim is Bob's son. Crippled by Scrooge's exploitation of his father, the child reveals the power of a selfish economic system that exploits society's weakest members. As the idealized child of the early-modern Carol, Tiny Tim becomes a victim of an ogre's denial of Christmas. He is the child within Scrooge repressed by Scrooge's negativity. For this "personalized" Scrooge, Bob Cratchit has little importance. Scrooge is changed by seeing himself, particularly himself as a child, not by confronting the social consequences of his behavior. Even Tiny Tim, the pivot of the tale, becomes more important as a projection of Scrooge than as a character in his own right.

The personalized Scrooge informs W. Pett Ridge's "New Christmas Carol" (1901), where he appears as Mr. Broadbent, a latter-day Bounderby who believes he has "nobody to thank but himself for his success."[48] At a reading of the *Carol*, he complains: "These things don't happen. . . . A man can't change at that age. He has fixed and settled himself by that time." But the reading recalls his childhood love of Dickens and introduces him to an inventor who has created a time machine that can take him back to his past. Broadbent revisits three Christmases where accidents caused his life to take a course different from the one he would have chosen. The remembrance of these Christmases makes him recognize that there are forces working in his life beyond his control. Humbled by this "science-fiction" dream-vision, he reconciles himself with his sister and her family and celebrates Christmas with them.

Appearing six years after H. G. Wells's *The Time Machine*, this up-to-date Carol personalizes Dickens' story. Broadbent has a misguided perspective on reality, a kind of existential dishonesty that causes him to lie about his life. His bad faith results in personal delusions, especially in the delusion that he is wholly responsible for his own success. Broadbent learns that he has forgotten his personal history; he does not learn, even though he is an industrialist, that he is responsible for social oppression. His conversion is effected by revisiting his past, not by confronting the present; it leads to a reunion with his family, not to changed relations with the Cratchits. Like the children's stories that called up nostalgic visions of childhood, the "New Christmas Carol" did not reform the present. It restored the past.

As a version of the *Carol,* Ridge's parody reduces the original to a three-stave story. Christmas Present and Christmas Yet-to-Come are deleted, and the pivot of Scrooge's conversion, Tiny Tim, who appears only in Staves 3 and 4 of the original, loses his structural importance in the tale. In the original tale Scrooge is restored to feeling by revisiting his past, so that he can empathize with Tiny Tim and recognize the oppressive realities of the present. His empathy with the oppressed children of Christmas Present, the urchins Ignorance and Want, extends his personal suffering to broader social concern. By omitting Staves 3 and 4, Ridge opts for the fantasy *Carol* where a time machine and personal memory, not social reality, transform Broadbent from selfish ogre into kind uncle.

Scrooge focuses the fairy tale, but he is a Scrooge who avoids the reality principle. His Christmas Present is not that of Stave 3. It is that of the final stave, when the curmudgeon becomes a child again, awakening "merry as a schoolboy [and] . . . quite a baby" (pp. 71–72) to discover that he has not missed Christmas. The emphasis in the fairy-tale version is that in R. L. Stewart's 1907 summary of the tale:

> In reading it one follows Scrooge—nay, one verily becomes Scrooge himself: feels with him the terrible power his ghostly visitants have over him, the softening influences of the various scenes through which he passes, the very pangs that are caused by the ghost's rebukes. One feels, too, how natural and how delightful it is when he is ultimately reclaimed, and when, in the first excitement of his new disposition, he jumps out of his bed, and hastily and confusedly putting on his clothes, orders the turkey for poor Bob Cratchit; nor can one help sharing the ecstatic delight with which he recompenses the boy and pays the "cab" to Bob's humble dwelling in Camden Town. One can easily believe that this sudden change in Scrooge's character is really the outburst of Dickens' own affection for Christmas.[49]

Stave 5, the shortest stave in the original, has become the key to the story, the source of almost all the detail in Stewart's description.

The first two sound recordings of the *Carol*, Bransby Williams's *The Awakening of Scrooge* (1905) and Albert Whelan's *Scrooge's Christmas Morning* (1905), both seem to have concentrated on the reformed Scrooge, encouraged perhaps by the space restrictions of the new medium. The title of one of the silent film versions, *The Right to Be Happy* (1916), similarly suggests an emphasis on Stave 5. The illustrators of the period also celebrated the Scrooge of the final pages. Four of A. I. Keller's eight illustrations for his 1914 edition, for example, depict scenes from the final stave, showing Scrooge buying the turkey, raising Bob's salary, smiling kindness to the people in the street, and knocking on Fred's door to request Christmas dinner (fig. 52). Reading the *Carol* as an idealistic fairy tale, early modern readers often seemed to begin with Stave 5. G. K. Chesterton's surprising characterization of Scrooge expressed a common desire to read the story as wish fulfillment: "Scrooge is not really inhuman at the beginning any more than he is at the end. There is a heartiness in his inhospitable sentiments that is akin to humour

Figure 52. A. I. Keller's 1914 picture of Scrooge arriving at Fred's for Christmas dinner depicts a popular subject in the illustrations of the early twentieth century. It celebrates the restoration of family ties as the crucial outcome of Scrooge's conversion.

and therefore to humanity; he is only a crusty old bachelor, and had (I strongly suspect) given away turkeys secretly all his life."[50]

Since 1843 every generation has had its carolers, people whose lives and works have been shaped by the *Carol.* In Dickens' own day, Thackeray recognized the story as a "blessing" and followed Dickens' lead in writing several Christmas books of his own. In later years Stephen Leacock, Lionel Barrymore, Bransby Williams, Frank Capra, Russell Baker, and even Franklin Roosevelt have been among the prominent carolers. The two most important carolers of the early twentieth century were Harry Furniss and G. K. Chesterton, an artist and a writer who resisted the simplifications that reduced the *Carol* to fairy tale and killed Tiny Tim. Their work affirms the child's Carol without suppressing the darker adult dimensions in its message.

As a caricaturist, Harry Furniss ran counter to the artistic taste of his day. The more established style was that of George Alfred Williams (fig. 53), who argued that Dickens "had suffered much at the hands of a school of caricaturists who saw only the distorted side of his writings without recognizing their more subtle and human phase."[51] He agreed with George Gissing, who thought that later, more realistic artists like Fred Barnard had been the first to do justice to Dickens' work.[52] But Furniss celebrated the caricatures of Cruikshank, Phiz, and Leech in his imitations of their work that appeared in *Punch* and other magazines. His ambitious edition of Dickens (1910), containing over five hundred pictures, is one of the great illustrated editions of the author's work, affirming and modernizing the graphic satire tradition of the original illustrators.

In his eight plates for the *Carol,* Furniss avoids altogether the sentimental scenes of the Cratchit family and Tiny Tim that were so popular with his contemporaries, and none of his plates depicts Stave 5. He concentrates on Scrooge, a gnarled and twisted man whose contorted body articulates his discomfort in the world, and five of the eight illustrations are based on scenes in Stave 1. The montage technique used in several of the pictures, clustering separate images into one illustration, suggests the way in which the text develops Scrooge's character by a series of images and his story by a sequence of tableaux. Juxtaposing the image of the body pinned by a stake of holly through its heart to images of the dramatic action of the story, such as Scrooge's confrontation with the charity solicitors, Furniss renders the point of view and style of the narrative as well as its plot (fig. 54).

The exaggerations of caricature also enable him to depict the simultaneous humor and seriousness of the story, as when he dwarfs Scrooge before an enormous doorway from which the face of Marley seems to be

Figure 53. George Alfred Williams's realistic rendering of Fred greeting his uncle Scrooge (1905).

Figure 54. Harry Furniss links story and style in this montage that illustrates, in part, the passage from Stave 1: "'Out upon merry Christmas! If I could work my will,' said Scrooge, 'every idiot who goes about with "Merry Christmas" on his lips, should be boiled with his own pudding and buried with a stake of holly through his heart!'"

Figure 55. Furniss's caricature exaggerates the amazing doorknocker and captures the humor in the ghost that Dickens' narrator described as surrounded by "a dismal light . . . like a bad lobster in a dark cellar."

Figure 56. Furniss's closing montage for Stave 1 depicts Scrooge turning his back on the madonna of the street, the mother huddled with her child in the doorway, whom the manacled ghost in the white waistcoat is unable to help. The dog slinking away from Scrooge in the lower right may be one of the blind men's dogs who lead their masters out of Scrooge's way when they see him coming down the street.

expanding like a genie released from a bottle (fig. 55). His final illustration for Stave 1 shows a bent and twisted Scrooge turning his back on the world of spirits – on the gentleman in the white waistcoat who, chained to a safe, reenacts the warnings of Marley, and on the huddled mother and child, the nativity of the streets, that Scrooge also refuses to acknowledge (fig. 56). Mixing fairy tale and serious social commentary, Furniss captures the children's story without reducing the *Carol* to sentimentality, and he reawakens the child in the adult reader.

Unfortunately, Furniss did not illustrate Scrooge's Christmas morning. He may have considered his black-and-white satiric art inappropriate for rendering the miser's awakened humanity. He comes closest to representing the sentimental side of the story in the frontispiece of Fezziwig's ball (fig. 57). The familiar scene of the dancers, led by the rotund head couple, is framed with an elaborate border of distorted caricature. At the edge of the picture, peering through this frame, stands Scrooge, analogous to the reader who experiences the tableaux of Scrooge's life through the frame of the narrator's commentary. These Christmas scenes within the frame humanize Scrooge with fellow-feeling, for they give him a life, a sequence of Christmases, not unlike that of the reader. After Scrooge's and the reader's lives are linked by the story, both are drawn back through the frame into the Christmas morning of the final stave. Even though Furniss does not attempt this concluding movement of the story, his frontispiece renders the levels of consciousness in the narrative that make this movement possible. Abjuring sentimental realism and its idealized images of Christmas past, he uses the grotesquerie in the irregular frame to elicit the energy and exaggeration in the enclosed picture, the tension between the two making the whole picture a rendering of present consciousness rather than nostalgic memory. Furniss's *Carol* might be described as a fairy tale for adults.

G. K. Chesterton also tempered the dominant realism of his time. Calling the realistic "adult" literature of his day a "disease,"[53] he celebrated the child and was himself described by Alfred Gardiner, the editor of the *Daily News* for whom he wrote a weekly column for many years, as possessing "the freshness and directness of a child's vision," seeing the world "as a child sees its first rainbow."[54] The *Carol* was formative in Chesterton's consciousness. Beside figuring in his important critical study of Dickens (1906), it reappeared in much of his work, particularly in Christmas columns for the *News*.

In "The Dickensian" (1909), he describes meeting a man on a holiday pilgrimage who is visiting the *David Copperfield* sites in Yarmouth.[55] This Dickensian laments that Daniel Peggotty's boat is not on the beach and

Figure 57. Furniss's frontispiece redoes Fezziwig's ball, the subject of Leech's frontispiece for the original Carol. *But in Furniss's version Scrooge's framing consciousness becomes a dominant element in the composition of the picture and in the vision of Christmas.*

complains that other *Copperfield* places are being destroyed to create a vulgar, modern seaside resort. Visiting the church with him, the narrator recalls the words of the angel at the sepulchre, "Why seek ye the living among the dead? He is not here; he is risen." So he admonishes the Dickensian: "But let us have no antiquarianism about Dickens, for Dickens is not antiquity. Dickens looks not backward, but forward; he might look at our modern mobs with satire, or with fury, but he would look at them. . . . We will not have them [Dickens' novels] all bound up under the title of 'The Old Curiosity Shop.' Rather we will have them all bound up under the title of 'Great Expectations.' Wherever humanity is he would have us face it and make something of it, swallow it with a holy cannibalism, and assimilate it with the digestion of a giant." For the narrator, and for Chesterton, reading Dickens was sacramental. But Chesterton's sacrament entailed a holy cannibalism, not simply swallowing a sugary idea of the past. Chesterton claimed that Dickens did not celebrate a medieval Christmas, or even a Victorian Christmas. He was very different from Irving in his celebration of the holiday. Dickens was a Christmas radical. "In so far as such an institution as Christmas was old," Chesterton asserted, "Dickens would even have tended to despise it."[56]

Rejecting nostalgic versions of both Dickens and Christmas, Chesterton did not affirm modernity for its own sake. He denounced an effete modernism that removed mystery from life, and "aesthetes" who appreciated Christmas with intellectual distance as a holiday of the people, and vegetarians who objected to eating turkey as part of the holiday feast. The "weakmindedness of modernity" implicit in these positions, he thought, turned celebration into cerebration.[57] By removing the cannibalism, modernity removed the mystery. Father Christmas makes the point with Chestertonian concreteness in "The Shop of Ghosts," a newspaper essay in which Dickens and Richard Steele talk with Father Christmas in the guise of a Battersea toyshop owner: "They say that I give people superstitions and make them too visionary; they say I give people sausages and make them too coarse. They say my heavenly parts are too heavenly; they say my earthly parts are too earthly; I don't know what they want, I'm sure."[58]

Intellectuals failed to understand Christmas, Chesterton asserted, because as ritual it "is really much older than thought; it is much simpler and much wilder than thought."[59] Nor could they understand Dickens, for "the mystery of Christmas is . . . identical with the mystery of Dickens. If we ever adequately explain the one we may adequately explain the other."[60] The modernists missed the essential Dickens, Chesterton declared, because with their preference for realistic literature, they were incapable of comprehending "the last of the mythologists," who "in fantasy and exaggeration . . . ritualize[d] something he [could] not express."[61]

At the heart of this Dickens myth are the great mythic characters, larger-than-life figures who, "if he did not always manage to make . . . men, . . . he always managed to make . . . gods."[62] They are static and unchanging. Thus Scrooge articulates the eternal capacity for sin and redemption. When Chesterton suggested that Scrooge had "given away turkeys secretly all his life," he was not denying the heartless taskmaster of the opening stave simply to affirm the popular, avuncular Scrooge of Stave 5. Rather, he was characterizing a mythic Scrooge whose spiritual pride and redeeming benevolence are ever-present and paradoxical parts of the same consciousness. Scrooge is an eternal paradox, a larger-than-life figure transcending the human components of his fictive personality.

In "The Modern Scrooge" (1909), Chesterton creates a latter-day version of this mythic figure.[63] Mr. Vernon-Smith, "of Trinity and the Social Settlement, Tooting," is a "modern and morbid" intellectual who has set out to civilize the urban poor. He condescendingly decides to read the *Carol* to his congregation of charwomen on Christmas Eve, because even though he knows that Dickens is "not literature of a high order, . . . not thoughtful or purposeful literature, [it is] literature quite fitted for charwomen on Christmas Eve." He preaches that Scrooge is out of date, telling the women "with progressive brightness, that a mad wicked old miser like Scrooge would be quite impossible now, but as each of the charwomen had an uncle or a grandfather or a father-in-law who was exactly like Scrooge, his cheerfulness was not shared. Indeed, the lecture as a whole lacked something of his firm and elastic touch." Vernon-Smith's social condescension and spiritual pride are undermined by the resistance of the charwomen, and probably also by the *Carol* that he has been reading to them. He leaves the settlement house unsettled. After he refuses charity to a beggar on principle, he is hit by a snowball in return, and then he finds himself in the midst of a wintry dream landscape. Finally reaching a snowy pinnacle, he sees below him a white world filled with boys leaping and playing. He knows that he must leap into the air and join them, and when he musters the courage to do so, he regains his childhood faith and loses his spiritual pride. In the streets of Tooting he is "taken up for a common drunk, but (if you properly appreciate his conversion) you will realize that he did not mind, since the crime of drunkenness is infinitely less than that of spiritual pride."

Chesterton offered an adult fairy tale, a Dickensian myth, telling truths of fantasy and imagination. "Literature is a luxury," he aphorized, "fiction is a necessity."[64] Though only a newspaper essay, his "Modern Scrooge" is a necessary fiction, a retelling of the myth in which Vernon-Smith/ Scrooge rediscovers in the streets of Tooting the mystery of the *Carol* that others have lost in the music hall or in the altered townscape of Yarmouth. That mystery involves transcending spiritual pride in childhood faith, replacing the wisdom of Trinity with the wisdom of charwomen, and knowing with a child's literalism that there are still men exactly like Scrooge who still fail to recognize themselves as Scrooge. The mystery can be celebrated in a leap of faith from a snowy pinnacle into a world of children's games. But the whole mystery can never be explained. That mystery is, finally, in "the great furnace of real happiness that glows through Scrooge and everything around him; that great furnace, the heart of Dickens."[65] For Chesterton and for all the other carolers, that mighty heart is heating still.

5

Always a Good Man of Business

The Carol between the Wars

And what a slogan Tiny Tim has given us – "God bless us every one!" We'll conduct a world wide campaign – we'll advertise in every magazine in the country! . . . What am I going to do? I'll tell you! I'm going to put Christmas on a business basis.

Scrooge in Kaufman and Connelly's
A Christmas Carol, 1922

Not in Moscow, Berlin, or Rome would such a story of rugged individualism, tempered by celestial interference, be apposite to the times. But in Washington, under the New Deal, it fits certain manifestations of governing philosophy very well indeed.

Arthur Krock on the *Carol*, 1934

After World War I the American humorist Robert Benchley pronounced the end of the Dickensian children's hour with his essay "Christmas Afternoon: Done in the Manner, if not the Spirit, of Dickens" (1921). His picture of the Gummidge family on Christmas afternoon (fig. 58) – the older generation laid low by overeating and besieged by an anarchic mob of children quarreling over Christmas toys – dispelled the prewar image of idealized childhood. One of the uncles remarks that the season should be renamed "the children's Armageddon season, when Nature had decreed that only the fittest should survive," and the narrator commemorates the end of the ordeal by paraphrasing Tiny Tim who "might say in speaking of Christmas afternoon as an institution, 'God help us, every one.'"[1]

If Benchley pronounced Tiny Tim dead, postwar critics conducted his funeral. Discovering that the narrator's assertion in the *Carol* that Tiny Tim "did *not* die" was a later addition to the manuscript (fig. 59), they suggested that Dickens might have originally intended the crippled child to die. At the very least, they argued, Dickens did not plan to make Tim's fate so definite. By adding the offendingly explicit assertion, compounded by the even more offensive italics, Dickens pandered to the desires of his audience and compromised the art of his story. "The fate of Tiny Tim," these purists argued, "should be a matter of dignified reticence. . . . Dickens was carried away by exuberance, and momentarily forgot good taste."[2] Art demanded that the text leave the question open.

The debate over Tiny Tim's fate raged in 1933–34 at the depths of the Depression. Such fine points as the appropriateness of italics seem grotesquely trivial at a time when, as one of the contenders pointed out, "we all know, or can easily find, plenty of Tiny Tims, many of whom unfortunately do die."[3] These divergent points of view illustrate the contradictions of the time and the gulf between the popular audience, for whom Tiny Tim never died, and some of the critics, who blue-penciled the child as an editorial and artistic mistake.

In a larger sense, Tim was a casualty of the world war. Wendy, in *Peter Pan*'s Neverland, sent her brothers to battle the pirates with the admonition: "These are my last words. Dear boys, I feel that I have a message to you from your real mothers, and it is this, 'We hope our sons die like English gentlemen'" (p. 562). But that traditional message, along with a whole generaton of young men, was left on continental battlefields between 1914 and 1917. The war ended Peter Pan's frivolous view of death as an "awfully big adventure," and it ended the Dickensian children's hour with its celebration of adults playing children's games. Yet there were

Figure 58. Gluyas Williams's modernist caricature of Benchley's postwar Christmas afternoon (1921). Illustration from "Christmas Afternoon" by Robert Benchley, in The Benchley Roundup, *edited by Nathaniel Benchley. Copyright 1954 by Nathaniel Benchley; copyright renewed 1982 by Marjorie Benchley. Reprinted by permission of Harper & Row, Publishers, Inc.*

those who did not suffer the loss lightly. If the *Carol* really commemorated the death of Tiny Tim, they seemed to reason, and if Dickens was the messenger, then Dickens was responsible for killing the Christmas child. Thomas Burke, an Irish journalist, asserted that "the supreme success" of *A Christmas Carol* "killed Christmas. . . . By drawing attention to it

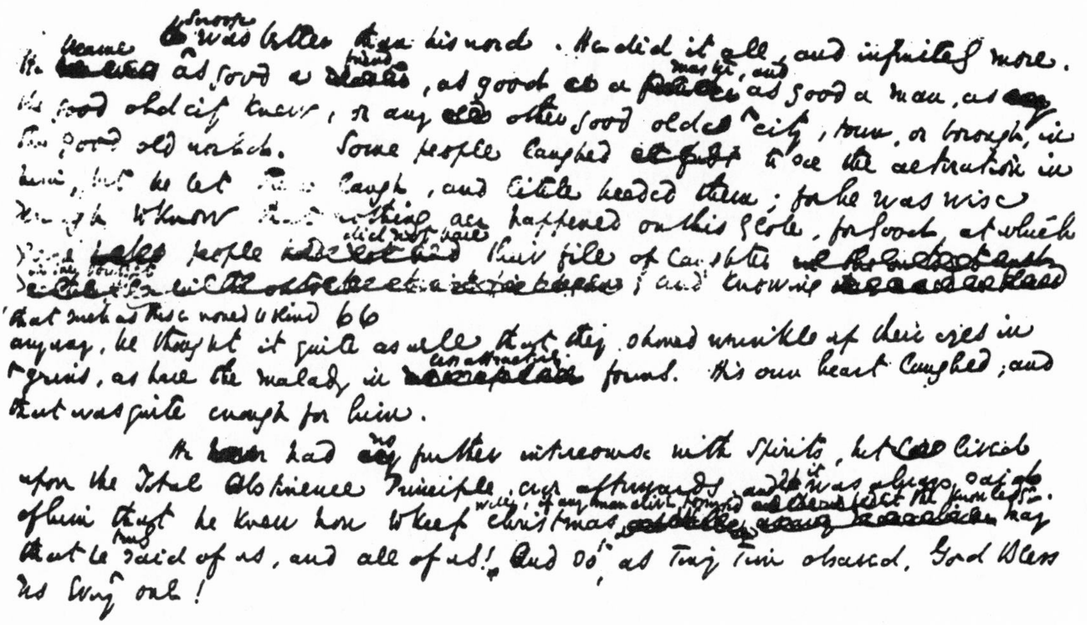

Scrooge was better than his word. He did it all, and infinitely more. He became as good a friend, as good a master, and as good a man, as the good old city knew, or any other good old city, town, or borough, in the good old world. Some people laughed to see the alteration in him, but he let them laugh, and little heeded them; for he was wise enough to know that nothing ever happened on this globe, for good, at which some people did not have their fill of laughter in the outset; and knowing that such as these would be blind 66 anyway, he thought it quite as well that they should wrinkle up their eyes in grins, as have the malady in less attractive forms. His own heart laughed; and that was quite enough for him.

He had no further intercourse with Spirits, but lived upon the Total Abstinence Principle, ever afterwards; and it was always said of him that he knew how to keep Christmas well, if any man alive possessed the knowledge. May that be truly said of us, and all of us! And so, as Tiny Tim observed, God Bless Us, Every One!

Dickens made it self-conscious, and so destroyed it. . . . He found it a festival and left it a function."[4] Even one of the Dickensians asserted that "Dickens did not know what Christmas meant," contending that he drained the holiday of all its spiritual significance.[5] In a bizarre inversion of tradition, the philosopher of Christmas became the scapegoat for the disillusion of the war and the economic suffering left in its wake.

Even the ebullient G. K. Chesterton qualified his optimistic prewar characterization of Scrooge as a fundamentally benevolent man who had "given away turkeys secretly all his life." After the war he linked Scrooge with Gradgrind, the calculating economist of *Hard Times:* "It is not only true that the new miser [Gradgrind] has the old avarice, it is also true that the old miser [Scrooge] has the new arguments. Scrooge is a utilitarian and an individualist; . . . he is a miser in theory as well as in practice."[6] Chesterton found the theoretical Scrooges of his own time more terrifying than the economic individualists of the mid-nineteenth century: "We have all seen the most sedentary scholars proving on paper that none should survive save the victors of aggressive war and the physical struggle for life; we have all heard the idle rich explaining why the idle poor deserve to be left to die in hunger. In all this the spirit of Scrooge survives." The aggressive intrusion of the modern welfare state into the lives of the poor outdoes even Scrooge for meanness, he continued. Scrooge "would not have thought it natural to pursue Bob Cratchit to his

Figure 59. The final paragraphs from Dickens' manuscript for the Carol *do not include the controversial sentence about Tiny Tim, which must have been added while the story was in production. Reproduced courtesy of the Pierpont Morgan Library, New York. MA. 97, pp. 65, 66.*

own home, to spy on him, to steal his turkey, to run away with his punch-bowl, to kidnap his crippled child, and put him in prison as a defective." The intrusive social theory that guides the modern dystopia, Chesterton suggests, is even more systematically cruel than Scrooge's neglectful laissez-faire individualism.

In a similar dystopian vision, published in the same year (1922), J. H. McNulty imagined the world of 1990 where diets have been rationalized with synthetic foods, where workers' lives, both public and personal, are controlled to make them more productive, where churches have been turned into business houses and places of amusement, and where Christmas has been abolished. This brave new world has "abolished all . . . sloppy sentiment," for in the aftermath of World War I, as McNulty's opening sentence reminds the reader, "Christmas was dead to begin with."[7]

Had the postwar disillusion carried over into the Carols of the Depression, one might expect to find Dickens' story used even more despairingly. As the exploiting capitalist, Scrooge would sit in his luxurious office, fat and self-satisfied, chewing on a cigar, and ignoring the suffering of the unemployed Cratchits outside in the streets. This tale would not end with Scrooge's reformation but rather with the death of Tiny Tim. The "ghost of an idea" that inspired Dickens in 1843 would have turned out to be the "spectre of Communism" that Marx had seen haunting Europe in 1848.

But the Depression did not turn Dickens' fable to such depressing uses. The British *Daily Worker*'s radicalization of the story, "Mr. Scrooge – 1932," is the exception rather than the rule.[8] "Scrooge still lives!" the *Worker* asserted. "Lives – and if it is possible for a Scrooge – grows fat! . . . The modern Scrooge is a monster, whose malice far surpasses that of his miserly namesake. His real name is Mr. Profit, Mr. G. Profit (G. for grab). . . . [He] give[s] to hospitals – and fill[s] them, too, with the victims of [his] rack-rented slums, [his] badly guarded machines, [his] worse ventilated factories, [his] rotten and adulterated food. . . . He has blossomed and grown fat. He has not reformed." The character who has changed, claims the *Worker,* is Cratchit, who has become "not a man, but millions – a class." The *Worker* Carol ends by echoing the prophecy of the original's Stave 3, when the Spirit of Christmas Present reveals the urchins Ignorance and Want: "Beware them both, and all of their degree, but most of all beware this boy [Ignorance], for on his brow I see that written which is doom." The Cratchit-class will fulfill this prophecy, the *Worker* Carol suggests, and the Spirit of Christmas Present

> will show Scrooge the most horrible sight of all – Scrooge. And having shown, smash him and his power for evil once for all. Rebuild the world.
>
> Already they are doing it, Scrooge. Your days are numbered.
>
> And they are not waiting. They are gathering in their thousands, and their millions.
>
> Demanding work and wages.
>
> Fighting hunger.
>
> Demanding the release of their comrades. Hunger has not crushed, nor will prisons daunt them.
>
> They are gathering, Scrooge. . . .
>
> I hope you had a rotten Christmas, Scrooge!
>
> And I hope next year sees you warmer – in hell – than this!

The incantory economic realism of the *Daily Worker* Carol marks it as an ideological anomaly among the Carols of the period.

The characteristic thirties Carol articulates instead a fantasy of liberation from the iron laws of economics. Readers of the period did not characterize Scrooge, as Edgar Johnson later did, as "nothing other than a personification of economic man."[9] Nor did they concur with the post–World War II radical who proposed that the story should be rewritten to present a revolutionary Cratchit who could not be bamboozled by a bowl of smoking bishop into allowing himself to be exploited.[10] These economic issues would dominate the readings of the *Carol* in the more comfortable fifties; they were pushed to the margins of the thirties version. In the center was a fantasy of freedom from economic necessity. Stephen Leacock characterized this thirties Carol when he asserted that "the point of the story" is that there is "a new world open to each of us at any moment . . . at the mere cost of opening the windows of the soul. It is of no consequence whether *A Christmas Carol* is true to life. It is better than life."[11]

Even the book itself exhibited its liberating power. Like the original *Carol,* whose hand-colored illustrations, two-color title page, and gilded binding belied the hard times of the hungry 1840s, several hand-set fine editions enlightened the darkest days of the Depression.[12] These leather-bound, boxed volumes exaggerated an irony noted by some of Dickens' contemporaries, who found the "genteel typography" of the 1843 volume too expensive for the poor.[13] Yet the modest luxuries in Dickens' volume,

Figures 60, 61. Everett Shinn's pictures for a popular 1938 edition of the Carol, *with an introduction by Lionel Barrymore, recalled Dickens' original text in the relationship between the celebratory color illustrations, such as the picture of Fezziwig's ball (left), and the marginal black-and-white drawings that depict the social messages in the tale (right). Courtesy of Henry Holt and Company.*

like those in the decorated Depression editions, represented the power of the story to deliver its readers from the daily necessity of hard times.

The Depression edition that may best recreate the physical presence of the original is one produced in 1938 with illustrations by Everett Shinn and an introduction by Lionel Barrymore, the most famous radio Scrooge.[14] Although it contained a dozen full-page color illustrations, numerous black-and-white pictures, and decorated end pages and cover, it sold for only $1.98, about the price for a full-length novel at the time. Its colored pictures give conventionally merry treatment to such well-established subjects as Bob carrying Tim through the streets or Scrooge confronting each of the spirits. But the more than thirty marginal illustrations, done in black and white and rendering less conventional sub-

jects, are the most distinctive part of this edition. In these pictures the frenetic gaiety of the colored rendering of Fezziwig's ball (fig. 60) is countered by such subjects as the madonna of the street at the end of Stave 1 (fig. 61), Igorance and Want in Stave 3, or the empty chair of Tiny Tim in Stave 4. Shinn and Barrymore celebrate the liberating fantasy of the story on its color pages, yet they catch its ground-in hard reality in the black-and-white margins. The contrast echoes the similar relationship of the black-and-white and color illustrations in Dickens' original.

The liberating power of the story is even more apparent in the film and radio "editions" produced during the period. A. J. P. Taylor has called the cinema "the essential social habit" of the Depression.[15] Even in such centers of economic misery as Liverpool and Glasgow, "as many as 80 per cent went to the cinema at least once a week."[16] Sixty million Americans made a weekly pilgrimage to the movies, which Will Hays, president of the Motion Picture Producers and Distributors of America, said served to "laugh the big bad wolf of the depression out of the public mind."[17] The underlying fantasy in the films of the period coincided with the story of Scrooge's liberation from the confines of his money-changing hole. Thus, the media versions of the *Carol* were, as Arthur Schlesinger, Jr., said of the movies generally, "near the operative center of the nation's consciousness."[18]

The printed editions of the *Carol* in the 1930s often revived the spirit of the original edition; the radio and film versions recreated the shilling seats for working people at Dickens' public readings. Gathering in the movie palaces to laugh away the frustrations of the time, the film audience could, as Thomas Caramagno has suggested, be "reassured . . . that as individuals they had not been rendered irrelevant by world-wide events, or by invisible, deterministic forces operating anonymously in a massive social system that seemed implacable, impersonal, and out of control."[19] In their collective fantasy the modern screen audience, like the mixed Victorian audiences at the readings, reaffirmed a belief in individual action, seeing in Scrooge's conversion a way to triumph over impersonal economic forces. The ideal community that Dickens envisaged in the theater and reading hall – one relating across class lines and sharing common feelings, hopes, and desires – gathered in the movie palaces to share the Carol as "common national property."

Although film historians generally consider British films of the period simply imitations of Hollywood models, the film versions of *A Christmas Carol* reveal distinctly British or American origins. Perhaps because the Carol was so deeply rooted in the British national consciousness, British film versions maintain established theatrical traditions in rendering the story. The Hollywood versions, on the other hand, develop an American Carol, articulating distinctively transatlantic dreams and aspirations. In the emerging global village created by the media, this American Carol becomes the dominant version of the story. Celebrating Scrooge's transformation as a conversion to an American business ethic of community service and rejecting the ingrained self-interest of Europe which had brought the world to economic despair, the American Carol liberated Scrooge and Cratchit with a New World new deal.

In a Christmas Eve commentary in 1934, Arthur Krock, columnist for the *New York Times*, suggested that *A Christmas Carol* contained the philosophic kernel of President Roosevelt's New Deal.[20] Noting that the president read the *Carol* aloud each year, thus adopting it as a kind of national Christmas scripture, Krock set out to interpret its pages as "propaganda for the whole program of the national conference on economic security." The teachings of Marley and the spirits may alarm "those who pray in fear for the return of the 'Good Old Days of 1929,'" Krock commented, "but for those who believe in more sharing than was the custom of industry in that lamented period, the moral is not frightening. While Scrooge reformed, and grew generous, the implication is plain that he kept enough wealth to remain a wealthy man, and there was no law to prevent that. He was not forced to engage in collective bargaining with Bob Cratchit; the raise was his own idea. The capitalistic system was seated more firmly in its place by Scrooge's realization of the happiness, as well as the wisdom, of sharing." If the story was not a "standpat document," Krock concluded, neither was it a revolutionary tract. The Carol, like the New Deal, presented an inspirational program of revitalized capitalism to lead all Americans together out of the wilderness of economic despair.[21] The common welfare was its business, and business the basis of its social optimism. In the period between the wars, *A Christmas Carol* was Americanized. In Hollywood, New York, and Washington, it became the Christmas manifesto for the brave New World.

In 1931 Aldous Huxley suggested that the primary difference between the modern Christmas and the Dickens Christmas was that the latter "did very little to stimulate consumption; it was mainly a gratuitous festivity."[22] In the century since *Pickwick*, Christmas had become a materialistic holiday, but the current hard times, Huxley argued, would force many to give up the exchange of expensive industrial goods and

Figure 62. The oval frame around Gordon Ross's version of the phantoms at the end of Stave 1 distances the Depression from this image of Victorian suffering. Courtesy of Limited Editions Club.

return to "the old, the gratuitous, the Pickwickian style." British Depression versions of the Carol often celebrate Huxley's theme. Dickens' text became a way to restore prewar Britain, a pretext for reviving a forgotten way of life.

For the 1934 Limited Editions Club volume, Gordon Ross enclosed his illustrations in oval frames, placing them on the pages of the book like oval portraits on Victorian parlor walls (fig. 62). Ross's subjects recall Leech's illustrations for the 1843 edition, but Leech's pictures are not framed. Their irregular outlines bleed into the page, melding with the text and articulating the ties between illustration and story. Ross's pictures, on the other hand, are windows into the past, framed visions of another time and place.

Looking through such windows was a way to reconnect past and present. Bridging the gulf created by war and depression, the newspapers filled their pages with accounts of the Dickens Christmas. Children of the 1860s called up the distant Christmases of their infancy for readers of the 1930s. Edwin Mead remembered an American reading of the *Carol* in Boston which he attended as a child, and Dickens' granddaughter recollected holiday celebrations with her grandfather.[23] Those who accepted journalistic invitations to "spend Christmas with Dickens" came away from the holiday agreeing with J. B. Priestley, who assured readers of the *Evening Standard* that "yes, there is a return to Dickens," and with Max Pemberton, who jubilantly reported that "thanks to Dickens Christmas still lives."[24] But W. R. Titterton scooped the competition when he published "What Is Christmas?" in the *Daily Sketch*, an account of an interview with Dickens reincarnate.[25]

The attempt was not to escape into the past but rather to transform the present with Dickensian optimism. Not so fortunate as to secure an interview with the author, Sir Philip Gibbs was forced to speculate for readers of the *Sunday Times*, "dejected by our present economic conditions," on what Dickens would say "if [he] wrote his 'Carol' now."[26] He would find in England "an almost miraculous change for the better," Gibbs proposed. The "ghastly wretchedness" in the material conditions of Victorian life was gone, and the nation had developed a social conscience. Dickens would be astounded because the message of the Carol had been heeded and "he would find us with all our faults – less selfish in regard to the happiness of our fellow men – more conscious at least of duties toward them." By the thirties the cynicism that sometimes colored the Carols of the twenties had been displaced by a Whiggish optimism.

The British Carol of the thirties is probably best represented by *Scrooge* (1935), the Julius Hagen–Twickenham Productions film directed by Henry Edwards.[27] Starring Seymour Hicks, the premier Scrooge on the London stage during the first third of the twentieth century, the film was praised when it appeared for its faithfulness to the original. But it was more faithful to the book as a book and to established conventions of dramatizing the Carol than it was to Dickens' original story. By celebrating the book and recalling familiar renderings of the tale, *Scrooge* alleviated the miseries of the Depression with the consolations of Christmases past.

The film announces its obligation to the past from its opening images. Beginning with a copy of the *Carol* being removed from a bookshelf and

Figure 63. Seymour Hicks's Scrooge confronts Donald Calthrop's Cratchit in the opening stave of the 1935 film Scrooge. *Calthrop is especially well cast as a living version of Leech's image of the clerk (see fig. 38). Courtesy of the Museum of Modern Art Film Stills Archive.*

opened to reveal the title and credits, the film affirms its commitment to the book. Even Dickens' original preface appears on the screen before the images of the story begin. In like manner, the film closes by showing the final page of the original edition with Leech's illustration of Scrooge and Bob sharing the bowl of smoking bishop. Thus, the book encloses the film, setting limits to the adaptation. The images of the story, especially Donald Calthrop's Cratchit (fig. 63), recall Victorian illustrations, both those by Leech and the immensely popular pictures by Frederick Barnard (1877). In *Scrooge*, the book of *A Christmas Carol* has become a kind of sacred object and the film a way of reaffirming its ceremonial importance.

This commitment to the book, however, does not extend to Dickens' original story. The film script is more faithful to the dramatic adaptation by J. C. Buckstone than to Dickens' text. Buckstone's *Scrooge*, written in the 1890s, was the most popular dramatic version during the early decades of the twentieth century, the basis for many music hall sketches as well as most stage productions.[28] This theatrical adaptation reduced the story to a one-act drama which took little more than an hour of playing time and concentrated on the first and last staves. The office scenes, especially the interactions between employer and clerk, were expanded somewhat, but the visits of the spirits were drastically cut. Marley was the only spirit remaining in the story, and he presented to Scrooge amputated visions of past, present, and future. Music hall versions reportedly condensed the story even more, cutting it to approximately half an hour and focusing solely on Scrooge. The two dominant stage Scrooges of the period, Bransby Williams and Seymour Hicks, performed in both theaters and music halls. So pervasive was Buckstone's script during the period that it virtually became *A Christmas Carol.*

The first half of the 1935 film is taken practically verbatim from the familiar Buckstone script. The film includes Bob's account of his family in the opening stave, a quarrel between master and clerk about coal for the fire, and Scrooge's lecture to Bob on economic prudence, all additions in the Buckstone text. Like the play, it also reverses the sequence of the original scenes, beginning with the charity solicitors followed by Fred's Christmas visit. The Scrooge who dominates these early scenes is so irascible that one of the solicitors, in one of several small details added by Buckstone to the story, apologizes as he leaves, thinking that he has caused Scrooge's irritability.

After Marley's visit the film departs from the Buckstone text, introducing the three spirits and expanding the visions over their minimal rendering in the stage version. Nevertheless, the Spirits of Christmas Past and Christmas Yet-to-Come have little visual presence in the film, Past appearing only as a vaguely human form outlined in light, Yet-to-Come simply as a shadow. Marley has no visual presence at all; he is merely a voice on the sound track.[29] The concentration remains on Scrooge, so that even the confrontation with Marley recalls the familiar one-man music hall productions by showing us Scrooge alone on the screen.

In 1929 the *Dickensian* criticized a dramatic adaptation of the *Carol* given at the newly formed People's Theatre in London, complaining that the forty-five-minute production, which devoted half its time to the office scene before the dream, was merely a redoing of the old music hall sketch.[30] But a few years later the same journal praised the film even though many of the criticisms brought against the People's Theatre could also have been leveled at *Scrooge.* The difference between the two versions may have been Seymour Hicks, the actor whose name in 1935 was virtually synonymous with Scrooge. On stage and in the music hall, he had performed the role two thousand times before recording it on film. Like the image of the book that opens the film, Hicks's Scrooge had the sanction of tradition.

Hicks's dominance in the picture is suggested by the title, *Scrooge,* and is apparent from the opening scenes. As Scrooge denies the charity solicitors and challenges his nephew, the camera watches from behind his back, his body a looming barrier to entering the visual world of the film.

He is a solitary figure who has turned his back on the world, meeting it with denial and irritation. In the only scene retained from the vision of Christmas Past, the separation of Scrooge from his fiancée, his solipsism is stressed by the significant addition of the word *alone* in Belle's bitter farewell: "May you be happy alone in the life you have chosen." However, as Scrooge changes he is visually linked with others. The camera moves closer to his point of view, seeing the world over his shoulder rather than blocked by his body. And in the final scenes, after his conversion, the camera shows us the world through Scrooge's face. Pretending to be angry with his clerk for arriving late to work, Scrooge turns his back on Bob and his face to the camera. While Bob sees his employer as the viewer has seen him early in the film, we watch the animation on Scrooge's face, his wry grin telling of his new beginning. The gradual shifts in camera angles through the film enable the viewer to participate in Scrooge's transformation.

The longevity of tradition behind Hick's Scrooge is suggested by his age. He is an old man. His disheveled white hair and tattered coat confirm his directive to his clerk, when he reminds Bob that he is his "senior by a great many years." He is not doddering but an old man of strong movements and abrupt speeches. He makes no punning proposal that there is more of gravy than the grave about Marley, for he is not a witty Scrooge. He is a negative force. His "bah, humbugs" convey anger and irritation rather than contrary exuberance. Nor does he wish, like the children's Scrooges early in the century, to play childish games. The games played by Fred and his friends in the film make Scrooge an outsider and the butt of their jokes. Their party ends – like several other scenes in the film – in a chorus of mocking laughter.

There is a curious discontinuity in the film between the world inside the dark and barren rooms to which Scrooge retreats – rooms which embody the emptiness and negativity of his lonely selfhood – and the world outside his apartments. Little in the street scenes or the Cratchit household bespeaks deprivation. The well-stocked markets, the shops where Bob buys his Christmas treats, and the extravagant Lord Mayor's feast suggest that Scrooge's mean way of life results from congenital miserliness rather than from experience in the world. There is no hint of his harsh and lonely childhood in the film, nor any signs of the suffering poor clustered around open fires in the streets. If Dickens' Scrooge makes himself mean by his bah-humbugging attempts to deny the suffering around him, Hicks's Scrooge seems to have been born mean. His miserliness has neither social nor psychological explanation. He is a miser without context.

The London this Scrooge inhabits fails to explain his character, for the film takes place in Bob Cratchit's London, a city defined by pastoral sentiment. The city in Dickens' text is seen from ground level, from the limited and mistified perspective of the pedestrian observer, but *Scrooge*'s camera sees London from above. Its opening shot, an image that reappears several times, is a pastoral "distant prospect" on a peaceful city swathed in snow and watched over by the dome of St. Paul's. For Hicks, the crucial moment in the story came in Bob's pastoral account of the cemetery where Tiny Tim's body will rest. Hicks describes crying on stage in his many performances as he listened to Bob telling his remaining children of that "green place" and assuring them, "I am very happy – I am very happy."[31] In the pastoral cycle which flings Scrooge "into the Garden of Agony and forces him to gather Weeds of Remorse and hug them to his withered bosom till the far-off summer comes," this moment is the seasonal turning point. Watching Bob's grief transformed to happiness, Hicks's Scrooge, moved to tears, speaks the narrator's recognition from the original text, "Tiny Tim, thy childish essence was from God!" and then he can enter Bob's Celestial City. His recognition of the transcendent power of Bob's crippled son recalls the Victorian Carol and its linking of Tiny Tim with the Christ child.

The spiritual power of Tiny Tim and Hicks's characterization of Scrooge connect the film to Victorian tradition. Just as Dickens invoked the old English celebration to give traditional feeling to his urban Christmas, so *Scrooge* invokes Carols past to celebrate its myth of Christmas present. In marked contrast to the insubstantial Spirit of Christmas Past and the shadowy Spirit of Christmas Yet-to-Come in the film, the Spirit of Christmas Present, played by Oscar Asche, is vastly corporeal (fig. 64). Of even more expansive girth than the figure in Leech's illustration, he enters the film eating large bites of turkey and throwing the bones to the floor. He embodies J. H. McNulty's observation about the spirit in the story: "The 'Ghost of Christmas Present' is not truly a ghost at all; he is too real."[32] This difference between Christmas Present and the other two spirits conveys the film's message that Christmas is present, alive and well fed in the 1930s.

The homage *Scrooge* pays to images of the book and to traditional treatments of the story does not carry over into its representation of Scrooge's past. Scrooge's earlier life is almost totally removed from the film. His unhappy childhood, his lonely schooldays, and his apprenticeship at Fezziwig's are all cut. Only the scenes with his fiancée are retained. Most significant, perhaps, is the removal of the Fezziwigs, the scene that provided the frontispiece for the original edition and that most fully articulated the story's connection with the traditional Christmas.

Figure 64. Oscar Asche, a corporeal presence as the Spirit of Christmas Present in Scrooge *(1935). Photo courtesy of British Film Institute.*

The Fezziwig party is displaced in the film by the Lord Mayor's banquet (fig. 65), an elaborate sequence based on a single sentence in the original text: "The Lord Mayor, in the stronghold of the mighty Mansion House, gave orders to his fifty cooks and butlers to keep Christmas as a Lord Mayor's household should" (p. 13). The film shows the fifty cooks, some basting rows of chickens roasting before an open fire, some mixing and tasting Christmas punch, and others testing sauces or icing cakes, including one very rotund chef whose stomach shakes like a bowful of jelly as he prepares the molded salads and desserts. This kitchen comedy, done with the pantomime and tempo of silent film, is intercut with scenes of the rich guests arriving for the feast, their carriages met by liveried footmen at the door, with pictures of the poor gathering around the Guildhall watching the celebration and reaching through the grates on the kitchen windows for gifts of food from the cooks, and, in sharp contrast, with images of Scrooge eating his solitary supper in an empty inn. As the sequence builds towards its climax in the singing of "God Save the Queen," a chorus that includes both the guests at the dinner and the poor in the streets, the montage suggests that only Scrooge is outside this national community that celebrates Christmas with common voice.

Unlike Fezziwig's party, the Lord Mayor's banquet is not located in Christmas Past. Rather than something lost, it is something retained, a

Figure 65. During the Lord Mayor's banquet in Scrooge, *the film cuts between this scene of the rich at their feast and images of the cooks preparing the meal, of the poor watching the festivities at the gate of the Mansion House, and of Scrooge eating by himself. The montage concludes by bringing all classes together in singing "God Save the Queen," a ceremony from which only Scrooge is excluded. Photo courtesy of British Film Institute.*

survival attesting to continuity between past and present. In the midst of the Depression, it presents a unified nation with all classes in harmony, an image repeated at the end of the film when Scrooge and Bob join together in church singing the common hymn. Though such sentimental religiosity bothered occasional freethinkers, the Carols of the thirties often substituted such scenes (see fig. 69) for the bowl of smoking bishop as a way of resolving the suppressed class conflict in the story.[33] These pious endings seem to restate, without Benchley's irony, his version of Tiny Tim's prayer, "God help us, every one."

As the British Depression Carol, *Scrooge* provided a fantasy of national unity, an image of an overfed Christmas Present sharing the Lord Mayor's excessive feast in a city where family feeling and religious harmony restore the contentment of the pastoral community. At the center of this urban idyll is an irascible and tattered old man whose unmotivated irritability isolates him from the rest of society. As the scapegoat for the repressed social anger and class conflict of the period, this negative Scrooge loses his anomalous power when he joins the communal chorus. At his nephew's Christmas dinner, he is only a doddering shell of his unregenerate self, for by joining the community he has denied the informing truth of his earlier life – that the hard-headed hard-heartedness of economic individualism makes each man a lonely protector of his own self-interest.

Although Scrooge tells Bob early in the film that their class interests conflict, the film does not pursue the implications of this view, either to Dickens' hungry forties or to the depressed 1930s. And the psychic energy needed to deny this economic reality reduces Scrooge to doddering imbecility. Though it resembles the original *Carol, Scrooge* is a gutted version. Ignorance and Want have been banished from its Depression present and at the end Scrooge is transformed into the senile celebrant of its unreality principle.

While the British Carol affirms age and tradition, the American Carol celebrates youth and energy. The American Scrooge is much younger than his British counterpart. A recent television version, *The American Christmas Carol* (1979), even cast Henry Winkler as Scrooge, the makeup of age only thinly disguising a youthful Fonz.[34] Part of an American Carol that emerges in the 1920s and 1930s, this youthful Scrooge is born of a different national mythology from that informing the British Carols of the period.

Until the 1920s the *Carol* had never been as popular in America as it was in Britain. It appeared shortly after Dickens' controversial account of his journey to America, *American Notes for General Circulation* (1842), and while the even more controversial American chapters of *Martin Chuzzlewit* were being serialized. As a result, the *Carol*'s American reception was chilled by resentment over the criticism in the other two books. Dickens was widely attacked in the American press for his lack of generosity to his hosts and for bias in collecting only unfavorable images of the United States. A copy of the *American Notes* was even ceremonially burned in New York. Although some American reviewers of the 1840s praised the *Carol* and suggested that it could make up for the sins of the other two books, none greeted it with praise as fulsome as Thackeray's declaration that the book was a "national benefit."

America's nineteenth-century Christmas dreams were more likely to call up the visionary sugar plums of Clement Moore's *The Night before Christmas* (1849) or the Santas in the illustrations of Thomas Nast (fig. 66) than to invoke Dickens' Christmas spirits. Attempting to define a cultural identity distinct from the mother country may have contributed to American readiness to adopt Moore and Nast over Dickens. Or the urban consciousness implicit in the *Carol* may have made it alien to the more rural imagination of nineteenth-century America. Whatever the reasons,

Figure 66. One of the many popular Santas by Thomas Nast that appeared in the Christmas issues of Harper's Illustrated Weekly Magazine *in the 1860s, 1870s, and 1880s. From* Thomas Nast's Christmas Drawings for the Human Race *(1890).*

they were transcended by the 1920s when Americans developed a healthy enough national ego to take Dickens' story and make it their own. In fact, in the period between the wars, the *Carol* was much more popular on the west side of the Atlantic than on the east, going through numerous American editions, versions, adaptations, and parodies. Its status in the New World may best be symbolized by its importance to the Roosevelts. The president read it aloud to his family each Christmas Eve, an event dutifully reported in the newspapers of the day, and he referred to it in his Christmas fireside chats with the American people. Eleanor Roosevelt later made a recording of the story which was commercially distributed. *A Christmas Carol* was one of the guiding texts of the New Deal.

As readers of the book, the Roosevelt family were a bit old-fashioned, even a bit British. The American Carol is not defined by the book; it is a media event. The most American version of the period is probably the radio play starring Lionel Barrymore (see fig. 71), who portrayed Scrooge over the airwaves annually from 1934 until the 1950s.[35] Each Christmas Eve, while the president was reading Dickens' story to the first family in the White House, Barrymore performed his Carol for the nation. Introducing one of Barrymore's annual performances, probably in the 1940s, Orson Welles characterized the audience as a family extended to national proportions: "There is, I think, in all America nothing more eagerly awaited or more firmly rooted in the hearts of the radio family that numbers millions than this yearly performance of *A Christmas Carol*."[36] Cut to little more than half an hour, this radio classic gave the story an American cast.

Barrymore's version facilitated the vicarious participation of the radio family by extending the idea of family in the story. Fred's role is virtually eliminated. He appears only in the opening stave, coming to Scrooge's office to wish him a merry Christmas. His mother, Fan, does not appear in Christmas Past to rescue Scrooge from the lonely school, he does not hold his Christmas party and play childish games, nor does the converted Scrooge go to his house for the Christmas feast. His role in the exposition is not so much that of family as that of a representative of Christmas tradition which Barrymore-Scrooge rejects with the assertion "I don't want any of your old customs." After Fred makes his eloquent defense of the holiday, Scrooge's ironic compliment in the original – "You're quite a powerful speaker, sir. . . . I wonder you don't go into Parliament" – is changed in the Barrymore version to "I wonder why you don't go into Parliament. You talk enough nonsense." In rejecting Fred's old customs, Barrymore rejects Old World "nonsense." His "bah, humbugs" carry a populist, antimonarchical, anti-European connotation. As father to the American radio family, Barrymore fosters the aspirations of the outsiders, the poor and downtrodden Cratchits whose good fortune replaces Fred's. Even in the condensed radio version, Bob is given a bigger role than in the original. He opens the dramatization as he mumbles the figures he is entering in his ledgers, offers threepence to the charity solicitors after Scrooge has refused them, and goes over lists of Christmas presents for his children. Later he is given a climactic scene to match Barrymore's conversion, when he mourns "my little son, Tiny Tim." When Scrooge is converted and restored to family ties, he becomes patriarch to an "extended family" that includes the Cratchits.

In the original story, Scrooge's nephew Fred and Bob Cratchit could be said to represent two aspects of Scrooge's denial of Christmas. By denying Fred, Scrooge cuts himself off from family, from his past and his loving relationship with Fred's mother, his sister Fan. By ignoring Bob and his family, Scrooge denies his social and economic responsibility as an employer and a man of means. British versions of the Carol generally keep quite distinct the resolutions of these two relationships. By attending Christmas dinner with Fred, Scrooge rejoins his family; by raising Bob's salary and caring for Tiny Tim, he accepts his social responsibility. Class distinctions keep the Cratchits from becoming "family" and avoidance of vulgarity prevents financial considerations from corrupting Scrooge's relationship with Fred. He does not become "low," like Magwitch in *Great Expectations*, making money the matrix of his connection with his nephew.

American carolers were not deterred by these British restraints. Perhaps the theme in the British Carol most alien to the American consciousness was the resolution that maintained the original class relationships between Scrooge and Cratchit, simply making Scrooge a more caring member of the well-to-do class. The American dream of success suggested that the story needed to end with the worldly elevation of an economic outsider. In some American versions, Fred is made more economically marginal – single and waiting for his fortunes to improve before he marries, for example – so that he can be taken into partnership by a reformed Scrooge. But more often, Fred's role is reduced or even eliminated so that the Cratchit family can become the vehicle for the romance of rising expectations. Rather than just concern and caring from a paternal and kindly employer, Americans favored profit sharing. Scrooge often ended up giving Bob a slice of the business. The American Carol celebrated more than the restoration of family ties. It celebrated the emergence of a new national family that transcended the class restraints of the European past. If the discomfort of the British Carol could be resolved by a return to social responsibility and stable class relationships, the discomfort in the American Carol was more radical and could only be resolved by making the opportunity for business success available to all members of a national family. The British Carol celebrates social stability; the American eulogizes economic opportunity.

Before the 1920s New World carolers seem to grope for these American themes. An 1877 dramatic adaptation, Charles A. Scott's *Old Scrooge: A Christmas Carol in Five Staves,* for example, appears to be searching for an outlet for Scrooge's youthful energy.[37] The play begins as a fairly straightforward rendition of the original, but by the end it has transformed the story into something foreshadowing screwball comedy. Scrooge becomes a romantic lead when he meets Belle again, now the widowed mother of Fred's wife. In an elaborate marital conclusion that is the outcome of Fred's Christmas party, Topper and Snapper, two of Fred's guests, are promised in matrimony to their sweethearts while Scrooge and Belle seem to be planning the consummation of the marriage they missed earlier. Another early American Carol, W. Pett Ridge's "New Christmas Carol" (1901), addresses the theme of business success, but its Scrooge, Mr. Broadbent, must learn the un-American lesson that his success is due more to accident than to individual effort.[38] Only in the 1920s do these American themes of youthful energy and business success become parts of a single coherent tale.

The American Carol got down to business in the expansive atmosphere of the 1920s. At a time of aggressive chamber of commerce boosterism and Babbitry, it is not surprising to find the John Hancock Insurance Company, in its 1921 greeting to its customers, purveying revisionist Tiny Tim: "We all join with Tiny Tim in his beautiful prayer – 'God bless us, every one,' and then we are reminded of the old saying that 'God helps (or blesses) those who help themselves.' There is no better means of self help to those we love than the great institution of Life Insurance, which enables us, by regular payments, to create a fund which will be paid to those we love at a time when, perhaps, they most need it."[39] These holiday sentiments seem restrained by comparison to those of the Metropolitan Casualty Insurance Company, which, in its promotion pamphlet *Moses, Persuader of Men,* celebrated the prophet as "one of the greatest salesman and real-estate promoters that ever lived."[40] A best-seller of the period, Bruce Barton's *The Man Nobody Knows* (1924), challenged the myth that Christ was a weak and delicate spiritual wimp, promoting Him instead as a Horatio Alger hero who rose from carpenter's son to business executive by "pick[ing] up twelve men from the bottom ranks of business and forg[ing] them into an organization that conquered the world."[41] Characterizing his hero as "the founder of modern business," Barton reduced the New Testament to a literal reading of Christ's words "Wist ye not that I must be about my father's *business?*"

As a latter-day scripture on business, *A Christmas Carol* became one of the sacred texts of the period. Its most outspoken prophet, A. Edward Newton, traveled to service clubs promoting it as "the greatest little book in the world." His message, given national circulation in the *Atlantic*, proclaimed that "Dickens gave Christmas a new meaning: from being merely a festival of the Church, kept to some extent by Church people, he made it a universal holiday, and he did this without in any way derogating its sacred character. What an achievement!"[42] Newton found the moral of the story in Marley's reply to Scrooge's observation "You were always a good man of business, Jacob." "Business!" Marley responds; "Mankind was my business. The common welfare was my business; charity, mercy, forbearance, and benevolence, were all my business. The dealings of my trade were but a drop of water in the comprehensive ocean of my business!" (*CB*, 20) If British readers like J. H. McNulty despaired that all the churches were being turned into houses of business, Americans found cause for celebration in the notion that houses of business were being turned into churches.[43]

Newton left to J. C. Aspley, however, the task of producing the red-letter edition of the *Carol* as latter-day gospel. In his 1928 version, *A Christmas Carol: The Story of a Sale*, Aspley glossed the original text with marginal notes to prove "it is the most fascinating story of a sale ever written."[44] Marley, "the sales end of the business," becomes the hero of this version, for even after seven years in the spirit world, he is able to concoct the "fine-spun strategy . . . to sell the idea of a Merry Christmas to 'hard-boiled,' cynical old Scrooge." Fred is an advance man who "opens [Scrooge] up for Marley," Marley's chains are a salesman's props to "hold [Scrooge's] undivided attention – fully as good as a pencil and pad," and the spirits who come after Marley "follow up" on his "call" and do not try to "close" the transaction too soon. Even the bounty of Christmas Present, the food and drink piled up around the spirit, "is sent by Marley's ghost to create desire." Although Tiny Tim prompts the marginal commentator only to aphoristic banality: "When you think of Tiny Tim and like Unfortunates, be thankful you have your health and use it," such apparently difficult moments as the vision of Ignorance and Want are turned to good account. "Ignorance and Want are Siamese Twins," writes the marginal commentator; "nowhere are they more in evidence than in the world of selling." Aspley's idealization of business is not simply a celebration of narrow self-interest. When Belle rejects Scrooge as

Figure 67. Marley appears by telephone rather than by door knocker in the dramatic modernization A Christmas Carol, *by George S. Kaufman and Marc Connelly. Herb Roth's illustration of the scene for the* Bookman *(1922) captures the parodic exaggeration in this prototype of the American Carol.*

her fiancé, Aspley reminds his readers: "The real Scrooge had been killed by Gain – even as the passion for gain is today blinding salesmen to greater opportunities of service." The model for such service becomes, not the Scrooge of Stave 5, but Marley the ghostly salesman who makes possible Scrooge's final stave.

The first full-blown "American Carol" appeared in 1922 in a dramatic parody by George S. Kaufman and Marc Connelly.[45] The short three-act play turned the story into a comic parable of business success. Scrooge, a manufacturer of doornails, fires his secretary on Christmas Eve for using a new dictaphone belt when she could have reused an old one. When he gets home from the office, the ghost of his former partner calls him up on the telephone (fig. 67):

> Hello. . . . Who? . . . Jacob Marley, my late partner? Don't try to be funny – he's been dead seven years. . . . WHAT? His GHOST? . . . No, I don't believe it. Get Conan Doyle to write a magazine article about it and I might listen, but I'm not in the habit of believing anything until I deposit it in the bank. . . . You'll give me proof? How? . . . Speak a little louder. . . . Yes, it's the voice, all right. . . . You left me a cuff link in your will? Yes, that's right. Anything else? (*As he listens he slowly turns toward the audience until he is facing Alexander Woollcott [the drama critic], who is wearing a new cravat in [seat] C-2. A look of horror comes over his face*) Marley, it is you!

Marley warns him of a visit from the Ghost of Christmas Present. The spirit gives Scrooge a cloak to make him invisible, and together they eavesdrop on the Cratchits and the former secretary, who talk about how they have been economizing on their small salaries, taking night-school courses to improve their job skills, and working at home to increase their income. When Tim enunciates his classic line "God bless us every one," the invisible Scrooge hears the ideal business slogan. He casts off the cloak, organizes the Cratchit family and the secretary into a new enterprise, Tiny Tim Products, and a year later they control the market. As the play ends, Tiny Tim, head of the successful firm, proposes to Miss Glitchwitchett, the secretary, Scrooge proposes to Martha Cratchit, and Bob and his wife plan to buy a new car. In parodic format, this play combines the elements of the American Carol: the focus on business, the youthful and energetic Scrooge who learns that altruism is good business, and the portrayal of the Cratchit family as exemplars of the American dream.

In the bullish twenties, the business Carol embodies Calvin Coolidge's aphoristic account of the times, "the business of America is business." Even after the crash, during the darkest days of the Depression, the celebration of business is not displaced by a critique of capitalism. Ashley Miller's 1928 play *Mr. Scrooge* takes some small steps in this direction.[46] The play keeps the vision of Ignorance and Want, and it portrays Scrooge as a cruel landlord who evicts tenants on Christmas Day. Cratchit has the beginnings of a revolutionary consciousness, asserting that "sometimes I am almost angry that there seems so little hope for just honest work. Why does Heaven give other men the power to withhold or bestow." Although the play suggests that it will prove that "the whole fabric of civilization is built upon the principle that men are brothers and must live together and work together," *Mr. Scrooge* does not revolutionize economic relationships in the final act. Its operative definition of "family" is conservative. Fred becomes the inheriting partner, keeping the firm firmly within the family and Cratchit remains an employee, though better paid. A few years later such limited modifications to Scrooge's self-interest would be inadequate to assuage Cratchit's social discontent. A new ideal of family would include Bob and his sons as appropriate heirs or partners in a new firm of Scrooge and Cratchit. The Coolidge doctrine would be revised to define the nation as a family and to make the nation's business a family business. By keeping the economic reforms within the confines of the family, this New Deal Carol, as Arthur Krock argued, stressed economic moderation. Like Roosevelt's program, the Carol allowed Scrooge to retain his wealth and at the same time keep alive the American dream: "The capitalistic system was seated more firmly in its place by Scrooge's realization of the happiness, as well as the wisdom, of sharing."

The 1938 Metro-Goldwyn-Mayer *A Christmas Carol,* produced by Joseph Mankiewicz and starring Reginald Owen as Scrooge and Gene Lockhart as Cratchit, provides a good illustration of this moderate version of the American Carol.[47] It promotes social change while maintaining economic continuity. Owen plays Scrooge as a much younger man than Hicks's miser. He takes his cue from Scrooge's words to the charity solicitor, "It's enough for a man to understand his own business and not interfere with other people's. Mine occupies me constantly." He is not obsessed with money; he is preoccupied with business. Even after the Spirit of Christmas Past has begun to soften his heart, he continues to justify himself by asserting, "Business is Business. I am a good businessman." And that is why, he implies, he has not had time to attend to the personal difficulties of his clerk. His sins are not so much sins of commission as of omission. The film does not include the scene where Belle accuses him of placing a golden idol before her. Nor is he shown as a cruel landlord evicting tenants on Christmas Day or as a hard moneylender refusing to extend a loan. His fault seems to be that he has too narrow a notion of business. When Bob overstays his time on Christmas Eve, Scrooge sarcastically counsels him: "Don't work overtime, you might make something of yourself." Behind this advice is not the traditional miser who begrudges his clerk a holiday on Christmas. Rather it is the single-minded businessman, the true believer in the American ethic of hard work leading to success. This Scrooge needs to learn that business can also be "an opportunity of service" to others.

Unlike the British *Scrooge*, this American film gives central roles to Bob Cratchit and Fred, who might almost be described as equal protagonists in the piece. The film begins with Fred and Bob, not with Scrooge. The opening scene shows Fred walking through the streets and stopping to slide on a patch of ice where some boys are playing. He offers a ride to a crippled child who is watching the others, and as he takes the boy on his back to slide, the film introduces its revised version of the most famous visual image of the Carol, that of Bob carrying Tiny Tim. As the two of them break the distance record for sliding, Fred exults, "We're a team, that's what we are." From this opening scene, Fred is a kind of second father to Tiny Tim, a double to Bob. Representing sexual energy and the family, he and Bob counter Scrooge's sexless devotion to business. When Fred arrives at Scrooge's office, Bob is there alone, and Fred opens a bottle of Christmas spirits so that he and the clerk may share a "loving cup" for the holiday. Before they can drink, however, Scrooge returns and interrupts the ceremony. They do not share the toast until the final scene of the movie. Indeed, the film might be seen as the story of this interrupted Christmas toast.

Scrooge prevents the toast because he refuses to celebrate family, either his own or the human family. His denial of Fred is part of a much broader denial of human generation. His vision of Christmas Past contains no memory of a lost love. He has no experience to enable him to understand Fred's desire to marry, nor does he recognize in the Cratchit family any human ideal. For Scrooge, only economic relationships matter. The circle around Tiny Tim – the prolific Cratchit family and the impending family of the erotically involved Fred and Bess – expresses a sexual energy and represents a model of human relationships as "family" beyond Scrooge's experience or comprehension. His devotion to business makes him a spiritual orphan unable to celebrate the family holiday. Changing his words from those in Dickens' original text, where Christmas is described as a time when "men and women . . . think of people below them as if they really were fellow passengers to the grave," Fred stresses the family theme when he characterizes the holiday as "the only time when men and women seem to realize that all human beings are members of the same family and that being members of the same family they owe each other some measure of warmth and solace."

As a film about family, *A Christmas Carol* plays down class differences. Scrooge and Bob, for example, are not portrayed as master and

Figure 68. An egalitarian Scrooge, Reginald Owen delivers Bob Cratchit's prize turkey himself in MGM's A Christmas Carol *(1938). Courtesy of the Museum of Modern Art Film Stills Archive.*

servant. Servants, in fact, do not appear in the film. The scene of the charwomen and undertaker's man selling Scrooge's possessions is cut, and even in the final stave Scrooge chooses to deliver Bob's turkey himself (fig. 68) rather than hire a man to do so. Bob is not of an ostensibly different class from his employer. He is a very bourgeois clerk. His home is more the model of a modest middle-class home of the thirties than that of a Victorian workingman. It has a separate entry hall, its rooms are well furnished and decorated – including pictures in oval Victorian frames on the walls – and Bob's well-dressed family drink their Christmas punch from matching glasses. In these comfortable surroundings, Mrs. Cratchit makes no objection to toasting Scrooge as the founder of their feast; in fact, she initiates the toast. Bob looks very well fed, and even though he has just lost his job, he shows little concern about his economic situation as he shops for Christmas food and presents. Nearly all the markings of class difference, much less class struggle, have been removed from this version of the story.

In the end this leveling Carol links financial and familial relationships. The visions of the loving Cratchit family, of the infatuated Bess and Fred, and of Fezziwig, whose business touches the personal lives of his employees, teach Scrooge a new ideal of business as service to others.

Figure 69. Eros and agape are melded in the church service montage for the MGM Carol *as the romance of Fred and Bess is linked to the adoration of the magi and the worship of the beautiful child. Courtesy of the Museum of Modern Art Film Stills Archive.*

After his reformation, Scrooge unites all the characters into one family. He makes Fred his partner, enabling him to marry Bess, he reemploys Cratchit at a higher salary, and he promises Peter a job when he is a little older. In the final scene this new "family-firm" gathers around the Cratchit dining table – the symbolic antithesis to the office of Stave 1 – to drink the Christmas cup denied in the opening scene.

At the beginning of the vision of Christmas Present, the spirit takes Scrooge to a Christmas service, a ceremony that pulls together the thematic strands of the MGM Carol (fig. 69). As the congregation sings "O Come, All Ye Faithful," the camera cuts from Bob and Tim, who raise their voices in adoraton of the divine child, to Fred and Bess, who look adoringly into each other's eyes. On the line "Word of the Father now in flesh appearing," a closeup of Tim hints at the power of the crippled child in this story. As the congregation sings "O come, let us adore Him," the camera shows an infatuated Bess looking into Fred's adoring face. This montage melds agape and eros, and when Tim, on the church steps after the service, whispers to his father about Bess, "She's very pretty," he offers a divine sanction to the earthly love of the couple and confirms Scrooge's observation during the service: "It's obvious they love one another. . . . They should be married." After everyone else has left, Fred and Bess slide on a patch of ice in front of the church, falling into an embrace in a snowdrift at the end. Just as Tim's blessing sanctifies the erotic, so this sacred slide, recalling the slide of Fred and Tim at the beginning, becomes a paradigm for the movement of the whole film. In love/play the couple form another "team," the beginning of another family to counter Scrooge's obsession with business. By becoming Fred's partner, Scrooge identifies his business energy with Fred's sexual energy, spiritualizing the firm by serving the next generation.

In Hicks's *Scrooge*, the miser is haunted by mocking laughter that chastens him into change. The businessmen on the street, the hags selling his clothes and bed linens, the revelers at Fred's party, and even Fred himself laugh at old Scrooge. In the Mankiewicz *Carol* Fred is too sweet to laugh at his benighted uncle. Instead of resolving into laughter, the party ends as Fred and Bess retreat amorously behind the curtain in the bow window through which Scrooge and the Spirit of Christmas Present have been observing the party. As the camera pulls away from the scene, Scrooge expresses his spiritual and erotic recognition in a mixture of meanings that echoes the mixture in the film as a whole when he laughingly asserts, "I love Christmas."

Mankiewicz's *A Christmas Carol* is one of several cinematic "classics" of the thirties that turned the novels of Dickens and other Victorians into romantic comedy. In MGM's *David Copperfield* (1935), J. Arthur Rank's *A Tale of Two Cities* (1935), Universal's *Edwin Drood* (1935) and *Great Expectations* (1934), and other films of the period, the studios raised Dickens' sentimental comedy to exorcise the misery of the Depression. This cinematic Dickens "revival" countered cultural fragmentation by establishing the common texts and by promoting the social idea that Scrooge and Bob Cratchit together sang the same hymn and shared a common culture. The sentimental Dickens rejected by the intellectuals of the twenties and thirties was the Dickens celebrated in these popular films.

When Edmund Wilson restored Dickens to intellectual respectability in his 1939 *New Yorker* essay "Dickens: The Two Scrooges," he found another Scrooge – and another Dickens – besides the one who ecstatically indulged his love of Christmas and who, in Chesterton's characterization, had secretly been giving away turkeys all his life. "Shall we ask what Scrooge would actually be like, if we were able to follow him beyond the frame of the story?" Wilson inquired. "Unquestionably, he would relapse into moroseness, vindictiveness, suspicion. He would, that is to say, reveal himself as a victim of a manic-depressive cycle, and a very uncomfortable person."[48] This Dostoyevskian Scrooge, Wilson suggested, was the creation of his divided author, a Dickens at war with himself, alternating between manic energy and morbid despair. Significantly, Wilson's image of the manic Scrooge was not drawn from Dickens' text. Rather, it came from the end of the 1938 film, from the scene of "Scrooge bursting in on the Cratchits" to bring presents to the children.[49] When he left the Cratchits' house, this divided Scrooge would return to vindictiveness and suspicion, like the audiences leaving the movie house after seeing the film to return to a world where Hitler, *Time*'s Man of the Year in 1938, was preparing to invade Czechoslovakia and Poland while Neville Chamberlain promised peace in our time. Wilson's two Scrooges embodied the contradictions of the day.

The two Scrooges disappeared unreconciled into the divisions of World War II. While Lionel Barrymore performed his annual ceremony on the radio, Field Marshal Montgomery concluded his Christmas Eve message to the Eighth Army on the battlefield with Tiny Tim's blessing. But the Dickens revival, begun by Edmund Wilson and the films of the thirties, was postponed. The centenary of the *Carol*'s publication in 1943 passed with little notice. Edward Newton reprinted his article on the "greatest little book in the world" for the occasion, and the BBC ran a forty-minute radio dramatization based on the Buckstone play, but wartime paper rationing made special editions impossible. The real celebration of the centenary had to wait until a Christmas Yet-to-Come when the war was over.

That Christmas came in 1946. Reaffirming the British commitment to the text, Penguin Books issued *A Christmas Carol* as its first postwar publication. They heeded the advice of a J. H. McNulty Scrooge who objected to changes and abridgments of his story, asserting that "if people really liked the story so much, it might sometimes be given in its entirety, like that other ghost story, Hamlet."[50] The Penguin is as close to a facsimile of the original as a book can be without actually being one. Bound in a hard-paper cover bearing the original decoration and just a bit larger than the 1843 edition, it includes the Leech illustrations, in color, and is printed in a typeface that the designers chose as the "nearest approach to the type in which the text was set." Even McNulty's Scrooge could have tolerated these sympathetic alterations in the appearance of his text. Penguin's choice of the *Carol* as its initial publication after the war and the care in the design of the edition bespeak the growing reverence for the book itself as a token of the past and as a symbol of an inherited common culture.

In America the Carol survived the war as film rather than book. For Christmas 1946 Frank Capra, the most important Hollywood director of the thirties, created, in his first postwar film, the apotheosis of the American Carol. Capra, like Dickens, combined artistic and commercial success. His popular comedies, especially *American Madness* (1932), *It Happened One Night* (1934), *Mr. Deeds Goes to Town* (1936), and *Mr. Smith Goes to Washington* (1939), expressed an inimitable style and vision enabling him to take top billing away from the studios for which he worked at a time when the mark of the studio was often more distinctive than that of the director. More than any other director of the period, Capra helped American audiences laugh away the Depression by articulating an American mythology. His films became the visual textbook for a nation understanding itself.

During the war Capra joined the war effort and explained to all Americans "why we fight." He returned to Hollywood after the war to form a new type of studio. Like Dickens experimenting with a new form of publication in *A Christmas Carol*, one in which the author kept control over the production of his book, Capra formed a group of writers, directors, and technical people to produce their own films cooperatively. Though the venture was short-lived, Liberty Films' first and most significant production was *It's a Wonderful Life* (1946), Capra's Christmas Carol.[51]

The film was based on "The Greatest Gift," a short story that Philip Van Doren Stern printed privately and gave to his friends for Christmas in 1943.[52] Stern's story has few resemblances to the *Carol*. It opens with George Pratt, a small-town bank clerk, standing on a bridge contemplating suicide. A stranger comes and stands beside him, and when George wishes he'd "never been born," the stranger grants his request, handing him a satchel filled with brushes to give away to the people he meets. George does not realize that his casual wish has been granted until he walks back to town. There the bank where he works is vacant and up for rent, and the light he left on is out. At his parents' home there are no mementos of him; there is only a childhood picture of his brother Harry, taken on the day he drowned because George was not there to save him. His parents are permanently embittered by this loss. Last of all, George finds his wife, unhappily married to an alcoholic. He returns to the stranger and pleads, "Change me back – please. Not just for my sake but for others too. You don't know what a mess this town is in. You don't understand. I've got to get back. They need me here." As the stranger returns George to life, he responds, "I understand right enough. . . . I just wanted to make sure you did. You had the greatest gift of all conferred upon you – the gift of life, of being part of this world and taking part in it. Yet you denied that gift." When George returns to town, he finds the light back on in the bank and his wife waiting for him at home. As he embraces her, he sees lying on the sofa the sample brush that he gave her in his vision.

George's brush with the supernatural and his transformation from despair to joy make "The Greatest Gift" a fairly conventional example of the Christmas story, a genre spawned by Dickens' *Christmas Books* and especially popular in the decades around the turn of the century. What Capra did in adapting the story to film, however, transformed the conventional into myth. He embedded the story in the history of the quarter-century between 1919 and 1946, giving it local habitation and name in Bedford Falls, USA. Then he melded this very American setting with the magic of the Carol mythology, turning George Pratt into George Bailey, a latter-day American Cratchit, making him the hero of the film, and adding Lionel Barrymore, the American Scrooge, as the story's villain. Capra's Dickensian vision and his Dickensian alterations to the story make *It's a Wonderful Life* the quintessential American Carol.

Stern's story becomes a frame, the first and fifth staves, for Capra's Carol. The stranger is elaborated into Clarence, a fledgling angel who hopes that this mission to save George will earn him his wings. A transatlantic Pickwick, Clarence is a child hidden in an old man's angelic skin. His old-fashioned clothes make him, like Pickwick, a representative of the past, of a prewar, pre-Depression America, but his fledgling status and the copy of *Tom Sawyer* that he carries with him reveal that he survives as an innocent child in a world driven to despair by adult traumas. The whimsical treatment of the supernatural in the film, complete with a very long shot of the heavens and some blinking stars recording the voices of God giving Clarence his orders, echoes the similar whimsicality of Dickens' spirits, especially Christmas Present, and transforms memories of the war into the metaphors of benevolence. Like the GIs who won their wings over Europe as they restored the American dream, Clarence will win his wings following god's orders to remind George Bailey that "it's a wonderful life."

As in the story, Clarence reveals to George the way the world would have been without him, but this distressing journey into darkness takes up only a small part of the film, placed toward the end in a position comparable to the vision of Christmas Yet-to-Come in the original *Carol*. The bulk of the film tells the stories of George's Christmases past and of the events in Christmas Present that have brought him to the bridge. Like

Scrooge, George is reminded of the positive things in his life on which he has turned his back – the parents who love him, the social impact of his building and loan business, his loving wife and children. By the time George sees what Bedford Falls would have been without him, these positive memories, like those the spirits bring to Scrooge, have already softened his suicidal despair. In the end he knows that his has been a wonderful life, and he returns to his wife and children to celebrate Christmas.

Just as Dickens rendered Scrooge's life symbolic of the dislocation and isolation of the displaced urban dweller of the 1840s, George Bailey's life is a nutshell American biography of the first half of the twentieth century. His childhood tells a story of self-help and social concern, showing young George as a soda jerk and delivery boy for the Bedford Falls drug store who saves his brother from drowning and prevents the druggist from dispensing harmful pills. George is enmeshed in his community, his life intertwined with the life of the town. Family troubles and difficulties at the building and loan frustrate his adolescent desires to go off to college and to see the world. He cannot even go off to war, for a childhood wound – the bad ear acquired when he saved his brother – has left him physically unfit for the army. Scrooge is wounded by childhood neglect, George by his involvement with others. Scrooge is frozen in isolation, George trapped in Bedford Falls, condemned to life as a provincial American innocent serving his fellow men.

World events play at the margins of George's life. As the camera pans a street scene, an incidental newspaper headline announces Al Smith's nomination or the stock market crash, and passing street people evoke the Depression with images of the down-and-out. At the center of the picture, world events are reduced to the scale of provincial America. The war provides opportunities for the local football star to become a war hero and for the small-time entrepreneur to get rich making military hardware. The struggle of the American economy to free itself from the failures of the international bankers becomes the melodrama of George's efforts to keep his building and loan afloat. And the twenties crash into the thirties as a whole high school prom in full evening dress splashes into a swimming pool hidden under a retractable gym floor. In this scene, the most wonderful echo of Dickens' Carol in the film, Capra turns the Fezziwig festivities into American madness (fig. 70). George's story is never secondary to the historical panorama against which it plays, nor are his troubles ever suggested to be simply the result of historical forces over which he has no control. The despair that George feels on the bridge may articulate such historic questions, but neither George nor the film makes the connection explicit.

Figure 70. James Stewart and Donna Reed become the top couple in Frank Capra's extravagant up-dating of Fezziwig's ball in It's a Wonderful Life *(1946). Courtesy of Wesleyan Cinema Archives.*

Probably the most important difference between George Bailey and Scrooge is that Scrooge is an outsider, a separate figure moving against the society which is the ground of his biography. George, on the other hand, is one of the people. His life is rooted in Bedford Falls. The moving figures in his story – his brother, who goes off to college as a football star and off to the war as a pilot hero, and his friend Sam, who becomes a successful plastics manufacturer – are in the background rather than the foreground of the picture. One of the messages of Capra's Carol is the Miltonic suggestion that George also serves, even though he only remains at home and waits on the people of Bedford Falls. George is an active progatonist: he saves his brother from drowning, the bank from failing, and the town from becoming a demoralized slum, but as a hero he is one of the people. He is Bob Cratchit, displacing Scrooge and taking the central role in the story.

Potter the banker, Capra's Scrooge, linked to his prototype by Lionel Barrymore, represents vaguely European forces that threaten George's America by hounding it to despair and suicide. George's small and shaky building and loan competes with Potter's bank, and Potter's financial machinations nearly bring down George's enterprise, just as the machinations in the European economy threatened to engulf the aspirations of many common Americans. Potter's real estate deals are directed at economic control, unlike Bailey's more limited ventures, which enable the little people of Bedford Falls to own their own homes and achieve the American dream. Potter's "Old World" exultation in power and control for their own sakes sharply contrasts with George's American ideal of business as service.

When he first appears in the film, Potter (fig. 71) arrives on the main street of Bedford Falls in 1919 in a horse-drawn coach bearing armorial decorations on the doors. He wears out-of-date, "foreign" clothes, his dress coat, high collar, and bowler hat recalling the formality of Europe, the antithesis to the shirt sleeves in the Bailey office. The pair of lions carved on the top rail of Potter's chair suggest a throne, and a bust of Napoleon decorates his office. Potter is much more than a business rival to Bailey; he represents the "economic royalists," the tyrannical, self-serving oligarchs of Europe against whom Americans have traditionally defined their liberty. He heads the draft board that sends American boys abroad to fight and die. On the home front, he tries to reduce George to the class categories of the Old World, calling him a "miserable little clerk" and trying to involve him in his corrupt enterprises. Had Potter the power to make Bedford Falls into Pottersville, he would, as he does, in George's vision, turn Bailey Park, the subdivision for the common man developed by George's building and loan, into a cemetery. He would bury American ideals in a European Potter's field.

Produced in the wake of the war, *It's a Wonderful Life* attempted to rediscover American ideals after the entanglement with Europe. Starring Jimmy Stewart, Hollywood star turned war hero, and directed by the nation's filmmaker, Capra's Carol, like Dickens', tried to reconcile past and present. To a rapidly urbanizing America, it recalled the ideal of the rural community. It reminded a nation celebrating war heroes and generals of its tradition of recognizing the heroism of the common man. And for a nation that had just won its wings in world affairs, it revived the residual image of America as an international child outside the corrupt quarrels of the adult nations of the Old World. While Capra's Cratchit reaffirms his belief in Bedford Falls, Capra's Scrooge is not changed by his contact with the wonderful life. The film ends with the people of the town rallying to save Bailey/Cratchit from Potter's machinations. Potter has disappeared. Capra seems to be asking whether the America that came of age during the Depression and the war can retain its naivete, youthful energy, and imagination in spite of its entanglement with Europe. At the end of the film George holds the copy of *Tom Sawyer* that Clarence has left behind, and the book seems to affirm that he can

Figure 71. George Bailey confronts America's Scrooge, Lionel Barrymore as Potter, the banker Scrooge of Bedford Falls, in It's a Wonderful Life. *Courtesy of the Museum of Modern Art Film Stills Archive.*

once again live an innocent and wonderful life in the restored house on Sycamore Street.

Some critics have found an essential flaw in the character of George Bailey. The suicidal despair that brings him to the bridge at the beginning of the film, they argue, is utterly inconsistent with his buoyancy and optimism in the rest of the picture. But other critics consider George's despair the natural conclusion to a life of failure. George Pechter, for example, argues that for readers who "accept the realities of George Bailey's situation – the continual frustration of his ambitions, his envy of those who have done what he has only wanted to do, the collapse of his business, a sense of utter isolation, final despair – and do not believe in angels . . . the film ends, in effect, with the hero's suicide."[53] The implausibility in the film, these critics contend, is not George's despair but his deus ex machina rescue from it. The fundamental discontent in the ending of *It's a Wonderful Life* that has evoked this critical controversy is the same as that which bothered readers of *A Christmas Carol* during the modernist decades. George's life, like Tiny Tim's, is caught in the dialectic of optimism and despair that divided the period. Perhaps, as the British Carols of the time suggest, the survival of the book gives grounds for continued hope. But if the text has disappeared, merging into the cinematic fictions of Capra's America and returning transmuted as a celluloid image of *Tom Sawyer,* is there reason for hope when the image of this ghostly text vanishes from the screen?

The Greening of Scrooge

Consciousness III sees not merely a set of political and public wrongs, such as a liberal New Dealer might have seen, but also the deeper ills that Kafka or the German expressionists or Dickens would have seen.

Charles Reich, 1970

When one observes that we devote a lion's share of our national budget to war and destruction, that capble scientists are tied up in biological and chemical warfare research that would make Frankenstein and his science-fiction colleagues look like Doctor Doolittle, we cannot avoid the question, do Americans hate life?

Philip Slater, 1970

Comparing *A Christmas Carol* with Herman Melville's "Bartleby the Scrivener," Pearl Solomon noted that in the American story the workingman takes the role that the master takes in the British tale: "Each is free to be a hero, set free by certain political, social, and ideological circumstances of their cultures to select their own paths." Scrooge uses his freedom to "embrace mankind as his business," while Bartleby severs all bonds with the human family in a "self-embrace . . . as representative an 'expression of the American mind' as the Declaration of Independence."[1]

This difference between Scrooge and Bartleby also described the difference between British and American Carols. Cratchit-centered, the American Carol celebrated a hero who challenged established authority. Although George Bailey's conclusion lacks the existential toughness of Bartleby's, he makes no détente with Potter – with traditional power – at the end of his story. His triumph is uncompromised by politics. In his wish-fulfilling version of the American Carol, Bailey/Cratchit reclaims his innocence while his Scrooge is vanquished and vanishes rather than reforms.

At the end of the British Carol Scrooge remained dominant, for his reformation testified to the ability of established authority to adapt and maintain its power. This authority was vested in the original text. Fearing that radio and television productions of the *Carol* would displace the traditional family ritual of reading the story aloud on Christmas Eve, British readers preferred facsimile and fine editions to film and radio adaptations, for such volumes celebrated the text and maintained its authority. British media versions followed the original more closely than American adaptations. While Disney translated Scrooge and Cratchit to Disneyland, Richard Williams in a 1971 British *Christmas Carol* animated the figures from Leech's original drawings.[2] Even small departures from the original could evoke an alarmed response from British traditionalists. When the Post Office took such textual liberties in an ad describing Scrooge ordering the Cratchits' Christmas goose with a convenient telephone, an irritated country clergyman complained in a letter to the *Times* that "every properly brought-up person ought to know that it was 'the prize turkey' that was hanging at the poulterer's shop."[3]

One of the most effective British Carols, and probably the best sound recording of the story, is the 1960 dramatic reading with Ralph Richardson as Scrooge.[4] Running a full hour, twice as long as many radio adaptations, and notable for its fidelity to Dickens' text, it renders the tale as traditional comedy, unifying the story with a motif of laughter. Its Dickensian narrator (Paul Scofield) recalls the point of view in the original text and reenacts the familiar family reading. While it tones down the sentimentality of the original – cutting such well-known moments as Tim's "God Bless us, every one!" – it has no Freudian overtones, no suggestions of a conflicted Wilsonian Scrooge. Yet its commitment to the traditional representation of the story gives a certain ironic doubleness to Scrooge's demand of the Spirit of Christmas Past: "Haunt me, haunt me no longer." For all its polish this rendering remains a reincarnation, a haunting from the past, that ignores the postwar implications of the tale.

For as World War II changed both Britain and the United States, it also changed the Carol. Historian David Snowman has decribed the period between 1945 and 1975 as one of the convergence of British and American cultures.[5] The prewar differences that engendered the distinct national Carols were superseded after the war by an emerging common culture. As the distinctions between officers and men, masters and servants, were discarded on the battlefields, the paternalistic class attitudes of prewar Britain gave way to a growing egalitarianism and Cratchit assumed new power in the British Carol. Jack Lindsay exaggerated this change in his 1950 description: "The whole point of *The Carol* lies in the handing over of Christmas as a symbol and expression of union to the worker Cratchit, and the cutting of it away from Scrooge the employer. If Scrooge is to be saved, he must go to the Cratchits; and his going (since it transforms him) transforms society."[6] This postwar cockney Cratchit has taken on the power of his prewar American counterpart.

While the British Cratchit was "Americanized," the American Scrooge lost his "Old-Worldliness." The Scrooge of *It's a Wonderful Life*, the "European" Potter, a displaced father-figure,[7] whose hard-headed business acumen reveals by contrast George Bailey's financial naivete, becomes an irrelevancy at the end of the film. He is not transformed; he is not even present at the final scene when the townspeople save the building and loan. His disappearance suggests that his parental role is over and that he and his European counterparts can no longer be blamed for the difficulties of their New World children. In the final image of the film, George, restored from his suicidal impulses, embraces his wife and children and accepts his parental role toward both his own family and the people of Bedford Falls. As he takes on economic responsibilities that were once Potter's, Cratchit and Scrooge are merged.

The Depression Carols, both British and American, had articulated a cultural desire to escape from the pressures of economic necessity into an idealized world where family unity replaced social division and distrust. The structural representations of these societal hopes – the Lord Mayor's banquet and the family reading preserving British tradition;

the New Deal projecting the promised American future – informed the Depression Carol's transforming vision. With the triumph of the allied democracies in the war, that vision should have become reality. But the war contained its own contradiction and the reality of human evil outlived Hitler. Although the Fascists were defeated, their pessimistic lesson about the nature of man persisted. Reviewing Capra's Carol for the *Nation*, James Agee challenged the film's prewar optimism. "I mistrust . . . any work," he wrote, "which tries to persuade me – or rather assumes that I assume – that there is so much good in nearly all the worst of us that all it needs is a proper chance and example, to take complete control." George Bailey, Agee contended, was an "exceptional man," a heroic Cratchit saving the helpless people of Bedford Falls, and he embodied the film's "chief mistake or sin – an enormous one – its refusal to face the fact that evil is intrinsic in each individual, and that no man may deliver his brother."[8]

As the deliverer of Bedford Falls, Bailey personifies the idealism implicit in the prewar Carol. But his triumph in this postwar film is at best ambiguous. Assuming his parental responsibilities at the end, George takes on Potter's former role, and in doing so he unconsciously accepts the belief espoused by his vanished antagonist that "evil is intrinsic in each individual." With the American Cratchit assuming the power of Scrooge, this film's ending marks the beginning of the postwar Carol. The hero of that story is Scrooge.

Dickens' first experiment with the "Christmas book," the *Carol* departed from the formula he used in his longer novels. In *Nicholas Nickleby, Martin Chuzzlewit,* and *David Copperfield,* he centered the novel on a young man coming of age who wondered, as David Copperfield does, whether he would "turn out to be the hero of [his] own life." With some variations, even *Oliver Twist* and *The Pickwick Papers* can be seen as versions of this quest for identity. The antagonist to the hero in these tales is often a greedy "uncle" or surrogate father, a figure like Ralph Nickleby or old Martin Chuzzlewit who frustrates the hero's quest. When the hero discovers his identity, defeats or transforms the interfering uncle, and establishes himself in the world, his quest is completed.

A Christmas Carol reverses the usual positions of protagonist and antagonist. The villain is given the central role and his negative presence obscures the quest story. Although attempts to place the Cratchits in the center of the Carol try to restore something closer to the usual Dickens plot, the figure who most resembles the Dickens hero is not Bob Cratchit but rather Fred, Scrooge's nephew. His suppressed story is that of a young man whose worldly advancement is frustrated by Scrooge's objections to his good humor, his marriage, his whole way of life. Scrooge's role in dashing his nephew's prospects is hinted at in Fred's wife's observation during the Christmas party that Scrooge must be very rich, and in Fred's reply that Scrooge's wealth is of "no use to him" because "he hasn't the satisfaction of thinking – ha, ha, ha! – that he is ever going to benefit US with it" (*CB*, 52). In *Nickleby* or *Chuzzlewit*, this economic conflict would motivate the plot. Some versions of the *Carol* try to bring this subtext to the surface by making Scrooge's interference in Fred's life more active. In these adaptations, Fred is often portrayed as engaged and putting off his wedding until he can afford to marry, while Scrooge becomes an active villain by denying Fred financial help and thus preventing the marriage. After his Christmas transformation in this plot of fortune, Scrooge, like old Martin Chuzzlewit, shares his money with his nephew, usually by taking him into partnership, and enables him to marry. These changes, as in the 1938 Hollywood film starring Reginald Owen, could make the Carol more conventionally acceptable to the popular audience, but they suppressed much of the complexity in the character of Scrooge.

Making the Carol the story of Cratchit also simplified its center. Some readers could take ideological consolation in the transfer of economic power to the workers, but in such tracts Scrooge was flattened into either a stereotypical capitalist or an incipient Owenite. And the Cratchits, as good as they are, for most modern readers are just not interesting. Despite attempts in the thirties and forties to enlarge the role of the clerk and his family, many readers would have agreed with T. P. McDonnell "that Cratchit was an insufferable bore, . . . a wimpering fool."[9] To admit this possibility and not reject the story altogether called for recentering the Carol in the problematic character of its villain-hero.

The central fact of Scrooge's life is his conversion, but he is remembered as the ogre of Stave 1 rather than the kindly grandfather of Stave 5. He has entered the language as a lower-case noun to describe the hard-hearted miser. The attraction of the villainous Scrooge may derive from the human fascination with evil that makes Satan more interesting than God. It also arises from his complexity. Scrooge can be reduced to a type – a miser, a cruel uncle, an ogre – but his character contains energy and complexity that belie such simplification. The divisions within him make him more even than "two Scrooges."

Some of the many versions of Scrooge appear in the various Carols of the story's first century. The *Carol*'s first readers were likely to see Scrooge as a representative of moral tradition, an emblem of "the Miser" whose preoccupation with money kills his altruistic impulses. Scrooge also engaged the sympathy of his first readers with a biography linking his experience with that of many city dwellers in the first half of the nineteenth century. Displaced from country into town and cut off from family and tradition, this Scrooge embodied their sense of urban anomie. As later Victorians consecrated the *Carol* with semireligious authority, Scrooge became a pilgrim, a fourth wise man seeking the "poor man's child" who would restore (and "restory") Christmas and the Christian message. At the turn of the century in the Carol as children's story, readers repressed the evil in Scrooge to focus on the kindly grandfather of Stave 5. Depression idealism discovered the potentially benevolent businessman whose reformation would break the chains of economic necessity. There is something of Scrooge in all these versions of his character. Defined by complexity and contradiction that make him both villain and hero, Scrooge embodies a tension between judgment and sympathy. Exploring this contradiction, Dickens countered the harsh sentences that hanged Fagin, Bill Sikes, and Ralph Nickleby and redeemed his own fascination with evil.

Postwar readers recognized in Scrooge a soulmate to Hermann Hesse's Steppenwolf. In that novel Harry Haller, tormented by the contradiction between man and beast within him, retreats from the world, fearing that his personality has been irreconcilably split. When he enters a visionary "magic theater," similar to the dream-world of Scrooge's Christmas spirits, he learns that he is not simply two selves, but rather a multitude of complementary and contradictory persons. Scrooge transcends the "two Scrooges," Edmund Wilson's Jekyll-Hyde characterization of him at the end of the 1930s, in the magic theater of Anglo-American culture during the thirty years after World War II. There he is performed as economic man, as a Freudian case history, as a creature of myth, as a spiritual father to the youth revolution of the late sixties and early seventies. Could Scrooge have worried, like Harry Haller, about the division in his personality, he might have been consoled in this series of transformations with Haller's recognition that "man consists of a multitude of souls, of numerous selves."[10]

Occasional Marxists of the thirties like T. A. Jackson had condemned Scrooge as a money-grubbing bourgeois, a capitalist "machine for meanly adding pound to pound, shilling to shilling, and pence to pence."[11] But most Depression readers resisted this cynical view. Choosing to see Scrooge as a misguided businessman who had forgotten his business ethics, they interpreted his reform as the restoration of an enlightened capitalism. They ignored Scrooge's internal contradictions by suppressing the economic principles that formed his character to favor those that transformed it.

The suppressed principles resurfaced after the war, when Scrooge materialized as "a personification of economic man." Edgar Johnson's best-selling biography of Dickens (1952) epitomized this view when it presented Scrooge as "the embodiment of all that concentration upon material power and callous indifference to the welfare of human beings that the economists had erected into a system."[12] Scarcity, self-interest, and materialism were the underlying assumptions of this capitalist ideology, the structural essentials of its worldview. Scrooge was more than misguided. He was the representative of the power elite, and his ideology systematically promoted his class interests.

David Snowman characterized the postwar period in England and America as one defined by affluence, when "nearly all members of both cultures have all their needs fulfilled."[13] Affluence probably encouraged the radical rereading of the Carol, for with scarcity no longer a daily concern, Scrooge could safely be seen as the representative of a class whose self-serving ideology was no longer necessary to calm fears of displacement and deprivation. In the context of affluence, even this calculated ideology was misguided, for it no longer constituted a rational response to economic reality.

John Kenneth Galbraith, in his classic book *The Affluent Society* (1958), described America in the mid-fifties as a society living in contradiction. Its social consciousness was grounded in an outmoded "conventional wisdom," a "tradition of despair" that defined the human condition as a competitive free-for-all in which each individual fought to secure enough scarce goods to survive.[14] But in affluent America, scarcity had disappeared. It was no longer necessary to maximize the production of consumer goods; indeed, the demand for these goods had to be artificially created. But as long as the assumption of scarcity held sway, the imbalance in the affluent economy could not be adjusted to allocate more resources to genuine public needs for schools, roads, or hospitals. It continued to produce even more unneeded things for private use. The economic problem was no longer one of scarce resources. It was a problem of a state of mind.

A century earlier, Dickens had challenged the same conventional wisdom from a similar perspective. Even without the abundance of postwar America to bolster his argument, Dickens was able to see the man-made contradictions in his economy. Scrooge was more than a simple miser. He was the monster created by the Frankenstein philosophy of Smith, Malthus, and Ricardo, the inevitable outcome of their laissez-faire principles. He was a theoretical miser. Reasoning from principles of scarcity, he sees the world as a struggle between the industrious and the idle, the producers and the parasites. His relations with others are defined by barter and sale. His only community is the marketplace.

From the opening page of the story, Scrooge's isolation is economically defined. He is described as Marley's "*sole* executor, his *sole* administrator, his *sole* assign, his *sole* residuary legatee, his *sole* friend, and *sole* mourner" (*CB*, 7, italics added). His "relationship" with Marley is one of contract and is really no relationship at all, for it leaves Scrooge alone. In one of his most memorable metaphors, the narrator characterizes Scrooge as "secret, and self-contained, and solitary as an oyster" (p. 8). To free himself for the market struggle, Scrooge has chosen solitude, bachelorhood, and separation from friends and family. Seven years after Marley's death, he has taken on no new business partner. His competitive position is economically "perfect," ideally embodying the principle of each man for himself. Alone he produces his world – right to its very weather: "The cold within him froze his old features, nipped his pointed nose, shrivelled his cheek, stiffened his gait; made his eyes red, his thin lips blue; and spoke shrewdly in his grating voice. . . . He carried his own low temperature always about with him; he iced his office in the dog-days, and didn't thaw it one degree at Christmas" (p. 8).

As a "manufacturer" of cold, Scrooge is metaphorically linked with the industrialists, the most vocal proponents of political economy, whose machines produced the hardware of the new iron age. "Cold" and "hard" are the adjectives applied both to the products of their industry and the iron laws of their ideology. "As dead as a doornail," Marley is a fit partner for an "old screw." He is chained to his life story, and he warns his surviving partner that an "iron cable" also binds him to a life of misdeeds and missed opportunities. A captive caged in a world of hardware – of locks, keys, cashboxes and "heavy purses wrought in steel" (p. 17) – Scrooge is as crippled as Tiny Tim, who bespeaks the crippling power of political economy with the iron cage he wears on his leg.

What Galbraith calls the "tradition of despair," Carlyle described as "the Dismal Science," a negative ideology whose central tenet, the vacuous laissez-faire, he translated as "let alone" or "do nothing." Fred instigates Scrooge's Christmas quest by posing a Carlylean question: "What right have you to be dismal?" he asks his uncle. "What reason have you to be morose? You're rich enough" (p. 19). If, as the economists argued, all value was economic, then no rich man should be dismal. But if, as Carlyle contended, men who recognized only economic value were spiritually diseased, then Scrooge was a terminal case of everlasting negativity. Scrooge denies anything that doesn't fit his ideology by "bah, humbugging" it out of existence. When he demands that Fred allow him to "leave [Christmas] alone" (p. 10), or when he tells the charity solicitors that he "wish[es] to be left alone" (p. 12), Scrooge asserts the negative central tenet of political economy. The emptiness of this "philosophy" appears in the countering image of Scrooge as a schoolboy in Christmas Past, "left . . . alone" (p. 28) by his neglectful father to celebrate Christmas by himself. At his Christmas party, Fred jokingly boasts that he "shook" Scrooge when he asked, "What right have you to be dismal?" Although Scrooge is not consciously aware of pursuing Fred's challenge, his Christmas Eve visions constitute an answer to Fred's question of how he can be rich and dismal at the same time.

Scrooge's most explicit statement of economic doctrine, his assertion that the poor who would rather die than enter the workhouse "had better do it and decrease the surplus population" (p. 12), articulates a callous Malthusianism. In *An Essay on the Principle of Population* (1798), Thomas Malthus mathematically linked population growth with the food supply, contending that as the number of people increased geometrically, the food supply grew only arithmetically. The remainder in this numerical problem was the "surplus population" whose inevitable misery reminded the rich of the necessity to be miserly. Well schooled in Malthusian mathematics, Scrooge automatically links food and sex. When Fred invites him to Christmas dinner, he responds in an apparent non sequitur by asking Fred why he got married. To Scrooge the logic is obvious, for food and fertility are the key factors in his Malthusian equation. The improvident Fred, by marrying, will bear children that he cannot afford to feed. Had he delayed his marriage until he could support a family, Fred could have avoided adding to the surplus population. That Fred's young wife is pregnant, even though their financial position is shaky, presents the nephew as one who wilfully challenges Malthus.

Scrooge is offended by Bob's fertility as well. Bob's large family is the one fact other than his wages by which Scrooge defines his "rampant" clerk. Bob's sexual imprudence confirms the Malthusianism that runs as a subtext in the relations between Scrooge and Cratchit. When he asks Bob, "You'll want all day tomorrow, I suppose?" (p. 14), Scrooge is ostensibly challenging Bob's right to a holiday. But his question is also an assertion, suggesting that anyone so sexually imprudent must inevitably "want." On this score, Bob, like Fred, is a living challenge to Scrooge's ideological rigidity, for although he wants, he is not miserable. Fred and Bob make Scrooge aware of his own rich misery and prompt the Christmas visions that bring Scrooge's subconscious fears to the surface of his mind.

The challenge to the assumptions of the conventional wisdom in the *Carol* is implicit, playing in puns and paradoxes like "want" and "left alone." In a way the whole story turns upon an economic pun. When, in the opening paragraph, the narrator declares that "Scrooge's name was good upon 'Change'" (p. 7), he tells in a single phrase of Scrooge's financial position and of his impending transformation. The *Carol* is the story of that change.

At the beginning Scrooge defines all relationships in economic terms. He immediately turns Fred's Christmas greeting, for example, into a discussion of the relative economic inequality between them, ignoring Fred's noneconomic value as Fan's son, as "family." Similarly, in Stave 1 Bob is wholly described as "my clerk, with fifteen shillings a week" (p. 11). He is not even named, for he has no value in himself, but only in his function as clerk. He does not become "Bob" until Stave 3, when a softened Scrooge sees him with his family at Christmas dinner. Then we learn his name and some details of his personal life as we share Scrooge's gradual recognition of his clerk's humanity. When the Spirit of Christmas Present blesses Bob's house, Scrooge thinks: "Bob had but fifteen 'Bob' a week himself; he pocketed on Saturdays but fifteen copies of his Christian name and yet the Ghost of Christmas Present blessed his four-roomed house!" (p. 43). Scrooge's confusion is ideological, for Bob, poor and yet happy, confutes Scrooge's economic principles. As a human being, Bob is much more than a fifteen-shilling clerk. Gradually Scrooge transcends his reductive view and accepts Bob as a priceless friend with whom to share a bowl of smoking bishop.

Bob's initial namelessness is matched by Scrooge's own. Scrooge has not altered the sign "Scrooge and Marley" in the seven years since Marley's death, and he answers to either name, for he sees himself simply as an economic function. As the charity solicitor suggests, he is "anonymous" (p. 12). The reductive laws of politial economy that turn Bob into a fifteen-shilling clerk turn Scrooge into a man totally defined by his business, which, he tells the solicitors, "occupies [him] constantly" (p. 12). To those caught within the conventional wisdom, the ideology is all-consuming, for its scientific laws purport to explain all social reality.

In "Traffic," an essay delivered at the dedication of the Bradford Exchange in 1864, John Ruskin asserted that political economy was not a science at all but rather a formulation of class prejudices. It failed to qualify as a science, he argued, because it did not take into account the most important branch of business, "the study of *spending*."[15] In its concentration on production and its total neglect of distribution, Victorian political economy codified the greed of the owners and producers into an apologia for the rich; its bias in favor of saving over spending gave the rich "miser" his theoretical defense. Ruskin challenged this theory from the perspective of affluence: "You gather corn: – will you bury England under a heap of grain, or will you, when you have gathered, finally eat? You gather gold: – will you make your house-roofs of it, or pave your streets with it? That is still one way of spending it. But if you keep it, that you may get more, I'll give you more; I'll give you all the gold you want – all you can imagine – if you can tell me what you'll do with it."[16] Giving the Bradford businessmen all the gold they could imagine, Ruskin challenged them to transcend their hoarding economics of scarcity to learn to live in a world defined by spending rather than production.[17]

Written twenty years before Ruskin's Bradford speech, the *Carol* contains a similar affirmation of the economics of affluence. Dickens would have agreed with George Bernard Shaw's comment "Whether you think Jesus was God or not, you must admit that he was a first-rate political economist," for he based his economic ideas on the New Testament paradox of saving and spending.[18] Like the servant who saves his one talent by burying it in the ground, the miser loses the worldly goods he fearfully hangs on to. Yet the servants who spend their talents are rewarded with more. Where "want is keenly felt," by economists as well as by the poor, there is misery. But where "abundance rejoices" there is an inexhaustible supply of loaves, fishes, and turkeys. The shops in *A Christmas Carol* are so full that "poulterers' and grocers' trades became a splendid joke: a glorious pageant, with which it was next to impossible to believe that such dull principles as bargain and sale had anything to do" (p. 13). As the narrator tallies the abundance of Christmas, he produces wonderful catalogues of the fruitfulness of the earth and the bounty of the marketplace. Even in a year of Irish potato famine, the Spirit of Christmas Present sits on a throne of plenty (fig. 72), surrounded by a cornucopia of "turkeys, geese, game, poultry, brawn, great joints of meat, sucking-pigs, long wreaths of sausages, mince pies, plum-puddings, barrels of oysters,

Figure 72. John Leech's illustration of the Spirit of Christmas Present celebrated the economics of affluence by surrounding the Spirit with a cornucopia of plenty.

red-hot chestnuts, cherry-cheeked apples, juicy oranges, luscious pears, immense twelfth-cakes, and seething bowls of punch" (p. 39). And on Christmas morning there are still prize turkeys waiting to be bought.

The abundance of Dickens' Christmas differed from that of affluent America. It was not measured in its ability to stimulate the consumption of gratuitous consumer goods. The reformed Scrooge who buys out the toy store for the Cratchit children is a creation of the twentieth century. The only gift Dickens' Scrooge buys is the prize turkey he sends to the Cratchits. Dickens' Christmas was literally a feast. The markets overflow with an abundance of food, not manufactured goods. Even in a poor household like the Cratchits', "everyone had . . . enough, and the youngest Cratchits in particular, were steeped in sage and onion to the eyebrows" (p. 46). If applesauce and mashed potatoes were required to eke out the goose, it was still "flat heresy" to suggest that the Christmas pudding "was at all a small pudding for a large family" (p. 46). That heresy was left to the dismal Malthusians; the Cratchits chose to rejoice in abundance. More than simply the centerpiece in the story, the Cratchits' Christmas dinner is also the central argument in Dickens' challenge to the conventional wisdom. It celebrates the fecundity and fertility that belie the famine and infertility of the Malthusian tradition of despair.

In a controversial passage in the revised 1803 edition of his *Essay on the Principle of Population,* Malthus graphically presented the implications of his theory in the parable of the beggars outside the banquet hall:

> A man who is born into a world already possessed, if he cannot get subsistence from his parents, on whom he has a just demand, and if the society do not want his labour, has no claim of *right* to the smallest portion of food, and, in fact, has no business to be where he is. At nature's mighty feast there is no vacant cover for him. She tells him to be gone, and will quickly execute her own orders, if he do not work upon the compassion of some of her guests. If these guests get up and make room for him, other intruders immediately appear demanding the same favour. The report of a provision for all that come, fills the hall with numerous claimants. The order and harmony of the feast is disturbed, the plenty that before reigned is changed into scarcity; and the happiness of the guests is destroyed by the spectacle of misery and dependence in every part of the hall, and by the clamorous importunity of those, who are justly enraged at not finding the provision which they had been taught to expect. The guests learn too late their error, in counteracting those strict orders to all intruders, issued by the great mistress of the feast, who, wishing that all her guests should have plenty, and knowing that she could not provide for unlimited numbers, humanely refused to admit fresh comers when her table was already full.[19]

The well-stocked markets, the Spirit of Christmas Present with his horn of plenty, and the Cratchits' Christmas feast are Dickens' graphic answers in the *Carol* to this well-known passage from Malthus. His polemical answer appears when the spirit reprimands Scrooge for mouthing the platitudes of the economists: "Forbear that wicked cant until you have discovered What the surplus is, and Where it is. Will you decide what men shall live, what men shall die? It may be, that in the sight of Heaven, you are more worthless and less fit to live than millions like this poor man's child. Oh God! to hear the Insect on the leaf pronouncing on the too much life among his hungry brothers in the dust!" (p. 47).

Nevertheless, the arguments for the conventional wisdom were strong in Victorian England. Although the spirit warns Scrooge not to draw his arrogant conclusions on the basis of numbers, the numbers seemed to support the economists. In the parliamentary reports, the newspapers, and the streets, the evidence of scarcity and suffering was everywhere. Dickens himself was the first to acknowledge the omnipresence of Ignorance and Want. Amid so much empirical evidence of scarcity, it was difficult to imagine the world with an infinite supply of gold, and most of Dickens' contemporary readers chose to ignore the questionable economic theory underlying the story. Only one reviewer, the economist Nassau Senior, writing in the Radical *Westminster Review*, detailed the ways in which the *Carol* violated the laws of political economy:

> In the *Christmas Carol*, Scrooge the Miser is so drawn as to leave an impression that he cheats the world of its 'meat, clothes, and fire,' which he buries in his own chests, whereas in truth he only cheats himself. He is the conventional miser of past times; and, when reformed by his dreams, he gives away half-crowns to boys to run quickly to buy turkeys to give away, and pays cabmen to bring them home quickly, to say nothing of giving bowls of punch to clerks. A great part of the enjoyments of life are summed up in eating and drinking at the cost of munificent patrons of the poor; so that we might almost suppose the feudal times were returned. The processes whereby poor men are to be enabled to earn good wages, wherewith to buy turkeys for themselves, does [*sic*] not enter into the account; indeed, it would quite spoil the *dénouement* and all the generosity. Who went without turkey and punch in order that Bob Cratchit might get them – for, unless there were turkey and punch in surplus, some one must go without – is a disagreeable reflection kept wholly out of sight.[20]

Dickens responded to this critique in *The Chimes* (1844), where he has Filer, the Scrooge of the second of his *Christmas Books*, castigate Trotty Veck with the admonition "You snatch your tripe, my friend, out of the mouths of widows and orphans" (*CB*, 95). The more explicit social message in *The Chimes* did elicit controversy, and the hard realities in the streets of the 1840s gave some credence to Filer's blunt version of the conventional wisdom. But the gentler social criticism in the *Carol* allowed its original readers to indulge in the heresy that there "were turkey and punch in surplus."

In the affluent society of the 1960s it was easier to imagine the world, as Ruskin did, with an infinite supply of gold, and the economics of abundance gained credence as an alternative to the tradition of scarcity. The Carol became the parable of this alternative, but Malthus's parable was not yet passé. It served to express the conventional wisdom. Caught between the two paradigms, sociologist Philip Slater observed that "Americans continually find themselves in the position of having killed someone to avoid sharing a meal which turns out to be too large to eat alone." Dickens would have shared Slater's analysis of the reasons for this contradiction: "The key flaw in the old culture is, of course, the fact that the scarcity is spurious – man-made in the case of bodily gratifications and man-allowed or man-maintained in the case of material goods."[21] Dickens knew that the person who imagined the world with an infinite supply had to give up the conventional wisdom and change economic priorities from production and saving to consumption and spending. By imagining Christmas from the perspective of affluence, he transformed the feast, in the words of his great-granddaughter, to "a universal jamboree of giving and getting."[22]

In his first performance in the postwar magic theater, Scrooge entered as economic man and exited freed from the preoccupations of economic necessity. His business no longer needed to occupy him constantly. Liberated by affluence, he could explore other dimensions of his personality.

Instead of the idealistic Carol of the thirties, the postwar social analysts discovered a dark Carol exposing the contradictions within capitalism. These economic realists often dismissed the supernatural parts of the story as mere machinery. Dickens had no more belief in ghosts, they argued, than the unregenerate Scrooge, and Scrooge's conversion represented nothing more than an exchange of "one set of economic values for another."[23] But since the doctrines of laissez-faire, as Edgar Johnson suggested, were based on a "curiously fragmentary picture of human nature,"[24] they prompted a reading of the *Carol* that "la[id] bare a partial truth at best."[25] Scrooge was more than an illustration of political economy, more than a grasping self-seeker, more than Bob Cratchit's oppressor. He was a sick man, and, as Leslie Conger pointed out, he "was suffering from his scroogianism more than anybody else."[26] In his second performance in the postwar magic theater, Scrooge changed from economic type to psychological case. His conversion was more than an example of economic reform; it was a miraculous redemption emerging "from the recesses of Scrooge's own mind."[27]

Economic and psychological readings were not necessarily incompatible. Beginning from the Freudian link between money and feces, for example, Michael Steig found in the *Carol* an expression of Dickens' "excremental vision," pitting Scrooge's anal-retentive miserliness – the "moral constipation" of an acquisitive society – against the openness of benevolence.[28] Scrooge's defensive anality dismisses the poor as "surplus population," yet when he sees himself as human waste in the corpse of Stave 4, he is convinced to let go of his corrupt anality. Thus, the paradox of saving and spending at the heart of the story's economic message also becomes its psychological dictum: keeping Christmas depends on spending oneself for others.

Steig's analysis presented the *Carol* as a precurser to Freud's *Civilization and Its Discontents*. More often, psychological interpreters treated it as a case from *The Interpretation of Dreams*. The story's abrupt transitions between tableau scenes, its doubling of Scrooge so that he watches himself in the visions, and its recurrent symbolic details cast the story into a dream mode. Dressed in nightgown and cap, Scrooge plays the dreamer. In his waking life he consciously limits his knowledge to his present business, but in the dream he liberates his subconscious repressions, recognizing his losses from the past and his fears of the future.[29]

In the essay "What Christmas Is as We Grow Older" (1851), Dickens described Christmas as a festival changing with the stages in one's life. To the child Christmas is immediate and complete, and for the youthful lover it is entwined with visions and hopes for the future. But for the adult in midlife, it becomes a time to remember the dead. "Of all the days in the year, we will turn our faces towards that City [of the Dead] upon Christmas Day, and from its silent hosts bring those we loved, among us" (*CS*, 23). The list of those recalled that climaxes the essay includes a Marley figure, "a friend . . . [whose] destined habitation in the City of the Dead received him in his prime," and a Tiny Tim, "a poor mis-shapen boy on earth, of glorious celestial beauty now" (*CS*, 23). Scrooge, to celebrate Christmas in midlife, must overcome his fear of death and visit the City of the Dead. When Fred forces him to remember Fan and the holiday itself

Figure 73. Some versions of the Carol add an extraterrestrial dimension to Stave 4 by taking Scrooge on a Dantesque journey to the inferno of his Christmas Yet-to-Come. Here Arthur Rackham (1915) shows "Old Scratch" welcoming Scrooge to the underworld.

reminds him of the anniversary of Marley's death, he unwillingly recalls the dead and begins his commemorative Christmas. One of the recesses in Scrooge's mind hides his fear of death. He humbugs the holiday to avoid meeting his memento Marley, but in midlife the confrontation is inevitable. The course of Scrooge's visionary life necessarily leads to the corpse and gravestone of the fourth stave. The television musical *The Stingiest Man in Town* (1955) and the film *Scrooge* (1970) even add a vision of Hell to Christmas Future, taking Scrooge literally to the City of the Dead (fig. 73). There, by confronting his fear, he is released from its power. A 1969 animated cartoon caricatured this fear/release reading of the story in a displaced "Steigian" interpretation. After an extra-large dose of the terrors of Christmas Future, its snuff-taking Scrooge overcomes his previous inability to sneeze with an especially therapeutic sneeze in response to a Christmas morning sniff of snuff.[30]

More than from his fear of death or Hell, Scrooge suffers from his repressed past hidden in another of the recesses of his mind. Although they might not approve of his bald assertiveness, many psychological critics would agree with the president of Screen Gems who claimed that "Dickens is a terrible writer. In the original, Scrooge was mean and stingy, but you never know why. We're giving him a mother and father, an unhappy childhood, a whole background which will motivate him."[31] Although this film never got produced, many other such interpreters have elaborated Scrooge's psychobiography as a way of explaining his denial of Christmas. The text hints that Scrooge was abandoned at school because of his father's dislike, that he cultivated solitude because of this neglect, that he loved his sister and was deeply hurt by her early death, and that his resentment of Fred is linked to his bitterness over this loss. By not providing a full explanation, Dickens may have been trying to avoid the case history. Allowing the specifics to be imaginatively filled in by individual readers, he makes the *Carol* a vicarious framework on which to fit a multitude of life stories. But psychological interpreters, like the president of Screen Gems, have often preferred detailed case history to suggestive biography.

Perhaps the best example of the psychological Carol is the 1951 film starring Alastair Sim.[32] Described by the *New York Times* as "heavy on the Freudian sauce,"[33] it presents Scrooge as neither the money-grubbing miser nor the irascible old curmudgeon. There are no scenes of him dunning his creditors or counting his money. Noel Langley's script also removes many of Scrooge's witticisms. He does not propose that Fred go into Parliament to exercise his oratorical ability, nor does he challenge Marley with the punning suggestion that "there is more of gravy than of grave about you" (p. 18). Sim's Scrooge is fearful rather than witty. He is vulnerable, troubled, and insecure (fig. 74). In the opening scenes the camera watches him from above, diminishing him into a cowering figure, terrified by the world. The stunning visualization of the phantoms outside Scrooge's window at the end of the first stave underscores his weakness,

Figure 74. Alastair Sim as the troubled Scrooge of the 1951 film A Christmas Carol. *Courtesy of the Museum of Modern Art Film Stills Archive.*

Figure 75. The older Fan who comes to release Scrooge from school in the 1951 film is more of a surrogate mother than a younger sister to the abandoned Scrooge. Courtesy of the Museum of Modern Art Film Stills Archive.

for he is linked with the powerless ghosts who are tormented by their inability to help the hungry mother and child. Unlike Seymour Hicks's hulking, irascible Scrooge, Sim's cringing figure bespeaks a disturbed rather than an angry man.

To explain this troubled man, the film expands the vision of Christmases past. His father's neglect results from bitterness and resentment, for Scrooge's mother died bearing him and his father blames the boy for her death. To accommodate this biographical addition, Fan is made older than Scrooge. When she comes to rescue him from the lonely school, she is not portrayed as a child representing the innocence of Christmas. She is more a substitute mother to Scrooge who has intervened for him to blunt the wrath of his father (fig. 75). Scrooge tells her, "I hardly know you now that you're quite a woman," and speculates that the mother he has never known must have looked like Fan. When Fan assures him that he is "never to be lonely, as long as I live," Scrooge's reply reveals his repressed fear: "Then you must live forever, Fan." But Fan dies giving birth to Fred, and Scrooge, like his father, blames his nephew for the loss of this mother surrogate.

The story of Scrooge's progress as a businessman counterpoints this personal biography. He begins as a clerk to Fezziwig, but when Fezziwig refuses to adopt machines because he sees business as "preserving a way of life" and not simply a way to make money, Scrooge joins one of his competitors. There he meets his fellow clerk and future partner, Jacob Marley. Together they rise in the firm, opportunistically gaining control when they buy out the other stockholders at a time of crisis. They also buy out old Fezziwig, his failure to preserve his way of life signaled as they replace his sign with one that reads "Scrooge and Marley." At the beginning of his business career, Scrooge's attachment to Fan seems to limit his absorption in the competitive struggle of the marketplace, but after her death, embittered by the loss, Scrooge gives himself totally to the exclusively male cash nexus.

The change is reflected in his relationship with Alice, his fiancée. When he believed that Fan would "live forever," Scrooge could love Alice and, in a scene added to the film, promise her that he would love her "forever and ever." But after Fan's death he finds the world a "hard and cruel place," and he breaks the engagement. He also ignores Fan's dying request that he take care of her boy. Turning his back on the feminine – on the nurturing realm of sister and fiancée – he retreats into his countinghouse.

Regina Barreca has described Scrooge's gradual conversion in this film as representative of the therapeutic process, depicting the "amount of psychological work necessary for his reclamation."[34] Linking the three spirits to the Freudian dimensions of personality – "the Spirit of Christmas Past . . . with Scrooge's id impulses (the emotional, irrational child), the Spirit of Christmas Present with his ego (the perceptions of the immediate world around him) and the Spirit of Christmas Yet-to-Come with his super-ego (to imagine the effects of his actions on himself and others; to consider moral implications of actions)," – Barreca points out that this Freudian Scrooge's release comes when he goes to Fred's Christmas dinner and begs forgiveness from Fred's young wife. Though the moment does not make realistic sense, it does complete the psychological pattern of the film: "The film audience understands, through a kind of sublimational pattern of associations, that Scrooge is begging forgiveness of all the women he has wronged. This young woman is a symbol of those others, forgiving Scrooge by proxy." To restore himself to wholeness, Sim's Scrooge must reunite the male and female halves of himself and allow the nurturing female side that he has repressed in bitterness and resentment to temper his business life.

The "feminization" of Scrooge in the film is apparent in the enlarged role given to Mrs. Dilber, Scrooge's cockney housekeeper. Her only scene in the original story is when she sells Scrooge's bed curtains to Old Joe, contending in macabre argument that taking such things from a dead man cannot be considered stealing. In the most effective rendering of this scene in any film, Kathleen Harrison presents Mrs. Dilber's underground logic to project a character as real as Sim's troubled miser. In a scene added to the film, she knocks at Scrooge's door on Christmas morning to awaken him from his redeeming dream and to bring him breakfast and shaving water. In this Christmas confrontation with him, she becomes the foil to reveal his transformation (fig. 76), replacing the boy in the street who usually informs him that it is Christmas Day. Scrooge's exuberance so terrifies her that she thinks she is dealing with a madman and tries to run out of the house to raise an alarm. But Scrooge convinces her of his sanity, raises her wages, and rewards her with a golden guinea and a Christmas kiss. She, too, represents the women that Scrooge has rejected. His reconciliation with her prepares his similar reconciliation with Bob Cratchit, just as his plea for forgiveness from Fred's wife precedes his reconciliation with Fred.

Scrooge's conversion in the film is a more "private" affair than in the book. The boy who fetches the Christmas turkey and the poulterer have smaller roles, and Scrooge does not go into the streets to spread Christmas cheer and make a large gift to charity. His internal change is

Figure 76. A surprised Mrs. Dilber (Kathleen Harrison) learns of her employer's (Alastair Sim's) transformation in the 1951 film. Courtesy of the Museum of Modern Art Film Stills Archive.

revealed in his changed relationships with Mrs. Dilber and Fred's wife. In the Sim Carol, Christmas is less a public holiday than a personal state of mind. Scrooge has been internalized.

All the characters in the psychological Carol tend to be seen as fragments of the complex personality of its internalized hero. Projecting Scrooge's hard-hearted selfishness, Marley comes to warn his former partner that he will suffer the same ultimate fate. Scrooge is so like Marley that he will answer to either name. If Marley represents Scrooge's actuality, Fred represents his potentiality. When Scrooge dismisses Fred in Stave 1, he represses that part of himself that will eventually earn him a reputation as a man who "knew how to keep Christmas well, if any man alive possessed the knowledge" (*CB*, 76). Fred's open-hearted joviality at the beginning matches Scrooge's at the end. Tiny Tim doubles the hero by embodying the child within Scrooge who is crippled by his repression of spontaneity and joy. In the miraculous psychology of the story, Scrooge converts to be "merry as a schoolboy" and cures Tiny Tim, sometimes overnight. The internalized Scrooge learns that the blame he projected on others is part of himself. Knowing this, he can suppress his Marley and liberate his Fezziwig. When the Christmas bells recall Belle, the fiancée he loved when he was "poor and content to be so" (p. 34) like Bob Cratchit, he can choose to be like his clerk, making himself "poor" again by helping others. In the psychological Carol, Scrooge is not the creation of social forces. He creates himself.

Philip Slater described such internalization as characteristic of the 1960s. "We interact largely with extensions of our own egos," he wrote. "We stumble over the consequences of our past acts. We are drowning in our own excreta. . . . We rarely come into contact with a force which is clearly and cleanly Not-Us. Every struggle is a struggle with ourselves, because there is a little piece of ourselves in everything we encounter."[35] For Scrooge, this recognition enables his transformation, his choice to live in the past, present, and future and embrace all his many selves. But Slater suggested that such internalization was more often paralytic than therapeutic, for "the capacity to give oneself up completely to emotion is almost altogether lost. . . . Life is muted, experience filtered, emotion anesthetized, affective discharge incomplete."[36] Paralyzed by his awareness of the contradictory impulses within him, the Steppenwolf is incapable of spontaneous feeling and action. Slater considered the drugs and sensation-retrieval techniques of the sixties attempts to counter these paralyzing effects of internalization. Even more appealing than drugs, he suggested, was "a more authoritarian social structure, which would relieve the individual of the great burden of examining and moderating his own responses. He could become as a child, lighthearted, spontaneous, and passionate, secure in the knowledge that others would prevent his impulses from causing harm."[37] If the therapy of the dream failed to liberate Scrooge from his cold paralysis, he could convert to a flower child and be liberated simultaneously from economic responsibility and psychological debilitation. In the next performance in Scrooge's theater of all possibilities, he seeks such liberation and becomes the flower-child revolutionary.

The economic and psychological Carols drew attention to a discontinuity within the story. A little soft-hearted charity did not appear to go very far in correcting the excesses of hard-headed, laissez-faire individualism.

It was also hard to believe that Scrooge could overcome the neglect and psychological distress of a lifetime overnight, no matter how therapeutic the spirits. So many readers noticed this discontinuity in the text that Elliott Gilbert defined it as "the Scrooge Problem." Caught up in the story, one could be "almost convinced by Scrooge's change of heart, . . . [but] there is a measure of discontent arising from the obvious disparity between the way in which moral and psychological mechanisms operate in the story and the way in which they seem to the reader to work in the 'real world,' a discontent focusing . . . on the unconvincing ease and apparent permanence of Scrooge's reformation."[38] The more effective the analysis of Scrooge's problem, the less convincing his conversion seemed to be.

Victorian readers were not so likely to feel this discontent, for as a conversion story, the *Carol* was a cameo treatment of a theme pervasive in the literature of the century from Goethe's *Sorrows of Young Werther* and Carlyle's *Sartor Resartus* to the novels of George Eliot and Tolstoy. Dickens himself treated conversion in many of his novels, and although Scrooge's change of heart is not described in its stages of natural growth as Martin Chuzzlewit's is in the longer novel Dickens was writing at the same time, most Victorians could accept the story as an allegorical or fabular rendering of the conversion theme. Only the odd rationalist or political economist demanded a more realistic treatment, and a few dour Evangelical Christians found their ideal of conversion demeaned in the carnal revelry of the tale. For most Victorians, the *Carol* embodied one of the profound desires of the time.

Twentieth-century critics have been less willing to suspend their disbelief, sometimes allowing a modern cynicism about the possibility of conversion to prompt their discontent with the text. Edmund Wilson explained away Scrooge's conversion as mental disease. Humphry House judged it unconvincing because it was "mere pictorial allegory without any pretense of belief in supernatural power, Grace, or anything like that."[39] Even so devout a Dickensian as G. K. Chesteron denied the reality of the conversion when he suggested that Scrooge had "given away turkeys secretly all his life."

In the late sixties and early seventies, solving the Scrooge Problem became the crucial critical issue. Several critics claimed that it was unreasonable to expect social or psychological realism from a religious allegory or a fairy tale, and argued that within its generic constraints the story successfully depicted Scrooge's conversion. Barbara Hardy showed that the treatment of Scrooge's change of heart was part of a whole tradition of conversion stories.[40] In its use of the double, the story resembled many other literary accounts of sudden conversion, while its presentation of Scrooge's life in condensed form related it to the more realistic treatments of George Eliot and Henry James. In the most comprehensive critical interpretation of the story, Robert Patten elaborated the Victorian reading of it as religious allegory.[41] With biblical allusion and symbolism, the spirits prompt Scrooge to realize that his denial of Christmas has inverted the biblical story; his journey as a nineteenth-century wise man ends in "the mock Adoration on a future Twelfth Night Epiphany" in Joe's den.[42] Although the story is playful, Patten contends that "the conversion it enacts is serious and permanent. To suppose Dickens had anything less at heart . . . not only mocks Dickens' entire strategy, but also denies the words of the story, and what lies behind them, the Word."[43]

The most timely solution to the Scrooge Problem was probably Gilbert's own, for he solved it by challenging rationalistic readings of the book. To classify the stages of Scrooge's developmental psychology or to speculate on the permanence of Scrooge's change, he proposed, was to remain "trapped in a rationalism that both Scrooge and Dickens have been at pains to overcome."[44] The *Carol* is neither a realistic account of Victorian society nor a psychological case study of Scrooge. The story does not explain his conversion and its causes. Rather, it is the myth of his recovery of "radical innocence." Realizing that he has lost this innocence when he has fallen out of eternity into time, Scrooge recovers it when he learns to live simultaneously in past, present, and future and falls back into eternity. Scrooge's conversion was the story. To experience that story was, for the reader, to experience conversion as well.

The Scrooge Problem was also solved by a changed attitude toward conversion. Noting that "among today's youth, the phenomenon of 'conversion' is increasingly common," sociologist Philip Slater described the typical converts from the communes and the colleges who gave up bourgeois money grubbing to become flower children: "In a brief span of months, a student, seemingly conventional in every way, changes his haircut, his clothes, his habits, his interests, his political attitudes, his way of relating to other people, in short, his whole way of life. He has 'converted' to a new consciousness."[45] Perceived as an extreme shift from one way of life to its opposite, the change was usually not so radical as it appeared. Slater chose a political analogy to describe the process: the student "appears to himself and others to have made a gross change, but actually it involves only a very small shift in the balance of a focal and persistent conflict. Just as only one percent of the voting population is needed to reverse the results of an American election, so only one percent

of an individual's internal 'constituencies' need shift in order to transform him from voluptuary to ascetic, from policeman to criminal, from Communist to anticommunist, or whatever."[46] The metaphor suggests the connection between the two Scrooges, between the psychological case and the economic type, the inner and outer man, the soltiary miser and the manic celebrant. It also provides a way to comprehend the contradictory complexity of Scrooge's character.

Simultaneously embodying all the possibilities for his character, this complex Scrooge is always himself and his opposite. He might be characterized in the two visualizations of him produced at the beginning and end of the sixties by the British caricaturist Ronald Searle (figs. 77, 78). In the 1960 volume, Searle's Scrooge is hawkish and gaunt, hiding within himself.[47] Huddled in a high-collared coat, his glassy stare suggesting inner concentration, this withdrawn Scrooge visually doubles his ghostly ex-partner. Ten years later, in his caricatures for the film *Scrooge* (1970), Searle depicts a much more public figure than the lean and secretive miser of his earlier work. Rather than hiding within himself, this Scrooge, much better fed than his predecessor, confronts the world with his denial of Christmas and removes his hat to make his denunciation more telling. For while Scrooge is "self-contained, and solitary as an oyster," he also

Figures 77, 78. Two Scrooges by Ronald Searle – left, *from* A Christmas Carol *(Perpetua Books, 1960);* right, *from the film* Scrooge *– suggest the dialectical polarities of Scrooge's character during the 1960s. © 1960, 1970 by Ronald Searle. Reprinted by permission of Tessa Sayle Agency.*

relishes the chance to shock the world with his misanthropy. He clearly enjoys the extravagant invention in his suggestion that "every idiot who goes about with 'Merry Christmas' on his lips should be boiled with his own pudding, and buried with a stake of holly through his heart" (*CB*, 10). Embodying opposite tendencies, miserly withdrawal and misanthropic confrontation, Searle's Scrooges contain the dialectical contradictions necessary for conversion. Only a slight shift in the constituencies of his personality turns him from his private to his public self, from a keeper to a spender.

As a dialectical character, Scrooge becomes a dynamic everyman. This status is not achieved by bland typicality or by allegory but rather by the contradictory genesis of his personality. He is simultaneously public and private, confrontational and secretive, active and passive, villain and victim. His presence is always doubled, his public appearance always shadowed by his opposite potentiality. Defined by contradiction, Scrooge embodied the consciousness of the sixties, described most tellingly at the time in Charles Reich's dialectic of the three consciousnesses in *The Greening of America* (1970).

Reich asserted that America was on the verge of a cultural revolution. Based on a historical analysis that described three dialectical stages to modern culture, Reich's revolution would transform America by consciousness raising, beginning with the conversion of the individual and changing "the political structure only as its final act."[48] Consciousness One, the thesis in this dialectical model, was the competitive jungle of economic individualism in nineteenth-century America. The antithesis to this individualistic thesis, Consciousness Two, was the hierarchical corporate state, largely put in place by the New Deal, which substituted the benevolent power of large economic and political institutions for the hegenomy of the individual. The coming synthesis, the revolutionary transcendence to Consciousness Three, would re-empower the individual, but with a new vision of human nature. Instead of the atomistic individual of Consciousness One, committed to pursuit of his economic self-interest in a mechanical system of laissez-faire, Consciousness Three will empower the individual as organic "self" to grow in a nurturing new social garden. In this liberating ecoculture, the flowering of the individual will also be the greening of America.

Although Dickens lived at a time when Britain was in transition from Consciousness One to Consciousness Two, Reich noted that he possessed an awareness "of the deeper ills" of society essential to the emergence of Consciousness Three.[49] Following this hint, Warren French described *A Christmas Carol* as Dickens' fabular version of "the greening of London town."[50] He traced Scrooge's growth from the suspicious economic individualist of Stave One to the statist of Consciousness Two who rejects Belle because of the opinion of the world, and finally to the liberated person of Stave 5 acting from an inner sense of worth. The internalized man of Consciousness Three, French's Scrooge is not changed by political pressure or by supernatural intervention. His greening is prompted "by his own vision."

The 1970 film musical *Scrooge* also presented the Carol as a tale of Christmas greening.[51] Featuring Albert Finney as Scrooge, Alec Guinness as Marley, and Edith Evans as the Spirit of Christmas Past, the film now appears very much a product of its time, but it incorporated so well the assumptions of its period that the London *Times*, preserver of British tradition, commended its "close proximity to the original."[52] Although its musical score disappointed the reviewers, most would nonetheless have agreed with Vincent Canby, who found the film "quite acceptable" as a version of the story, and with Christopher Hudson, who described Albert Finney as "the definitive Scrooge of our times."[53]

Scrooge sums up the assumptions of the postwar Carol. Transcending its British origin, it is the postmodern Carol of the global village. It melds the British music-hall one-man show with the pizzazz of the Hollywood musical, ending with a high-kicking cockney chorus on the Busby Berkeley model. It adopts the "egalitarianism" of the American Carol: class distinctions between Scrooge and Cratchit are replaced by generational distance, and Bob's wish for Tiny Tim is that he will become a millionaire. It also assumes the interiorization of Scrooge. Without dwelling on his psychobiography, it treats the story as the emergence of his selfhood. The doubling and feminization of the psychological Carol here link Scrooge's death with Tiny Tim's and cast a woman as the spirit of Scrooge's Christmases past. The spirits project Scrooge's inner being. They do not show him the ills of society; they show him himself.

Finney's Scrooge embodies the dialectical contradictions that make his conversion possible. A miser with hands dirtied from handling money, he celebrates his misanthropy in the opening scenes with a rasping recitaton of "I Hate People." The song's Swiftian summary of human corruption lists "scavengers," "sycophants," and "flatterers," and "fools," "pharisees," "hypocrites," "swindlers," and "frauds." Scrooge concludes that "people are despicable creatures!" But instead of withdrawing from humanity as a result of this unsettling conclusion, he seeks out opportunities to make life miserable for others. Repressed and withdrawn, he is also aggressively assertive. He is an active, confrontational misanthrope. Even his physical appearance is ambiguous. Neither young nor old, to one critic he appeared "prematurely aged," while another thought him "too full of face for a man of withered soul."[54] Although he enacts a fantasy of Scrooge, Father Christmas, and Santa Claus all rolled into one, he also fits Pauline Kael's characterization as "glum and realistic."[55] These ambivalences in Finney's character suggest his dialectical complexity.

As a representative of Consciousness One, he recites the litany of laissez-faire. He excuses himself from Christmas charity, pleading that he pays taxes to aid the poor. Then, going a step further than his original, he expresses resentment at being "forced" to pay such taxes. They interfere with his first duty to his own self-interest. To this morose economic individualism, Leslie Bricusse adds an intense puritanism. Scrooge religiously affirms hard work as "the only reality" and attacks the "indolent classes / Sitting on their indolent arses." Rather than objecting to Bob Cratchit's holiday on economic grounds – that he must pay him a day's wages for no work – he is offended by Bob's hedonism. "The trouble with you, Cratchit," he says to the clerk, "is that all you think of is pleasure." Finney's Scrooge has always denied himself pleasure. At Fezziwig's party, he does not dance with his fiancée, because he has refused to learn how to dance, even though "Isabel, who clearly adored Ebenezer, tr[ied] with great love and understanding to bring him out of his shell and introduce him to a world of pleasure and happiness that his many inhibitions made it hard for him to accept."[56]

Isabel fails to free him from his puritanism. She later leaves him because he adds to his Consciousness One inhibitions the institutional fears of Consciousness Two. When she tells him that he loves money more than he loves her, his rebuttal – "How shall I ever understand the world? . . . There is nothing on which it is so hard as poverty, and there is nothing it professes to condemn with such severity as the pursuit of wealth!" – articulates his confused attempt to define himself by the world's expectations. His success in this endeavor over a lifetime makes him an institution. At the beginning of the film the chorus of street urchins, liberated harbingers of Consciousness Three, taunt him as "Father Christmas." They do not see him as an eccentric iconoclast but as the representative of the established order, a Father Christmas of the old consciousness, a "miser," a "skinflint," "the meanest man in the whole wide world." Rather than promoting the holiday, Scrooge and his repressive society devote all their energy to preventing it from happening. Leave your stocking out for Christmas, the urchins sing, "and he'll steal it."

The greening of Scrooge begins when he abandons the assumptions of scarcity to adopt the perspective of affluence. His transformation turns on several phrases that articulate the creed of the new consciousness. Countering his puritanical belief that happiness is not something man should strive for, and his Consciousness Two sensibility that allows society to define his reality, Scrooge must learn Isabel's message that "happiness is whatever you want it to be." The revolution does not begin with a change in the political structure, but rather with a new consciousness that accepts happiness and pleasure as worthy personal goals.

Pleasure is not in expectation or delayed gratification. It is in the "here and now." This catchphrase of the sixties runs through the film, for as Scrooge is liberated from the fears of scarcity that have driven him to hard work and miserliness, he celebrates living in the present. Christmas Day is any day lived in the here and now. Tiny Tim usually sings one of the traditional Christmas carols, but in *Scrooge* he wishes that the beautiful day he dreams about will be "here and now." And Scrooge, when he finally stops hating people and promises to "be better somehow," learns to "like life here and now!" In the vision of Hell in Christmas Future – when Scrooge sees his eternal destiny as Satan's clerk working in a freezing office, "the only man in Hell who's cold" – Marley expounds the pop theology of the film: "Let's talk about Heaven a minute," he says to Scrooge. "Heaven – you idiot – you're in it on earth!" Hell may have eternal presence; Heaven exists only in the here and now.

Scrooge's guide to the here and now, the Pablo for this yuletide Steppenwolf, is the Spirit of Christmas Present, his mentor in what Reich calls learning "how to live." The spirit converts by kindness, on the pleasure principle, abjuring such strong-arm fear techniques as visions of Ignorance and Want. His most potent persuader is the milk of human kindness, a chemical he dispenses liberally to turn on the populace to the spirit of the day (fig. 79). When Scrooge shows signs of backsliding, a few sips of the milk are sufficient to make him ecstatic and to keep him receptive to the philosophy of this tinseled Timothy Leary. "I like pouring the wine," he sings to tune Scrooge into his version of the Christmas spirit, turn him onto the pleasures of the here and now, and convince him to drop out of the puritanical established culture.

The usual class distance between the miser and his clerk is replaced by generational differences in *Scrooge*. Instead of being pitted against the surplus population of the poor, Finney's Scrooge wars against youth. His antagonists are a gang of cockney street children who collect pennies from the older generation for not disturbing the peace with their singing. Scrooge's institutional power does not intimidate them. They do not run from him in fear like the caroling boys in other versions of the story. When Scrooge tries to chase them away from his door, they taunt him by calling him "Farver Christmas," and when Cratchit smiles at their insolence, Scrooge warns him that he has "a dangerous sense of humour." Scrooge later marks his conversion by joining these youthful revolutionaries. Dressed in a Santa Claus suit that he has borrowed from a shop

Figure 79. Scrooge, portrayed by Albert Finney in the 1970 film musical Scrooge, *goes on a Christmas high after drinking the "milk of human kindness" from the spirit's goblet. Courtesy of the Museum of Modern Art Film Stills Archive.*

window, he leads the mob down the street (fig. 80), praising the spirits and their youthful allies and singing the secular hymn "Thank You Very Much." When they meet a church choir singing traditional carols, so envious are the choirboys to see "that those in Scrooge's party [are] having much more fun than they [are, that] they surge down the church steps, almost trampling the choirmaster underfoot in their eagerness to fall in behind Scrooge."[57] Liberating the holiday from its established sacred customs and from its otherworldly theology, the Christmas Revolution is well underway and Scrooge/Santa has become its Lenin. The Con-

Figure 80. Dressed in a Santa suit liberated from a shop window, Scrooge leads his youthful followers in a demonstration of Christmas power, in Scrooge *(1970). Courtesy of the Museum of Modern Art Film Stills Archive.*

sciousness Two "Farver Christmas" has been turned into a secular Santa of the streets, de-institutionalized, and raised to Consciousness Three.

Not all the critics of the period were convinced of Scrooge's liberation. Some thought his change into Santa Claus cheapened the holiday into materialistic indulgence. Gene Shalit complained that the film "ruined the redemptive core of the story" and turned Scrooge into a "tinseled tinkerer who equates Christmas with goods and things."[58] But from a New-Age perspective, Scrooge could be seen as one who had given up the miserly view of money as a means of narcissistic self-aggrandizement to adopt the economics of affluence. Buying toys for all the children of the streets and promising to hire the best doctors to cure Tiny Tim, he uses money for the pleasure it will give.

Yet the materialism of film's ending reveals a residual discontent, for it displaces the biblical subtext of the *Carol*. The traditional carols sung by Tiny Tim and the waits in most versions of the story are here replaced by the secular, music-hall "carols" of Leslie Bricusse. Rather than Christ's nativity, these songs celebrate "December the 25th," "Happiness," and "The Beautiful Day." Tiny Tim does not return from church "good as gold," hoping that his handicap has reminded others of the Christ child. Instead he sings in the streets, earning tenpence ha'penny and the commendation from Bob: "Another fantastic coup by young Timothy Cratchit, the financial wizard! At only seven years of age, the youngest millionaire in the vast Cratchit empire!" The banalities of pop culture and the business motifs of the American Carol have supplanted the biblical subtext of the original. The "old theology" of the visit to Hell is included ony to be discredited by the theology of the here and now.

In this Carol for the secular city, the discontent finally centers on the question of whether the Christmas story itself is believable. The Christmas story in question, however, is not the story of Christ's nativity but the mythology of Father Christmas/Santa/Scrooge. A believer, Tiny Tim affirms "that story we've been told [that] Christmas is for children, young and old," but the street urchins are more cynical. They know that Father Christmas is a skinflint and they distrust the Christmas mythology. When Scrooge reforms, he promises to change their version of his story, "to start anew" and "make quite certain that the story ends on a note of hope." But the absence of the biblical subtext in *Scrooge* makes this strong amen difficult. The underlying mythology of the film celebrates Christmas as a festival of pagan recurrence, of the annual cycle of restoration from the depths of winter cold. Without the biblical story there is no escape from this cycle, no possibility for a final amen. Celebrating the here and now, *Scrooge* fails to fall into eternity and becomes a retelling of the recycling of Scrooge from old Father Christmas into youthful Santa Claus. It is trapped in time, in the problematic cycle that repeats itself every "December the 25th."

The Scrooge Problem could be reformulated as the Carol Problem. Caught in the contradiction between a one-time conversion story and a retelling of a familiar tale, *A Christmas Carol* attempts to merge two irreconcilable texts. As conversion story it begins when the anniversary of Marley's death prompts Scrooge's midlife crisis, progresses through the review of Scrooge's life, and ends with his liberated awakening on Christmas morning. That such a Damascus road experience happens only once in a lifetime is implicit in the strong linearity of this tale, with its definite beginning, middle, and end. But as a retelling the text reminds us of the *Carol*'s status as story by starting a second text after the opening paragraphs with a new beginning: "Once upon a time – of all the good days in the year, on Christmas Eve – old Scrooge sat busy in his counting house"

(*CB*, 8). The formula recalls the many similar stories we have heard, but most of all it reminds us that we have heard this story before and that this is a retelling. For the purposes of the retelling, we must forget Scrooge's former conversions to begin the cycle once again with the unredeemed hero, otherwise "nothing wonderful can come of the story." As retelling, the *Carol* necessarily contradicts the finality of its conversion theme. The story ends in contradiction, in the paradox of its hero/villain expanded to explain the world. Our tears of joy celebrate simultaneously the conversion and the inevitable human need to retell the tale again next year.

While the counterculture celebrated Scrooge's greening, there were those who did not specially want it to happen. They focused instead on his reversion and the inevitability of the story's retelling. Thomas Meehan's "A Christmas Carol, Revised and Updated for 1969" tells of Scrooge as a soft-headed New York business executive who begins singing carols early in the fall and gives all of his employees disproportionately large Christmas bonuses.[59] He reverts to Scroogishness when three very modern Christmas spirits – Holly, Belle, and Carol, in bunnyesque, diaphanous nightgowns – reveal his life to him. They show him his past when his cruel father Adolph gave him only a single lump of blue coal for Christmas, his present as the cynical Cratchit family exult in their employer's naivete, and his future when he becomes a Salvation Army Santa begging in the streets. Retracting the Christmas bonuses, and cutting Bob's salary by 37 percent, he becomes "as mean, miserly, and generally unpleasant as any old skinflint could possibly be, . . . for Ebenezer Scrooge . . . had at last learned the modern meaning of Christmas. In short, late in life, he'd become as mean-spirited as those around him. . . . Or, as Tiny Tim later put it when cringing at the very mention of Scrooge, 'God help us, Every One!'" Verbally echoing Dickens' text, Meehan's parody casts doubt on the conversion by emphasizing the retelling.

Marion Markham explains away Scrooge's conversion as the result of fraud. His detective story "What Really Happened to Scrooge?" describes the investigation of Inspector Mudrick of Scotland Yard into the case of Scrooge's transformation.[60] Although he suspects nearly everyone, even Tiny Tim, whose "pleasant smile and cheerful manner [are] obviously a clever cover for his real feelings," Mudrick finally arrests Scrooge's housekeeper, Mrs. Potter, who has used her psychic powers as a former medium to "produce" the spirits and terrify Scrooge into an altruism from which she will benefit. Yet when the truth is known, Scrooge refuses to press charges, because help is so hard to get. Instead he decides to pretend that he is a changed man so that he can save on his tavern bill by getting invited out to dinner. Like everyone else in the story, with the possible exception of the detective, Scrooge has become a fraud.

The most interesting of these reversion parodies, Russell Baker's "The Ghost of Christmas Endless," purports to be an interview with a latter-day Scrooge who has left England in 1931 to escape taxes and settled in a trailer park in Passaic, New Jersey.[61] There he complains that he was just a "typical nineteenth-century businessman," not a misanthrope, and that he was totally misrepresented by that "monstrous hack, Dickens." But his fundamental complaint is that Dickens misrepresented the truth by telling a story with beginning, middle, and end. "It wasn't that things turned out so badly," he says, "but that they just didn't turn out at all. Instead they just went on, as things always do. We always expect things to turn out, and they don't. You close the story with Tiny Tim saying 'God bless us every one,' and you think it has turned out, but instead it goes right on." In Baker's version Tim has gone on to become a rich book-maker, Fred to abandon his wife and take up painting in Samoa, Mrs. Cratchit to open a goose carry-out shop, and Scrooge to become a small-time complainer in a trailer park in Passaic. By reducing the conversion story to ridiculous triviality, Baker's Carol becomes wholly a "retelling." It doesn't turn out; it goes on. Lacking mythic contradiction, Baker's Scrooge makes us aware of the power of his original by calling attention to his absence in Passaic. Baker's article elicits our desire for the conversion story with beginning, middle, and ecstatic end, to transcend the unrelieved triviality of things just going on.

The *Carol* is not only about Scrooge's conversion. It is itself a conversion experience. Lesley Conger describes rereading the story for the first time as an adult and being brought to tears at the moment when Scrooge leans out of his window and learns from the boy in the street that he has not missed Christmas Day.[62] Following closely on Scrooge's visit to the City of the Dead in Christmas Yet-to-Come, this moment of therapeutic release, for Scrooge and for the reader, becomes the moment of purest joy. Even when rereading the tale, we anticipate this moment of ecstasy.

The therapeutic effect of the story does not derive from the dream itself but from its telling. Some modern versions of the *Carol* – like the recording made by Ronald Colman (1949) – cast Scrooge as the narrator, for in the telling Scrooge brings to consciousness the story's therapeutic power. But a negative, humbugging Scrooge has difficulty engaging the sympathy of the reader. He is too definite a caricature, too extreme a case. In the original, Dickens' narrator acts as intermediary between Scrooge's dream and the reader. Just as the spirits act as Scrooge's therapists, making the significance of his life apparent to him, so the narrator acts as the therapist-teller of the tale who vicariously engages the reader with its healing power. He has both judgmental distance on the negative Scrooge and a sympathetic desire to share his transformation. He can describe Scrooge's coldness and isolation with irony, but he can also share Scrooge's sense of regret and loss.

Nevertheless, the narrator does not fully understand his subject. Presenting Scrooge as the cold and withdrawn miser in Stave 1, he neglects his energy and wit, his enjoyment of word play, cleverness, and confrontation. When he tells us that "Scrooge was not much in the habit of cracking jokes" (p. 18), we question his report, for we have already heard several of Scrooge's witticisms. The narrator's misrepresentation of his subject suggests his reasons for telling the story and heightens its therapeutic effect. Ignoring the complexities in Scrooge's character, he simplifies him into a polarized figure, the ogre transformed into godfather from children's fairy tale. This polarization heightens the conversion story, but it suppresses the narrator's adult knowledge that Scrooge, like himself, lives in contradiction. The narrator's identification with the contradictory Scrooge is most apparent during the vision of Belle's family in Christmas Past. As he watches the younger children chase the older daughter, who resembles her mother at the time of her engagement to Scrooge, the narrator adopts Scrooge's wish as his own: "What would I not have given to be one of them! Though I never could have been so rude, no, no! I wouldn't for the wealth of all the world have crushed that braided hair, and torn it down; and for the precious little shoe, I wouldn't have plucked it off, God bless my soul! to save my life. As to measuring her waist in sport, as they did, bold young brood, I couldn't have done it; I should have expected my arm to have grown round it for a punishment, and never come straight again. And yet I should have dearly liked, I own, to have touched her lips, to have questioned her, that she might have opened them; to have looked upon the lashes of her downcast eyes and never raised a blush; to have let loose waves of hair, an inch of which would be a keepsake beyond price: in short, I should have liked, I do confess, to have had the lightest license of a child, and yet to have been man enough to know its value" (p. 36). Our post-Freudian perspective may make it impossible for us to share the innocence of this Victorian wish, but this is the essential desire of the text: to transcend the contradiction of innocence and experience. Christmas itself becomes the metaphor to reconcile age and youth; the *Carol*, the means to achieve simultaneously a fresh experience and a retelling. To ask whether Scrooge's conversion is permanent or convincing is to view the story from a mortal perspective.

Figures 81, 82. Two of Alan Tabor's iconographic illustrations (1916) capture the movement of the story as embodied in the narration. The image of Scrooge observing himself as a child (left) pictures a self-conscious figure trapped in introspection, metaphorically represented in the dark and dreary rooms that Scrooge inhabits. When Scrooge opens the windows of his soul on Christmas morning (right), he gives up brooding introspection, becomes one with himself, and reconnects with the world outside.

To open the window with Scrooge and learn from the boy in the street that we have not missed Christmas Day is, at that moment, to achieve the narrator's wish and see the world from the perspective of eternity (figs. 81, 82).

For Dickens, writing *A Christmas Carol* was itself a conversion experience. Bogged down in the swamps of the Eden colony in the American sections of *Martin Chuzzlewit*, he longed to escape the oppressive greed and violence of that text. His account of the inspiration for the *Carol*, which came in a flash while he was visiting Manchester to speak to a convocation of workingmen, describes a moment of recognition and release similar to Scrooge's awakening. The story's affirmation of the goodness of common humanity offered a dialectical alternative to *Chuzzlewit*,

SCROOGE at the WINDOW
"What's to-day, my fine fellow?" said Scrooge.
"To-day!" replied the boy.
"Why, Christmas Day."

countering the rapacity of its fallen world. Georgina Hogarth, Dickens' sister-in-law, never remembered seeing him more excited by his writing. He "wept and laughed and wept again" as he worked over the *Carol*'s pages. And when he completed the manuscript, he "broke out like a madman" to celebrate the holiday.[63]

Biographers have found bits of Dickens' life and character in many details in the *Carol*.[64] Scrooge's lonely childhood and the darkened schoolhouse are reminders of the blacking warehouse where Dickens felt abandoned as a child. Fan, the sister who rescues Scrooge from his scholastic exile, recalls Dickens' own sister Fanny. Fred's enthusiasm for the holiday and the Spirit of Christmas Present's magnanimity as a Christmas host recall Dickens' love of the holiday and his enjoyment of celebration. But Dickens identified himself with the converted Scrooge. In an 1855 letter to his assistant editor, W. H. Wills, he wrote: "Scrooge is delighted to find that Bob Cratchit is enjoying his holiday in such a delightful situation; and he says (with that warmth of nature which has distinguished him since his conversion), 'Make the most of it, Bob; make the most of it.'"[65] In writing the *Carol*, perhaps, Dickens transcended the two Scrooges to make the most of the many contradictory Scrooges within himself.

Bread and Circuses

The Carol Now

Were Charles Dickens writing this book in 1984 and did it in America, he would be dealing with economic justice in America and the paradoxes of those things.

Gregory Moser, 1984

I think we have to change our views. So let's be fair to Scrooge. He had his faults, but he wasn't unfair to anyone.

Edwin Meese, 1983

It is a strange phenomenon that at Christmas, there always seems to be a Scrooge on the scene.

Thomas P. "Tip" O'Neill, 1983

Figure 83. Oliphant; © 1987 Universal Press Syndicate. Reprinted with permission. All rights reserved.

And what of the Carol now? Scrooge is alive, to begin with (fig. 83). Among the many recent editions of Dickens' little book are *The Annotated Christmas Carol* (1976), wonderfully enhanced with illustrations and explanatory comment by Michael Patrick Hearn; an edition showing the puppets created by Peter Fluck and Roger Law in scenes from the story (1979); an edition with provocative expressionist photographs by Marcel Imsand (1984); the exciting and original visualization by Michael Cole (1985); as well as newly illustrated versions by Trina Shart Hyman (1983), Michael Foreman (1983), and Greg Hildebrandt (1983).[1] Notable among recent performance versions of the Carol are dramatic adaptations by Israel Horovitz for Baltimore's Center Stage (1979), by Barbara Field for the Guthrie Theatre in Minneapolis (1975), and by David Richard Jones for the New Mexico Repertory Theater (1987); Roger O. Hirson's teleplay for the George C. Scott *Carol* (1984); Thea Musgrave's impressive operatic version for the Virginia Opera Association (1979); and Jon Deak's avant-garde chamber music version with a libretto by Isaiah Sheffer, premiered at the Twentieth-Century Consort's Smithsonian Institution concert in 1986.[2] The "Carol industry" has been so productive in recent decades that Philip Bolton, bibliographer of the dramatic versions of Dickens, concludes that "'The Carol' now knows the zenith of its popularity on stage. The annals of its being dramatized are unlike those of any other narrative from Dickens's pen: only in the last twenty years, have the great bulk of plays, films, radio, and television dramas accumulated. Until about 1950, at least seventy-five productions had occurred. Indeed this is a goodly number. But since 1950, there have been well over two hundred twenty-five (225) additional live stagings, filmings, radio dramas, as well as TV plays."[3] And Bolton's figures are conservative.

Besides the "straight" dramatic adaptations catalogued by Bolton, the Carol has become text and subtext for the center ring in an annual Christmas circus. Thinly disguised as Mister Magoo or Maddie Hayes, Scrooge turns prime time into Christmastime, and during the commercial breaks he pushes Scrabble games and waterbeds, or hosts a Christmas party where he urges his guests to mingle and enjoy a Big Mac. Dickensian festivals at such unlikely places as Westbury, Rhode Island, and Galveston, Texas, feature Scrooge and Tiny Tim, while the traditional Dickens Festival at Broadstairs, the author's favorite holiday retreat in Kent, recently presented Scrooge as a talk-radio host offering advice on money problems from "the world's most famous miser." In community and children's theaters, annual Carol pantomimes confront slapstick

Figure 84. Drawing by D. Reilly; © 1985 The New Yorker Magazine, Inc.

Scrooges with space-age special effects, while on the stage at Radio City Music Hall Scrooge arrives in a real horse-drawn carriage to disperse the Rockettes and scatter Christmas cheer.

The story has become more than the "most institutional" work of English literature, as the Dickens scholar Philip Collins described it.[4] It is a frame for our experience (fig. 84). The sportswriter Hal Bock characterizes the confrontation between Kareem Abdul-Jabbar and rookie Patrick Ewing as an "NBA Carol" pitting "the ghost of centers past . . . and present . . . against the ghost of centers future."[5] Senator Pete Domenici, chairman of the Senate Budget Committee, gives a Dickensian turn to the ongoing battle of the budget when he analyzes the nation's financial situation as the problem of "budgets past, budgets present, and the ghosts of deficits forever."[6] Politicians run the perennial peril of being identified as Scrooges (figs. 85, 86). Not long after Mayor Ed Koch of New York accused President Reagan of being a Scrooge for supporting the elimination of state and local tax deductions on the federal income tax, Koch himself earned the appellation for asserting that some of the homeless people on New York's streets were there by choice.[7]

On television the Carol melds so seamlessly with media mythology that translations of it can be seen as "The Andy Griffith Show," "WKRP in Cincinnati," "Fame," "Family Ties," "Moonlighting," and, perhaps most aptly, "The Ghost and Mrs. Muir." In a television tour de force, Rich Little, performing an electronic public reading, does the characters in dif-

Figures 85, 86. Caught between Dickensian alternatives of past and future, President Ronald Reagan would discover that Edwin Meese had cast himself as the Spirit of Christmas Present. Above: *drawing by Tony Auth © 1983* The Philadelphia Inquirer. *Reprinted with permission of Universal Press Syndicate. All rights reserved.* Below: *drawing by Jim Berry reprinted by permission of NEA, Inc.*

ferent voices, refracting W. C. Fields as Scrooge, Paul Lynde as Cratchit, and Robert Goulet, Anthony Newley, and Tom Jones as street singers.[8] Meanwhile, the Saturday cartoons feature Bugs Bunny as nephew Fred tormenting a Yosemite Sam Scrooge or, in a most apt animation, translate Scrooge's stinginess into the irritability of short-sighted Mr. Magoo. The apotheosis of these animated transformations is probably *Mickey's Christmas Carol,* a 1983 translation of Dickens into Disney.

The collaboration is instructive. Who, we might ask, could better translate Dickens for our time than Walt Disney? As popular artists, each was at the center of his era, remaking the materials of the collective imagination into celebrations of cultural identity. Difficult childhoods spurred both men to become adult retellers of children's fables and fairy tales. Yet behind their public masks as avuncular storytellers, both Dickens and Disney had Scrooge-like qualities. Edmund Wilson psychologized Dickens as divided between "two Scrooges," and Richard Schickel has characterized Disney as "a man who fundamentally – and with good psychological reason – mistrusted the human animal, rejected intimacy and discovered early that he could rely completely only upon himself."[9] Although *Mickey's Christmas Carol* did not appear until well after Disney's death, a product of the studio rather than the master, Dickens' story ran like a thread through Disney's career. Sooner or later Mickey Cratchit was bound to confront Scrooge McDuck.

Disney's Carol was born in the Depression, that nexus of the American Carol, and Mickey was its Cratchit. But Mickey had to grow into the part. E. M. Forster said of the mouse in 1934: "No one has ever been softened after seeing Mickey or has wanted to give away an extra glass of water to the poor. He is never sentimental, indeed there is a scandalous element in him."[10] But Mickey, like his creator, softened with success. Although Disney began cartooning by drawing a "capitalist bloated and wearing a vest decorated with dollar signs standing in opposition to a laboring man,"[11] he ended his career a Goldwater Republican animating the American dream. If Mickey in the early 1930s was a rodent version of Huckleberry Finn, by the end of the decade he had been civilized into a beast-fable George Bailey.

Disney's first telling of the Carol, however, did not cast Mickey in the Cratchit role. It told instead of another rodent, Cedric Mouse, a clock repairman oppressed by his slave-driving employer, a human Ebenezer Scrooge. Published in 1957, this story vaguely hearkened back to the Depression, "those days [when Cedric] . . . was lucky to have a job of any kind."[12] When Scrooge refuses to give time off on Christmas Day, Cedric quits his job so that he can spend the holiday with his wife and fourteen children. Cedric's courage gives Scrooge bad dreams. That night the grandfather clock in his bedroom shows him a future Christmas when his "name has turned into the worst of insults," a synonym for greed and selfishness. Horrified by this prospect, Scrooge reforms, takes gifts to Cedric and his family, and invites them to live happily ever after in the grandfather clock. At the end of the story "father mouse . . . closed his tiny book and put away his spectacles. . . . One of the little mice sitting around the candlestick piped up. 'Daddy, that sounds very much like a Christmas story I once overhead the people downstairs reading. Their story was by Charles Dickens." The Disney version is simplified for the mice upstairs. Although it purports to be a tale of both mice and men, its human characters are shadowy background figures. Disney's sentimental version of the American Carol comprehended Cratchit. It had difficulty defining Scrooge.

Disney discovered his Scrooge in the figure of Donald's crotchety Scotch uncle, Scrooge McDuck. An "economic royalist" from the old country – a relative of Capra's Potter – McDuck softened Scrooge's selfishness into Scotch tight-fistedness. In fact, his "vices" were Disney's virtues, the parsimony and industry that turned Depression struggle into later success. Appropriately, Scrooge McDuck's film debut came in a didactic short, *Scrooge McDuck and Money* (1967), a project devoted to teaching young people the virtues of free enterprise. The myopic economic ideas that drove Dickens' Scrooge into irritability and isolation became in the Disney version marketable skills for Scrooge as economic consultant.

To sell *Mickey's Christmas Carol,* however, the studio needed more than Scrooge and Cratchit. Counterparts for all the Dickens characters had to be found in the Disney menagerie. Minnie was a natural for Mrs. Cratchit and Donald for nephew Fred. Some of the other characters presented difficulties. As one of the animators put it, "There was a challenge in every character in this picture because the part the character was playing sometimes didn't meet up exactly to the part the character was. . . . Goofy is a fumbling, bumbling idiot, . . . but he had to play Marley, who has to scare Scrooge somehow. . . . That was a big problem. . . . I think we handled it successfully."[13] As they watched Goofy's ghostly pratfalls, the audience didn't agree. Although one reviewer thought the film had too much Dickens and not enough Disney, most found Dickens' short novel shortchanged in the thirty-five-minute cartoon. As Disney beast-fable, *Mickey's Christmas Carol* caught only a small shadow of its original, a shadow no bigger than that cast by Jiminy Cricket on the hearth.

Attempts to retell the Carol in the vocabulary and grammar of another story system almost inevitably lose in translation. Scrooge is never quite

Scrooge in his guises as Yosemite Sam or W. C. Fields or Scrooge McDuck. The most apt of the animated translations is probably *Mister Magoo's Christmas Carol* (1962), in which Magoo's nearsightedness is used to represent the blindness of Scrooge's ideology.[14] Disney's version suffers from more than the inevitable problems of translation. Whatever power the Disney myth once had, by 1983 it had largely dissipated. In 1938 *Snow White and the Seven Dwarfs* had lightened the dark corners of some grim fairy tales and in doing so had articulated the triumphant idealism of the Depression, the same idealism that produced the American Carol. But unlike Dickens, whose vision deepened in the course of his career, Disney's seems to have become more superficial. The later Disney films, including *Mickey's Christmas Carol*, probe no depths, make no significant contemporary interpretation of the stories they translate. Richard Schickel suggests that this tendency in Disney "to diminish what he touched" is the result of a kind of aesthetic imperialism. "He came always as a conqueror, never as a servant," Schickel remarks. "He could make something his own, all right, but that process nearly always robbed the work at hand of its uniqueness, of its soul, if you will."[15] *Mickey's Christmas Carol* recreates only the shells of its originals. It is a hollow retelling both of Dickens and of the American Carol.

In rubbing the rough edges off Mickey and Scrooge McDuck to make them fit a homogeneous success story, Disney removed the conflict between rich and poor that informed Dickens' story and that lies at the heart of our current version of it. Instead of retelling the Carol, the studio retailed it, reduced it to commercial property to be peddled like the "Bah Humbug" necktie for those who think "the yule season is nothing more than a pain around the neck," or the diamond bracelet that Barney's of New York placed around the neck of the Cratchit's goose in their Christmas window.[16] Such displays may continue the sixties suggestion that affluence has made obsolete the economic conflict that created Scrooge and Cratchit. But if diamonds have become a yuppie Tiny Tim's best friend, we have also rediscovered in our time others who have not shared Tim's good fortune. The belief in affluence that turned the sixties Carol inward and concentrated attention on Scrooge's psychological maladjustment has given way to economic uncertainty. Our Scrooge has left the therapeutic couch to engage in political debate and social action.

The great *Christmas Carol* controversy of 1983, with "Edwinezer Meese" as its Scrooge, sets the issues.[17] The controversy began on December 8, when Edwin Meese, then a presidential counselor, characterized as "purely political" allegations that there were hungry children in America. The people lining up at soup kitchens were there "voluntarily," he claimed, "because the food is free and . . . that's easier than paying for it." Democrats immediately stood up to defend the poor, calling Meese's comments "disgraceful," "unkind and mean-spirited." Tip O'Neill led the critical opposition by concluding that "at Christmas, there always seems to be a Scrooge on the scene."[18]

Meese did not consider the "Scrooge" label an albatross hung around his political neck, but rather as something closer to a diamond bracelet. In a speech to the National Press Club, he contended that whatever hunger problem there was in America was inherited from Christmases and administrations past. That the Reagan policies had created hunger was just "mythmaking." As for Scrooge, Meese asserted that he too was "the victim of a bad press." Scrooge was really a generous employer who provided handsomely for his clerk: "If you look at the facts, . . . Bob Cratchit was paid 10 shillings a week, which was a very good wage. . . . Bob, in fact, had good cause to be happy with his situation. He lived in a house, not a tenement. His wife didn't have to work. . . . He was able to afford the traditional Christmas dinner of roast goose and plum pudding." Meese concluded by urging his audience to "be fair to Scrooge. He had his faults, but he wasn't unfair to anyone."[19]

The journalists quickly took up Meese's challenge to "look at the facts." Besides pointing out that Cratchit's salary was fifteen, not ten, shillings, they consulted economic historians who challenged the notion that Bob's salary was "a very good wage," even with the extra five shillings. His Christmas dinner, the historians pointed out, took nearly his whole week's pay, an income "below the level of most working class families of the time."[20] Literary critics also disputed Meese's reading of the story. Nina Auerbach observed that Dickens was making the case that society's responsibility to the poor was to be "generous and humane," not just fair.[21] Newspapers were soon inundated with letters coming to similar historical and critical conclusions, and suggesting that Meese wished to return America to the exploitation of the industrial dark ages.

Meese's playful apology for Scrooge purported to present new historical evidence of Scrooge's generosity, but his version of the *Carol* was not really grounded in facts. Rather, it was based on the belief that Bob's wages couldn't be low because they were set by market forces. "The free market," Meese declared, "wouldn't allow Scrooge to exploit poor Bob. . . . The fact that Bob Cratchit could read and write made him a very valuable clerk and as a result of that he was paid 10 shillings a week."[22] Meese's supply-side version of the *Carol* is one of many contemporary "apologies" that recast the unconverted Scrooge as the hero of the story and dispute his need for conversion.

Scrooge has long had defenders. Modernist intellectuals usually preferred his energy to Cratchit's sentimental passivity, and psychological readers, particularly in the fifties and sixties, defended Scrooge as the victim of neglectful parents and a harsh childhood. But contemporary apologists take a different tack. Scrooge does not require defending, they assert, because he is right. He is, in fact, a model of social responsibility. Industrious and frugal, he is an example to the poor of the way to escape poverty, and his hard work provides jobs for others. Scrooge's new apologists have difficulty only with his conversion. They find the case for charity at the end of Dickens' story a misguided or even dishonest attempt to obscure the real issues.

This ideological apology first appeared in 1937. J. H. McNulty's satiric Scrooge contended that he did not underpay Cratchit. Fifteen shillings was a market wage and also a moral wage, for it did not encourage Bob in such extravagances as overeating. "Every supposedly harsh act of mine," McNulty's Scrooge concluded, "was a hidden act of kindness."[23] For idealistic readers of the thirties, this apology clearly undermined the credibility of its narrator by ironically revealing the sophistry of his after-the-fact rationalizations. But by the mid-seventies this apology turned serious. In *Defending the Undefendable* (1976), Walter Block backed Scrooge against the Keynesians who blame the miser for "unemployment, changes in the business cycle, and economic depressions and recessions." In the "infamous 'paradox of savings,'" Block asserts, the Keynesians teach "young students of economics [that] although saving may be sensible for an individual or a family, it may be folly for the economy as a whole."[24] Block shows how the Scroogian virtue of hoarding contributes to capital formation, job creation, and the overall health of the economy. His unreformed Scrooge is an economic hero.

James McCaffrey similarly supports the unconverted miser in the *Mensa Bulletin* (1981), appropriately characterizing the debate as one between the apologists of head and the defenders of heart.[25] The unreformed Scrooge, McCaffrey argues, is "a truly good man. . . . Years of hard work, self-denial, and thrift on Scrooge's part had provided Bob with this good job with a respected man whose name was synonymous with financial integrity." The harsh judgment of Scrooge that has become an institutional part of our Christmas results from the anger he provokes by telling the truth and from envy of his riches. In fact, the attitude that prompts us to villify the unreformed Scrooge and celebrate the convert, McCaffrey suggests, contributes to some of our major social problems: "The senile-mad Scrooge is a model we hold up to our children every Christmas. 'Spend your money now! Have a good time today and don't worry about tomorrow!' These are the lessons of *A Christmas Carol*. Is it any wonder that kids today prefer the instant gratification of drugs and booze to the delayed rewards of the drudgery of study?"

Even Russell Baker has whimsically whitewashed the supply-side Scrooge. In a 1983 commentary, Baker characterizes the *Carol* as "the story of a man of principle . . . a lineal descendant of the 17th-century Puritans" who is "corrupted by a series of supernatural events."[26] Dickens stacked the deck against Scrooge, Baker suggests, and by depicting him as "a dyspeptic, foul-tempered, tight-fisted geezer while conveniently ignoring the honorable tradition from which he springs," he caricatures the productive supply-sider and promotes Christmas as a "festival of consumption." Such a book, Baker concludes, "with its gloating contempt for the man faithful to unfashionable principles, . . . is not recommended for impressionable children."

Nor for gullible adults, contends Jeffrey St. John more seriously in the magazine of the John Birch Society.[27] Unlike W. H. Auden, St. John believes that literature makes things happen. He describes the *Carol* as the textbook of "welfare-state liberalism" and he discovers Dickens in league with Franklin Roosevelt to lead Anglo-American culture down the path of delusion by denouncing "the business class as composed of heartless and cruel people." The president read the *Carol* annually, St. John points out, because it preached his doctrine "that the poor had by the very state of their destitution an automatic claim on the productive, without qualification or the consideration that their poverty might be the product of their own refusal to practice the work ethic. . . . What Mr. Scrooge earned by his own effort is automatically open to claim by those who have less. The only justification for that claim is need. This premise pervades almost all of Charles Dickens' books." And this principle, St. John suggests, influenced the Fabian Socialists in Britain and the New Dealers in America and has governed Anglo-American politics for the last century and a half. But now times are changing. "We are on the verge," St. John optimistically concludes, "of questioning those ideas for the first time since Dickens died."

Brock Brower seems to agree.[28] Seeking a subject for an eighties Christmas story, he rejects the Carol formula as passé: "You can't do Dickens either. . . . How do you get anybody to listen now beyond 'Bah! Humbug!'? You can't do monetarist change of heart, squirearchical benevolence." The contemporary Carol celebrates instead squirearchical self-interest, as in Louis Auchincloss's "Marley's Chain: A Christmas Story" (1980).[29] Convinced that his successful career and comfortable life have formed for him a Marleyan chain, Leslie Fairburn, a Virginia country gentleman, art collector, and diplomat, decides to cash in his comforts and marry a woman committed to social causes. When he confesses his plan to an old friend, a widow who has secretly loved him for years, she forces him to see his mistake and to realize that he really wants to marry her and continue his comfortable life even if it means extending the chain: "Whether he had redeemed himself or added the heaviest golden ball to the chain of his damnation he did know. But he also knew that he no longer cared."

Throwing off the chains of Dickensian conscience may not be easy. The first step, recognizing our own self-interest, is often difficult. The second step – not caring – may, even for supply-siders, be nearly impossible. The Dickensian chains, the altruistic and interventionist assumptions behind the *Carol*, have a firm hold on our sense of the story. Linked to memories of a fatherly FDR, of Lionel Barrymore's annual reformation, of Ronald Colman reading Scrooge on scratchy old recordings, our subconscious assumptions surface as we acknowledge Scrooge in nightgown and cap as our Christmas secret sharer and yearn for his transformation. These chained assumptions let us identify a captionless silhouette of a lame child on his father's shoulder as Tim and Bob Cratchit. And they enable Garry Trudeau to satirize George Will as a journalistic Scrooge without ever mentioning Dickens' story or even showing us Will (fig. 87). His cartoon merely depicts Will's assistant working, Cratchit-like, at his high desk to make its point about Will's outmoded thinking.

Our unconscious interventionist assumptions make the supply-side Carol easy to mock. In Richard Lingeman's topical 1984 parody, the narrator becomes "Uncle Ronald" and tells the story of "an honest, hard-working businessman" and his clerk, "a lazy, worthless agitator type who was always trying to organize the workers into a union, . . . an almshouse chiseler . . . getting money from poorhouses under the system of socialism that was prevalent in England before Mrs. Thatcher turned the country around."[30] This Scrooge employs Cratchit out of pity for his crippled son, even though he suspects the boy of faking the gimpy leg to collect for disability. But when Cratchit successfully tricks Scrooge into

Figure 87. Doonesbury; © 1986 G. B. Trudeau. Reprinted with permission. All rights reserved.

some Christmas benevolence and convinces the workers at the factory to strike, Scrooge "move[s] his blacking business to India, where the work ethic [is] still strong." Lingeman's exaggerations evoke the familiar Scrooge whose avarice is not heroic.

Whether despicable or heroic, the supply-side Scrooge is the Scrooge of our time. The new apologists and the Carol traditionalists now seem to agree that the *Carol* is not primarily a religious or Christian story, but rather a profoundly secular treatment of the economics of Christmas. Its frames of reference have become so "institutionalized," so much a part of our cultural perception, that it requires a revolution of consciousness to recognize their century-old influence.

The controversy over the economics of the *Carol* could be seen as a debate waiting to happen ever since 1843. When Dickens wrote his "sledgehammer" for "the poor man's child" in the midst of the contentious 1840s, he must have expected some challenge to his economic message, for the social and economic issues raised by the *Carol* were intensely topical at the time. Although Thomas Hood, in his review of the *Carol*, facetiously referred to "Mr. Fizziwig [*sic*] at his Benthamite Ball, in his warehouse adapted to the greatest happiness of the greatest number," he did not probe the political themes of the story.[31] Only the economist Nassau Senior commented at any length on Dickens' economic theory.

Since the 1840s other readings of the *Carol* have taken precedence over the economic. Its moral and religious messages engaged later Victorians; its social idealism countered the darkness of the Depression; Scrooge's psychobiography preoccupied the 1960s. When the economic message embedded in the story was acknowledged in the 1950s it was seen from the transcendent perspective of affluence as a critique of the outmoded economic principles of a bygone age. To the affluent society, the important issues raised by the story involved Scrooge's more middle-class dilemmas, his unhappy childhood, his psychological maladjustment, and the self-imposed sensory deprivations that denied him a full life.

When everyone is perceived as more or less comfortably middle-class, economic concepts lose their consequences. Affluence took the edge off the Cratchits' poverty, and they became the social exception rather than the rule. The invisible war of the sixties was the War on Poverty. The images of those for whom it was fought, the American poor, were displaced on television by images from the visible war in Viet Nam. Only recently have pictures of the hungry and homeless reappeared, recalled to life by a national debate on economic principles that echoes the debate of Dickens' own time. The economic controversy the *Carol* might have fomented in the 1840s has been enjoined in the 1980s.

When Edwin Meese asserted that the poor in the soup lines were not really starving, he recalled the notorious Malthusian parable of the beggars outside the banquet hall. Malthus shocked charitable Victorian readers with his suggestion that the way to deal with poverty was to deny it and leave the poor to fend for themselves – or die. Meese also seemed to be suggesting that we could eliminate hunger by removing the vacant covers from the well-stocked American table and ignoring those huddled outside in the streets. These Malthusian images prompt a shock of contradiction by linking two contrasting rhetorics. Statistical analysis and the laws of political economy it supports may prove that hunger is not real or that charity is an illogical way to respond to it. Such arguments are convincing only when stated with numerical abstraction. The rhetoric of images, on the other hand, of the poor outside the banquet hall or the homeless standing in soup lines, presents particulars that undermine the abstractions to become persuasive exceptions that disprove the numerical rules.

The supply-siders of the 1840s, the ascendant liberals of Dickens' day, garnered volumes of statistics to support their causes. They campaigned for the New Poor Law, the first major reform of the welfare system in two centuries, proving with numbers that the free labor market it promoted would diminish poverty. They fought for free trade and led the opposition to the Corn Laws, protective tariffs on grain, by arguing that a free market in agriculture would lower the price of bread. Let the economy alone, they contended, and free markets would produce the greatest happiness for the greatest numbers.

The opposition challenged their "let alone" philosophy and countered their statistics with images of the suffering poor in the streets of the new industrial cities. In the oppressive monotony of Coketown in *Hard Times* or the fetid ruins of Tom All Alone's in *Bleak House*, Dickens imaged the concrete results of the economists' equations, and he challenged the competitive atomism of the marketplace model with a more organic ideal. He pictures that ideal in the unselfish doctoring of Alan Woodcourt in *Bleak House*. Like Carlyle, Dickens believed that charity could cure the fragmented condition of England. Society could be made whole by relations of duty and responsibility, for in the healthy body politic the active caring of the well-to-do would inspire the loyalty of the poor.

The contradictions between numbers and images inform our debate about economics as they did in the 1840s. Neoconservatives assume that the War on Poverty was won, and they attack their liberal opposition for not acknowledging the victory. Ironically, in their belief that abundance and an expansive economy have provided more than enough for everyone, the neoconservatives carry on the liberal assumptions of the affluent sixties. The late Michael Harrington characterized them as "new Gradgrinds" who prove by statistics that "poverty has disappeared and no one noticed."[32] Meanwhile, up-to-date liberals have adopted a traditionally conservative stance. Their relativistic concept of poverty defines as poor

Figure 88. This "Street Carol" drawn by "Phiz" for a Christmas issue of the Illustrated London News *in 1851 reveals the underside of the Victorian Christmas.*

a fixed percentage of those at the bottom of the economy and seems to assure that the poor will always be with us. They confirm the presence of poverty now in revelatory images of the hungry and the homeless that recall similar pictures from the hungry 1840s and the Great Depression (fig. 88).

Harrington challenged both liberal and conservative positions. He countered conservative optimism with ecological realism. Writing in the wake of the oil crisis, he asserted that "resources are not infinite. If everyone at bottom is brought up to a minimal level of decency, those at the top can, and should, pay." But, like the neoconservatives, he challenged relativistic definitions of poverty. "A serious definition of poverty," he stated, "has to be as absolute as death." He proposed that we not try to characterize poverty in strictly numerical terms, but seek instead a broader cultural definition. Following the lead of Peter Townsend, he suggested that poverty be defined as lacking the resources necessary to permit participation in the activities, customs, and diets commonly approved by society. Taking this perspective, Harrington speculated that there were as many as forty million American poor in 1984.

In spite of fundamental differences in approach, both sides in the current debate seem to agree that contemporary America, like Victorian England, is two nations: a nation of the well-to-do beside a subculture of outsiders who, for psychological, educational, geographic, and economic reasons, form an ongoing "culture of poverty." We disagree about the causes of this division, about the numbers of the poor, and about solutions. But we are haunted by the images of the poor. For the Victorians, the crude woodcuts of children working in the mines and factories became the iconographic shorthand depicting the "second nation." Our poor are revealed in pictures of the hungry in the soup lines and the homeless huddled in doorways and sleeping on subway grates and under bridges.

The images of those marginalized in our society inform the serious Carol of our time. Thea Musgrave's 1979 opera *A Christmas Carol,* for example, represents a transition from the psychological Carols of the sixties and early seventies to the "socio-economic" Carol of the eighties. Musgrave expands Belle's rejection of Scrooge into a first-act curtain scene revealing the miserly fiancé torn between his fear of poverty and his love of Belle. This Scrooge, a figure too sympathetic for some of the critics, who thought him "un-Dickensian," is psychologically realized. "I had to make sure my audiences wouldn't just say 'what an old horror' and have no sympathy for him," Musgrave explained. "In that case, why go to the opera? You have got to love your hero."[33]

But sympathy for Scrooge did not mean inattention to Cratchit. Unlike the sixties versions, which often ignore or deprecate the clerk, the opera presents a Cratchit family pinched by poverty and resentful of Scrooge's power. Sharp-tongued Mrs. Cratchit is unrelenting in her refusal to toast

Scrooge on Christmas or to acknowledge him as the founder of their feast. "People are poor because they are stupid and lazy and drown themselves in drink," she sings, smashing her glass on the table. She sarcastically mimics Scrooge's gradgrindian rationale that blames the victims for their poverty. "They deserve to be poor!" she concludes. "Let them be punished for their poverty" (act 2, scene 2). The Cratchit children, included in Musgrave's version of the vision of Ignorance and Want, join the two urchins who emerge from under the spirit's robes to "scream and crawl all over [Scrooge], crying out for money or food. In their desperation and hunger they are rough and vicious. Scrooge tries to push them off, but they cling to him all the more. Finally, Scrooge throws them violently to the ground. Tiny Tim is hurt and dies" (act 2, scene 3). This Tim is not the victim of simple neglect; he is killed by an act of willful suppression. Bob, "bitter and desperate" and reduced to beggary by unemployment, haunts the streets. He attacks the rich for spurning him and turning him into the gutter. "They show no mercy, no generosity, even to save a little child," he sings, concluding that "it is clear that poverty is a crime" (act 2, scene 4). Even Christmas cannot overcome the animosity between the poor clerk and his rich employer. Musgrave's poor are not the free-spirited street people of the sixties. They are the hungry and homeless outsiders of the eighties.

The opera simultaneously resolves psychological and social issues. Recalled to his better self by recognizing the love he has rejected in Belle, Scrooge brings together the scattered parts of his life – Fred and his wife, the Cratchits, and "the other waifs and orphans" – to celebrate Christmas by sharing a prize turkey. His psychological recovery creates a new community.

The Goodman Theater's controversial 1984 production of the *Carol* in Chicago enjoined similar social issues in a different way. Its Scrooge, Frank Galati, characterized the play in the psychological terms of the sixties, suggesting that it gave lessons "about the good way to be in the world, . . . to be fully present: to see, smell, relish the experience of being alive."[34] But the production, with its twenty-seven-member interracial cast, presented Chicago with a social vision, an image of itself as a city where a white Bob Cratchit carried a black Tiny Tim on his shoulder. "There is no issue more on the minds of people in this city than racism," Gregory Mosher, artistic director of the Goodman, explained. "This doesn't directly translate into a political statement, but it's there in front of your eyes: 27 people creating a play together, oblivious to everything racial."[35] While one unhappy theatergoer complained, "I really don't want to see this. Charles Dickens wrote Tiny Tim as a little English boy," and others called for reviving productions from the past, Brad Hall, the production's Cratchit, described the unsettling version as "a good thing for Chicago."[36] But it may not have been a good thing for the Goodman. For the 1985 season, the theater returned to a more familiar version.

Several attempts during the last decade to create a black Carol have been similarly problematic. *Comin' Uptown*, a 1979 musical written in the wake of *The Wiz*, danced its way downtown to Broadway with an all-black cast starring Gregory Hines as a streetwise, high-stepping Scrooge.[37] In his final number, "Born Again," Hines brought the theater to life with ecstatic dancing and with his orders for Christmas gifts from a Chinese take-out and a Jewish delicatessen, the only places open on Christmas morning. But in the earlier scenes Hines's role as a bent old Harlem slumlord tied his feet and dampened the energy of the production. While *Comin' Uptown* did not let Hines be Hines until its final number, it also did not let its black Scrooge be Scrooge. The Harlem of the play, a community drawn together by gospel music and symbolized in the church and recreation hall that Scrooge threatens to close, lacks the contradictions of Dickens' London. It does not attempt to celebrate Christmas and cut-throat capitalism at the same time. Gospel has triumphed over greed before the curtain has even risen. Because this Scrooge does not articulate a contradiction within his black community, the issues are no longer life-and-death issues. Tiny Tim does not die and return to life, and Belle is not lost forever. When Christmas comes uptown, Scrooge regains the girl who has been waiting for him for thirty years.

The tension missing in *Comin' Uptown* is also absent in Robert Guillaume's *John Grin's Christmas* (1986).[38] Set in a black Bedford Falls – an idealized small town with break dancers rather than carol singers on Main Street – this television adaptation recalls the American Carols of the thirties and the psychological Carols of the sixties. Its Scrooge, a black toy manufacturer who refuses to donate toys to the poor, is the product of a traumatic childhood. Orphaned when he is unable to save his family from their burning house, John Grin becomes the boy-of-all-work in an orphanage where he washes dishes, windows, and floors. He longs to be adopted as some of the other children are, but instead he is "sold" into apprenticeship and his habit of hard work is turned into a selfish survival skill. Although his personal history might be seen as a symbolic rendering of the black experience in America, John Grin appears to be the only person in his community psychically wounded by his past. Even the Tiny Tim of this version is not crippled by his fatherless home or unemployment. So we are not surprised when the camera pulls back to reveal that Christmas Future's vision of a black community of cardsharps, layabouts, and small-time hoods has been staged. Like John Grin, we know that the real black community is that of Grin's hard-working clerk, who spends Christmas Eve preparing cost estimates for his employer, or that of Timothy, who spends the evening doing some extra odd jobs to earn a present for his mother. John Grin was never outside this community at all, for he too believes and practices the gospel of hard work. After rewarding his assistant with a partnership in the firm and Timothy with a place in the training program, he sends a truckload of dolls to the poor and joins a gospel chorus in "Joy to the World." Whatever tension there was between this Scrooge and his community has easily worked itself out.

Tension may be missing in these black Carols as a result of a reluctance to confront the contradictions within the black community or to explore its problematic relationship to the dominant white culture. When a black Scrooge is allowed to be Scrooge, he will become one indication of the acceptance of blacks into the mainstream of American life. That we do have a successful "feminist" Scrooge indicates how much closer women are than blacks to achieving cultural equality.

In the text of Dickens' *Carol* women are absent or inconsequential figures. Scrooge has no mother, his sister Fan is significant only as the messenger who comes to take him home from school and, later, as the dead mother of Scrooge's nephew Fred. Mrs. Cratchit is a shadowy figure without a Christian name, and the other women – Mrs. Fezziwig, Scrooge's fiancée, Fred's wife, and the young women at Fred's Christmas party – are defined only in relation to men. Scrooge has chosen the isolation of the male business world and suppressed his feminine impulses toward human relationship. He has rejected marriage for money and, forgetting the love he once had for his sister, he begins his Christmas by turning away her son, his nephew Fred. From this perspective, Scrooge's conversion requires his "feminization," an acknowledgment that his male isolation must be complemented by female relationship and dependency. Modern versions often articulate this theme more explicitly by making some or all of the ghosts female, by developing Scrooge's relationship with Belle, and by giving more prominence to the sexual energy of Fred and his wife (or fiancée) and the prolific Cratchit family. In such versions, even though Scrooge is "feminized," the story usually does not have a "feminine ending." Scrooge does not give all his goods to the poor and, except in a few eccentric versions, he does not marry. He remains in control of his relationships. He dispenses his charity selectively, and even with Fred or Cratchit as his business partner, he still controls the firm. The difference is that the firm now has a generational future. It will become "Scrooge and Son." If patriarchy has been qualified, it has also been sustained.

The feminist Carol requires more than Scrooge's feminization. He must become woman. Although World War II prompted a dramatic production with an all-female cast, a version with a female consciousness did not appear unil the 1980s in the form of a Christmas parody on television's "Moonlighting."[39] A mature version of the American Carol – with Scrooge, not Cratchit, as its hero – this retelling inverts the gender of its originals – the *Carol* and *It's a Wonderful Life* – by casting women in the important male roles.[40] Its Scrooge, Maddie Hayes, owner of the Blue Moon Detective Agency, has earned her anti-Christmas title by asking her employees to give up some of their holiday to complete a project. When the workers complain, led by Ms. Dipesto, the story's Cratchit, Maddie asks, "What ever happened to gratitude? These people do have steady jobs, and benefits, and Christmas bonuses. . . . I was the one who scrimped and saved during the lean times. . . . I was the one who made sure they had a job in the morning when they got here." She has all the economic egotism of the supply-side Scrooge, but she is unsettled by her Marley. The ghost in Maddie's life is Aunt Ruth, sick and dying in a hospital just a few blocks from her office. Maddie has been so busy that she has not gone to visit her. When Aunt Ruth dies, Maddie, guilty and angry, storms out of the office wishing that she had never taken over the business. She retreats to a bar where she meets Albert, her guardian angel, who makes her wish come true.

Maddie has really wished for a world where she wouldn't be burdened with her assertive femininity. Albert shows her just such a world. Without Maddie, women are left to manage womanly businesses. Ms. Dipesto directs a greeting card company, not a detective agency, frivolously requiring her employees to speak in verse. Detective agencies are again run by more traditional detectives, and the Blue Moon, in a witty reflexive allusion, has been taken over by the Hart Agency from a television series that "Moonlighting" displaced. Sexual relations also conform to more conventional gender expectations, and Maddie is replaced in her problematic liaison with David Addison by Cheryl Tiegs, playing herself as the accomodating female ideal of a male-dominated world. This second "real-world" intrusion adds satiric bite and complicates the status of the fantasy, raising questions about the relationship of "Moonlighting" to social reality. When Maddie overhears Addison confess – on the day of his marriage to Tiegs – that he "really admired [Maddie, because] she had this softness about her, warmth. . . . She was really a special girl," she regains her will to live as the problematic woman she is. Back in the office, she rearranges the work schedule to allow a Christmas holiday and, affirming her sexuality, she embraces an accepting David Addison. This assertive embrace in the final frames of the film – like the image of Scrooge embracing Tiny Tim that often ends more traditional versions of the Carol – expresses iconographically the "resolution" of the story. Maddie does not need to deny her sexuality to assume a dominant economic role or to distinguish herself from the accommodating Tiegs, but she may need to become the aggressive partner in bed as in the boardroom. The ambiguity in this final image fixes in freeze-frame the irresolution of the social issues it articulates. The episode's title, "It's a Wonderful Job," also embodies this uncertainty in its diminished echo of Capra.

If "Moonlighting" presents a feminist Carol, the 1984 film *A Christmas Carol,* starring George C. Scott as Scrooge, might be seen as the new-historical Carol.[41] From the psychological Carol this version takes a Scrooge whose "father holds him a grudge," apparently blaming the boy for his mother's death. But Scott's Scrooge is more than a victim of psychological abuse. He is a tormented man caught in the social contradictions of his time and ours. When Scrooge rejects Belle, for example, he does not do so out of simple miserliness or meanness. His action is the result of a difficult decision over whether to use a small inheritance to seed a business or to marry. He chooses the former and establishes himself as a grain dealer. In Victorian terms he has opted for Malthusian prudence. In contemporary terms he could be characterized as deciding between family and career, a far more ambiguous and difficult choice than that between marriage and miserliness.

Scrooge's occupation as a grain dealer also attunes the film to historical and contemporary issues. His business is directly linked to hunger. In the opening scene, after he has struck a particularly hard bargain, one of his competitors asserts, "If we pay your price, bread will be dearer . . . the poor will suffer." But as a supply-sider Scrooge knows that market forces produce happiness, not misery. Watching the Cratchit family toast him as "the founder of the feast," he expatiates on the justness of their characterization: "He's made a point, . . . Bob Cratchit has. . . . Without me, there would be no feast . . . no goose, at all. My head for business has furnished him employment."

Scott's Scrooge is not consciously malevolent; he is ideologically blind. His problem is that he does not see the suffering around him. The Spirit of Christmas Present tells him: "I'm beginning to think you've gone through life with your eyes closed. Open them. Open them wide." The film makers nicely suggest Scrooge's blindness by inverting an image

Figure 89. The homeless in many contemporary versions of the Carol update Dickens' vision of Ignorance and Want and recall images like Gustave Doré's drawing of the Victorian poor sleeping under a bridge by the Thames in London: A Pilgrimage *(1872).*

from the original. As Scrooge slinks home through the dark and misty streets in Dickens' text, the narrator remarks that "even the blind men's dogs appeared to know him, and when they saw him coming on would tug their owners into doorways and up courts, and then would wag their tails as though they said, 'No eye at all is better than an evil eye, dark master.'" In the film, Scrooge becomes the "dark master" (*CB*, 8). When his way home from the office is blocked by a group of carolers, he uses his stick to find his way through the crowd.

More resistant to change than Dickens' Scrooge, Scott's ideologue erects intellectual defenses against the messages from the spirits. He rationalizes his hard-heartedness with economic theory. To break down this willful ignorance, the Spirit of Christmas Present doubles the vision of Ignorance and Want. To the two urchins hiding under his cloak, the spirit adds a second vision of a crowd of homeless people huddled under a bridge for shelter (fig. 89). Scrooge protests that he does "not want to see them" and tries to divert the spirit into a discussion of the abstract economic issues: "We'll have some give and take . . . come to some meeting of the minds. . . . I'm a reasonable man." But the spirit refuses to suppress the image of the homeless family huddled around an open fire and engage in discussing numbers. He leaves Scrooge to his contradictions and evasions. When the spirit vanishes, Scrooge is thrown back into his economic isolation. "What have I done to be abandoned like this?" are his final words to the disappearing spirit.

The vision of society's abandoned under the bridge reverses the movement of the drama and draws together the social and psychological strands in Scrooge's life. When he is abandoned by the spirit, Scrooge realizes that he has chosen the life he most fears. He too is abandoned, cut off from his fellows by willful ignorance and isolating economic ideology. This self-imposed isolation repeats his abandonment by family and fiancée earlier in his life.

Confessing that he "was in love once," Scrooge returns to his family, to the nephew that he has denied, and admits that his diatribes against Christmas were all humbug. Humbug, too, were the economic doctrines that prompted him to excoriate Fred for marrying imprudently and for allowing personal factors to interfere with his business sense. When Fred hired Peter Cratchit for a wage above the market rate, Scrooge complained that "[Fred's] doing this to spite me, you know. . . . Employing the son of my employee at an exorbitant wage." But at the end of the film, an abandoned Scrooge doubles Bob's salary "for a start," thus imitating his imprudent nephew. Instead of choosing defensive isolation to suppress the pain of desertion and loss, Scrooge celebrates his "abandonment" and restores his community with the Cratchits and Fred.

If Scott's *Carol* is a new-historical attempt to identify the sources of Scrooge's discontent in the economic ideology of his time and ours, then the last of the eighties versions, the film *Scrooged* (1988), is an explosive deconstruction of the Carol.[42] Directed by Richard Donner and starring Bill Murray, the film draws together nearly all the diverse elements in the eighties Carol and succeeds in blowing them up.

Murray plays Frank Cross, a television network executive, one of several Scrooges of the eighties whose power comes from controlling the media.[43] He is the Scrooge of the Information Age. The hard surfaces of chrome and glass in his executive suites recall the hardware of Scrooge's iron age, but Cross's world is not merely hard, it is also reflective. Frank Cross is the controlling image in a narcissistic world of images.

This world of images brings together fragments of many earlier versions of the Carol and nearly all the contemporary possibilities for the story. In some of the best scenes in the film, *Scrooged* returns to its Pickwickian urtext when Carol Kane, playing the Spirit of Christmas Present as a post-feminist goblin, batters Murray, a Madison Avenue Gabriel Grub, from narcissism to self-awareness. In the midst of ever-present television monitors that show passing pieces of Mister Magoo's and other earlier Carols, Cross's life story recapitulates Scrooge's story as television fantasy. Neglected by his family in a working-class suburb in New Jersey, he was raised by Howdy Doody, an orphan of the first television generation; he leaves home, goes to New York, and himself becomes the man inside the dog suit on a children's television show; he gives up his Belle (Claire Phillips, played by Karen Allen) to climb the corporate ladder as a television executive; and by the time of the film he is constantly occupied by his job, as he lives in a private suite behind his offices and spends twenty-four hours a day producing television images. The culmination of his life promises to be his up-coming production of *Scrooge,* the glitziest version of the story ever, with Buddy Hackett as Scrooge surrounded by a cast of celebrities (Jamie Farr, for example, as Marley and Mary Lou Retton as Tiny Tim) and a chorus of Las Vegas showgirls. But a colleague whom Cross has fired for questioning his plans (Eliot Loudermilk, played by Bobcat Goldthwait) threatens to destroy this finale when he returns to the studio, drunk and crazed, during the production of *Scrooge,* intending to assassinate his former boss.

Beside this unreal world of television Carols is a second Carol, a story whose controlling images come from the real world of the eighties rather than from television. If Cross is to be transformed and escape the destructive world of images, it will be by engaging with this real-world Carol. If Eliot Loudermilk is the film's first Cratchit, its second Cratchit is Cross's black secretary (Grace Cooley, played by Alfre Woodward), and the film's only Tiny Tim is her mute son (Calvin, played by Nicholas Phillips). Grace is an assertive Cratchit as she stands up to her boss and cares for her disabled child. Similarly, Cross's one-time fiancée, Claire, has denied the unreality of Cross's world of images and chosen to work as the director of a shelter for the homeless. When Frank leaves his office and his production of *Scrooge* to confront these realities of the streets, of Grace's difficult circumstances, of Calvin's voicelessness, and of the lonely men in Claire's shelter, he opens up the possibility that the Carol can be saved from narcissistic self-destruction.

Early in the film Frank has chosen an ad to promote *Scrooge* that shows the mushroom cloud of nuclear explosion and hypes the Christmas program as the greatest event since Hiroshima. In television's world of empty images where power alone has meaning, there is no difference between the image of a nuclear bomb and the divine image. Both represent ultimate power. When only the ratings matter, then any image serves that gets the numbers. The danger is that the Carol will be lost in the holocaust.

The Carol's power depends on transcending its art to reshape the real world. In the reflexive world of television, *Scrooge* is a restatement of its former images. If it is to become *Scrooged,* it must enter the real world and become history. When Frank leaves the studio for the streets, he seeks the transforming truths that will save him from narcissistic self-destruction and make his life a Carol. When the streets come to the studio during the production of *Scrooge*, they threaten and eventually halt the performance. The transforming power of the story makes Calvin talk and revives Claire's love for Frank, but it does not save *Scrooge*. Frank stops that program in the middle to lecture to the television audience on the theme that "the miracle of Christmas can happen every day." As he continues, Frank becomes Bill Murray lecturing the movie audience as the final credits roll on the screen and the lights come up in the theater. The moviegoer is left with the reality of the theater, littered with popcorn boxes and candy wrappers, and the voice of the satirist desperately pleading, "It would help if people treated each other with more consideration – you know it as well as I do." In this nuclear chain deconstruction, *Scrooge* exploded, then *Scrooged* exploded, then, in Christmas Present, Bill Murray speaks and the screen goes dark. After this holocaust, is there a Carol Yet-to-Come?

Scrooge was Dickens' words, to begin with. But Scrooge was better than his words, and more, infinitely more. The text of *A Christmas Carol*, penned by Dickens in a few months in 1843, was only the beginning of the larger culture-text of the Carol written over the last century and a half and still being written today. John Lucas has said that the power of Dickens' text derives from its "compressed intensity," a quality shared with Blake's *Songs of Innocence and of Experience* of suggesting more than it states.[44] Reaching beyond its words, this expansive text probes our cultural memory, explains the particulars of the changing present, and prompts our hopes and expectations. Its power is creative.

As memory, the Carol recalls more than its previous tellings. It is more than the sum of its Christmases past. We cannot remember when we first knew the story. It is allied in our consciousness to our awareness of day and night, winter and spring, rooted to the elemental wish that the fearful ogre become fairy godfather. Tiny Tim and Scrooge in fairy tale reenact Beauty and the Beast; as the archetype of the *senex* and *puer*, the old man and crippled child, they express human life at its temporal extremes.[45] In ghost story these mortal figures transcend youth and age, innocence and experience, to perform a supernatural drama on Hamlet's stage where time and eternity meet. Like Coleridge's Ancient Mariner, we have a compulsive need to retell this story, to search in the ritual of telling for things lost or forgotten. As memory, the Carol is myth.

But as the ever-present tale of Christmases present, the Carol is fiction. Frank Kermode draws the distinction: "Myth operates within the diagrams of ritual, which presupposes total and adequate explanations of things as they are and were; it is a sequence of radically interchangeable gestures. Fictions are for finding things out, and they change as the needs of sense-making change. . . . Myths are the agents of stability, fictions the agents of change."[46] Dickens' contemporaries made sense of the Carol as a survival. They rediscovered in it the traditional rural Christmas in the new context of the industrial city. For later Victorians, troubled by Darwin and doubt, the Carol became latter-day scripture, a retelling of the biblical nativity. In the twentieth century, the Carol has ministered to cultural needs to recover childhood innocence, to affirm social stability in the midst of economic distress, to find sources of personal fulfillment and happiness, and to reconcile economic individualism with the social good. Each of these texts responds to the needs of its place and time, ignoring or suppressing other possibilities. Yet alternative texts remain beneath the surface of the fiction. Their unresolved tensions may emerge to generate next Christmas's telling.

The culture-text of the Carol is composed of all the possibilities in the mind of its re-creators. It is not limited by its original formulation or by all its past versions. It is open to the yet unspoken potentialities of Christmas Carols Yet-to-Come. If we could imagine all the possibilities beforehand, we would reduce the fiction to myth. But as we change, the Carol is ever-changing. We continue to learn from Scrooge with each reappearance.

Ted Koppel introduced the discussion following the television showing of *The Day After,* a visualization of America after a nuclear attack, by asking his viewers to look out their windows. "It's all still there," he remarked. "Your neighborhood is still there; so is Kansas City and Lawrence. . . . What we've all just seen is a sort of nuclear version of Charles Dickens' *Christmas Carol.*"[47] But in asking his viewers to confirm their survival by looking out the window, Koppel revealed the radical difference between the two texts. The nuclear nightmare that is the text of *The Day After* contains no assurance of its retelling. Told once, that story may never be told again. But the Carol creates its own retelling. At the end of the tale, over the bowl of smoking bishop on Boxing Day afternoon, Scrooge and his newly promoted clerk share accounts of their holiday. "Marley was dead," Scrooge begins. He goes on to tell of the three spirits and of celebrating the day with his nephew Fred. Then he ends, as good as his word, by beginning again over a bowl of smoking bishop. After the first "reading" of the Carol, we remain in consciousness of Scrooge forever. Tiny Tim does not die. The story of Scrooge and Marley, Scrooge and Bob Cratchit, Scrooge and the spirits, Scrooge and Tiny Tim is unending. And so, as Tiny Tim observed,

GOD BLESS US, EVERY ONE!

Notes

CHAPTER 1. THE CAROL AS CULTURE-TEXT

EPIGRAPHS: Hewitt brief quoted in E. T. Jaques, *Charles Dickens in Chancery* (London: Longmans, Green, 1914), 30–31; president of Screen Gems quoted from the *Knoxville Journal* in the *Dickensian* 65 (1969): 112–13.

1 See below, chap. 5, p. 163.

2 The first report of the Children's Employment Commission (1842) had shocked the nation with its accounts of the conditions in the coal mines, especially with its crude wood-block illustrations. The second report (1843) revealed that conditions for children were even worse in several other industries, including the needlework sweatshops in London. Perhaps the most telling parts of the reports were the verbatim interviews in which the children described their life and work.

3 Letters to Dr. Southwood Smith, 6 and 10 March 1843, in Madeline House, Graham Storey, and Kathleen Tillotson, eds., *The Letters of Charles Dickens* (Oxford: Clarendon Press, 1974), 3:459, 461. (Hereafter this edition will be cited as *Letters*.) He used the hammer metaphor not simply to describe something that was hard-hitting, but also to characterize a work that came out all at once rather than in parts.

4 Kathleen Tillotson speculates on this possibility in *Letters*, 3:461*n*.

5 John Forster, *The Life of Charles Dickens* (New York: Dutton, 1927), 1:287.

6 Ibid., 1:286.

7 Dickens wrote to Forster on 11 February 1844: "I found the *Carol* accounts awaiting me. . . . The first six thousand copies show a profit of £230! And the last four will yield as much more. I had set my heart and soul upon a Thousand, clear. What a wonderful thing it is, that such a great success should occasion me such intolerable anxiety and disappointment!" (*Letters*, 4:42).

8 Dickens to C. C. Felton, 2 January 1844, *Letters*, 4:2.

9 *Fraser's Magazine* 29 (February 1844): 169.

10 For an account of the piracy, see E. T. Jacques, *Charles Dickens in Chancery* (London: Longman's, Green, 1914) and S. J. Rust, "Legal Documents Relating to the Piracy of *A Christmas Carol*," *The Dickensian* 34 (1938): 41–44.

11 F. Dubrez Fawcett, *Dickens the Dramatist* (London: W. H. Allen, 1952), 78.

12 *The Athenaeum*, 17 February 1844: 157.

13 Letter to John Forster, 21 February 1844, *Letters*, 4:24.

14 Quoted in Edgar Johnson, *Charles Dickens: His Tragedy and Triumph* (New York: Simon and Schuster, 1952), 1:34.
15 Letter to Forster, 18 January 1844, *Letters*, 4:24.
16 Letter to Thomas Mitton, 7 January 1844, *Letters*, 4:17.
17 *The Illustrated London News*, 10 February 1844: 83.
18 Forster, *Dickens*, 1:302.
19 This view of the text as a creation of its readers has been developed by a number of literary theorists. Paul B. Armstrong, for example, states the point in these terms: "A text is not an independent object that remains the same regardless of how it is construed. It is not autonomous but 'heteronomous.' While a literary work transcends any individual interpretations, it exists only in and through its 'concretizations'" ("The Conflict of Interpretations and the Limits of Pluralism," *PMLA* 98 [1983]: 345). What Armstrong describes as the transcendent, heteronomous text, I call the culture-text, the sum implicit in its many versions or concretizations.
20 *Dickens and the Scandalmongers* (Norman: University of Oklahoma Press, 1965), 116–17.

CHAPTER 2. BRINGING CHRISTMAS TO THE CITY

EPIGRAPHS: Southey, *Letters from England*, ed. Jack Simmons (London: Cresset Press, 1951), 362; Dickens, *SB*, 220.
1 *The Sketch Book of Geoffrey Crayon, Gent* (New York: New American Library, 1961), 193, 180, 220.
2 Ibid., 180.
3 Frank S. Johnson has suggested that Sandys' collection may have incidentally influenced the *Carol:* "It is known that Dickens corresponded with Sandys who, in the introduction to one of the Carols 'Old Christmas Returned' suggests the idea of a rich miser and his conversion by the Spirits of Christmas. Tiny Tim's well-known 'God bless us every one' is given in Sandy's [*sic*] Carol of the 'Holy Well' as follows: – 'He said God bless you every one / And Christ your portion be'" (*The Dickensian* 28 [1932]: 8).
4 *Coningsby; or the New Generation* (Harmondsworth: Penguin, 1983), 459–60.
5 Harry Stone, *Dickens and the Invisible World: Fairy Tales, Fantasy, and Novel-Making* (Bloomington: Indiana University Press, 1979), 125. Stone goes on to discuss the reasons why the *Carol* is so much better than its prototype. For another useful discussion of the links between the tale of Gabriel Grub and *A Christmas Carol*, see John Butt, "Dickens's Christmas Books," in *Pope, Dickens, and Others* (Edinburgh University Press, 1969), 127–48.
6 Michael Wolff and Celina Fox point out that such traditional perspectives on the city continue to dominate perspective in the illustrations of the city in such news magazines of the period as the *Illustrated London News*. Humor magazines like *Punch*, however, take a more urban perspective and view the city from amid the crowd on the streets. See "Pictures from the Magazines," in H. J. Dyos and Michael Wolff, eds., *The Victorian City: Images and Realities* (Boston: Routledge and Kegan Paul, 1973), 2:559–82.

7 "Dickens, Griffith, and the Film Today," in *Film Form: Essays in Film Theory* (Cleveland: World, 1949), 216–17.
8 F. S. Schwarzbach, *Dickens and the City* (London: Athlone Press, 1979), 10.
9 Ibid., 52.
10 In *The Dickens World* (London: Oxford University Press, 1941), Humphry House showed that this "modernization" of Dickens' worldview is apparent in all his work and that the change in orientation comes roughly after *The Old Curiosity Shop* (1841). House suggests that the change was not in Dickens' consciousness alone, but rather represented a change in the consciousness of the age coincident with the development of railways.
11 *The Christian Remembrancer*, January 1845: 301.
12 *Knickerbocker Magazine*, March 1844: 276.
13 *The Northern Star*, 21 December 1844.
14 *Knickerbocker Magazine*, March 1844: 276.
15 *Letters*, 3:459.
16 *Letters*, 3:461.
17 Fuller discussion of the parliamentary report as a source for the *Carol* can be found in Michael Slater's essay on *The Chimes*, "Dickens's Tract for the Times," in Michael Slater, ed., *Dickens 1970* (London: Chapman and Hall, 1970), 99–123, and in Kathleen Tillotson's notes to the letters to Smith (*Letters*, 3:461*n*). Michael Steig suggests that Edwin Chadwick's 1842 *Report on the Sanitary Condition of the Labouring Population of Great Britain* also contributed to the "excremental vision" of the *Carol*. See "Dickens' Excremental Vision," *Victorian Studies* 13 (1970): 48–49.
18 *Second Report of the Commissioners, Children's Employment Commission* (1843), F 30, no. 288.
19 *Second Report*, f 210, no. 534.
20 Philip Collins, ed., *Dickens: The Critical Heritage* (New York: Barnes and Noble, 1971), 162–63.
21 The much more intense and intrusive politics of *The Chimes* is carefully documented in Michael Slater's essay "Dickens's Tract for the Times."
22 This reservation appears in a few of the reviews. Kathleen Tillotson also cites Samuel Rogers's unusual reaction after reading his presentation copy of the story: "The first half hour was so dull it sent him to sleep, and the next hour so painful that he should be obliged to finish it to get rid of the impression. He blamed Dickens's style very much, and said there was no wit in putting bad grammar into the mouths of all his characters, and showing their vulgar pronunciation by spelling 'are' 'air,' a horse without an h: none of our best writers do that" (*Letters*, 3:609*n*).
23 C. Z. Barnett, *A Christmas Carol* (New York: Samuel French, n.d.), 3.
24 Ibid., 4.
25 The comment of Dickens' fellow novelist Mary Russell Mitford to an Irish friend represents a common contemporary view: "I like Dickens's Christmas Carol, too, very much – not the ghostly part, of course, which is very bad; but the scenes of the clerk's family are very fine and touching." Quoted in R. Shelton Mackenzie, *Life of Charles Dickens* (Philadelphia: T. B. Peterson, 1870), 157–58.

26 The best-known objection to the overindulgence in the *Carol* is Ruskin's (see p. 59). The objection also appeared in several contemporary reviews. Bon Gaultier [Theodore Martin] in *Tait's Edinburgh Magazine*, "reported" a Christmas Carol, presumably by a Scotch Calvinist, raising this issue in response to Dickens (see n. 22, chap. 3).

27 Collins, ed., *Critical Heritage*, 148. Jeffrey was echoing the concluding sentence to "A Christmas Dinner" in *Sketches by Boz* (1836), where Dickens wrote of the celebration: "And thus the evening passes, in a strain of rational good-will and cheerfulness, doing more to awaken the sympathies of every member of the party in behalf of his neighbour, and to perpetuate their good feeling during the ensuing year, than half the homilies that have ever been written, by half the Divines that have ever lived" (*SB*, 224).

28 Edward Wagenknecht, ed., *Selected Letters and Journals of Fanny Appleton Longfellow* (New York: Longmans, Green, 1956), 105.

29 Letter to C. C. Felton, 2 January 1844, *Letters*, 4:2–3.

30 Edgar Johnson, *Charles Dickens: His Tragedy and Triumph* (New York: Simon and Schuster, 1952), 1:468.

CHAPTER 3. FOUNDER OF THE FEAST

EPIGRAPHS: F. D. Maurice, *Christmas Day and Other Sermons* (London: J. W. Parker, 1843), 6; Thomas Carlyle, *Two Notebooks*, ed. C. E. Norton (New York: Grolier Club, 1898), 215.

1 "Dickens and Father Christmas," *Nineteenth Century*, December 1907: 1016.

2 Dickens' four other *Christmas Books* were *The Chimes* (1844), *The Cricket on the Hearth* (1845), *The Battle of Life* (1846), and *The Haunted Man* (1848).

3 "Dickens' Last Christmases," *DR* 52 (1972): 373.

4 Introduction to *Charles Dickens: The Public Readings* (Oxford: Clarendon Press, 1975), xxv.

5 Carlyle quoted in Martha L. Burnson, "Novelists as Platform Readers: Dickens, Clemens, and Stowe," in David Thompson, ed., *Performance of Literature in Historical Perspective* (Lanham, Md.: University Press of America, 1983), 651.

6 London *Times*, 2 January 1854.

7 Letter to Mrs. Watson, quoted in Norman and Jeanne Mackenzie, *Dickens: A Life* (Oxford: Oxford University Press, 1979), 260.

8 Longfellow, letter to Charles Sumner, 8 December 1867, in Andrew Hilen, ed., *Letters of Henry Wadsworth Longfellow* (Cambridge, Mass.: Harvard University Press, 1982), 5:191.

9 For a detailed discussion of the reading texts, see Collins, *Public Readings*.

10 Quoted in Collins, *Public Readings*, xxxi.

11 Quoted in Raymond Fitzsimons, *The Charles Dickens Show: An Account of His Public Readings, 1858–1870* (London: Geoffrey Bles, 1970), 72.

12 Quoted in Collins, *Public Readings*, 2.

13 *Pen Photographs of Dickens's Readings* (Boston: J. Osgood, 1871), iii. The account of the *Carol* reading comes from chapter 2, pp. 23–36.

14 Charles Dickens, *A Christmas Carol: The Public Reading Version,* ed. Philip Collins (New York: The New York Public Library, 1971), xx.

15 Fitzsimons, *The Charles Dickens Show,* 19.

16 Quoted in *A Christmas Carol,* New Amplified Edition, edited by Henry E. Vittum (New York: Bantam Books, 1966), 103.

17 "Charles Dickens in Relation to Christmas," *The Graphic,* 25 December 1870; reprinted in the *Dickensian* 5 (1909): 80.

18 Collins, *Public Readings,* 4.

19 "About the *Christmas Carol* and Dickens in Boston," *Unity* 110 (December 1932): 234–35.

20 Margaret Oliphant, "Charles Dickens," *Blackwood's Edinburgh Magazine* 109 (June 1871): 689.

21 Ibid., 677.

22 Letter to Charles Eliot Norton, 19 June 1870, in Ruskin's *Works,* ed. E. T. Cook and A. Wedderburn (London: 1903–12), 37:7. *Tait's Edinburgh Review* for February 1844 caricatured the criticism of Dickens' Christmas as vulgar overindulgence in the following lines:

> He cannot away
> With a Church holiday,
> Unless it be made a perpetual cram. . . .
> What's Christmas, indeed,
> But a season to feed:
> Why should it be more in the Christian's eye!
> 'Twas made but for this;
> But to revel and kiss
> And spoil one's digestion with brandied mince-pie.
> With pleasure unfeign'd,
> This lesson I've gained
> From the new "Christmas Carol," invented by Boz,
> And I mean never more
> To be sober, before
> I have emptied the cellar, entirely that's poz.

23 "Press, Religious," in Sally Mitchell et al., eds., *Victorian Britain: An Encyclopedia* (New York: Garland, 1988), 632.

24 *The Christian Remembrancer,* January 1845.

25 *Novels of the Eighteen-Forties* (Oxford: Oxford University Press, 1961), 128.

26 *The Works of Robert Browning* (London: Smith, Elder, 1912), 4:41, lines 1296–99.

27 The narrator takes on this issue in the final lines of the poem, balancing his act of joining into the hymn with an apology for his use of light verse:

> I have done: and if any blames me,
> Thinking that merely to touch in brevity
> The topics I dwell on, were unlawful, –
> Or worse, that I trench, with undue levity,
> On the bounds of the holy and the awful, –
> I praise the heart and pity the head of him,
> And refer myself to THEE, instead of him,

Who head and heart alike discernest,
  Looking below light speech we utter,
  When frothy spume and frequent sputter
Prove that the soul's depths boil in earnest!
May truth shine out, stand ever before us!
I put up pencil and join chorus
To Hepzibah Tune, without further apology,
  The last five verses of the third section
  Of the seventeenth hymn of Whitfield's Collection,
To conclude with the doxology. [lines 1343–1359]

28 For a Tractarian reaction to the *Carol*, see the *Christian Remembrancer*'s remarks on pp. 99–100 below.
29 *Christmas Eve with the Spirits* (London: Bull, Simmons, 1870), 87.
30 *The Disappearance of God* (Cambridge, Mass.: Harvard University Press, 1963), 5.
31 Nonesuch Dickens, *Letters* (Bloomsbury [London]: Nonesuch Press, 1937–38), 3:125.
32 *Hood's Magazine*, January 1844: 74–75.
33 *The Secular Pilgrims of Victorian Fiction: The Novel as the Book of Life* (Cambridge: Cambridge University Press, 1982).
34 *Charles Dickens: The Man and His Work* (Boston: Houghton Mifflin, 1912), 2:276–77.
35 "Dickens Time and Again," *Dickens Studies Annual* 2 (1972): 170.
36 *Dickens and Melville in Their Time* (New York: Columbia University Press, 1975), 80.
37 "Passing of the Christmas Ghost Story," *The Bookman* 50 (1919): 260.
38 *Charles Dickens: His Life and Work* (New York: Doubleday Doran, 1934), 140.
39 Michael Slater has called attention to an *Oxford English Dictionary* definition of "cut" in dancing, meaning "to spring from the ground and, while in the air, to twiddle the feet one in front of the other alternately, with great rapidity," (Charles Dickens, *The Christmas Books* [Harmondsworth: Penguin, 1971], 1:259*n*).
40 *A Kind of Power: The Shakespeare-Dickens Analogy* (Philadelphia: American Philosophical Society, 1975), 39.
41 Graham Holderness ("Imagination in *A Christmas Carol*," *Etudes anglaises* 32 [1979]: 32) describes the allegory in this way. Most critics locate whatever allegorical force the story has in the three spirits, describing them variously as representing Memory, Example, and Fear (Edgar Johnson) or Nostalgia, Pity, and Fear (Barbara Hardy). Jane Vogel, however, finds a much more extensive pattern of Christian allegory in the story; see her *Allegory in Dickens* (University, Ala.: University of Alabama Press, 1977), esp. 70–73.
42 Field, *Pen Photographs*, 36.
43 *A Christmas Carol, in Three Staves* (Boston: W. H. Baker, 1874), 248.
44 London *Times*, 27 December 1859: 7.
45 S. J. Adair Fitz-Gerald, *Dickens and the Drama* (London: Chapman and Hall, 1910), 195.
46 *The Gentleman's Magazine*, 21 February 1844: 170–71.

47 For a discussion of this type in Victorian literature, see George Landow, *Victorian Types, Victorian Shadows* (London: Routledge and Kegan Paul, 1980), 66–94.

48 For a detailed account of the theology of the social gospel movement in the United States, see Janet Fishburn, *The Fatherhood of God and the Victorian Family: The Social Gospel in America* (Philadelphia: Fortress Press, 1981).

49 For a discussion of Dickens' use of the Christian love feast, see Thomas L. Watson, "The Ethics of Feasting: Dickens' Dramatic Use of Agapé," in Thomas A. Kirby, ed., *Essays in Honor of Esmond Linworth Marilla* (Baton Rouge: Louisiana State University Press, 1971), pp. 243–52.

50 A Victorian version that reduced the story to the Cratchit's Christmas was *Their Christmas Dinner* (New York: G. R. Lockwood, [1884]); later such versions include *The Cratchits' Christmas* (Waverley, Mass.: Millpond Press, 1912) and *Tiny Tim's Christmas Dinner* (Los Angeles: A. E. Bell, 1927).

51 Scrooge has, in fact, consciously rejected a paternal role. When his sister Fan died, he apparently had a chance to become a second father to her orphaned son, Fred, but turned his back on the opportunity.

52 Leslie Fiedler has remarked of Tiny Tim: "His image has remained in the years since Victoria, when so much else has been desacralized, an icon as 'sacred' in its way as that of the Christ Child at his Virgin Mother's breast; though also as vulgarly cheerful-tearful and as commercially viable as the Easter Seal cripple-of-the-year, which descends directly from it." See "Pity and Fear – Images of the Disabled in Literature and the Popular Arts," *Salmagundi* 57 (1982): 67.

53 Quoted in Collins, *Carol*, 201*n*.

54 Field, *Pen Photographs*, p. 35; Kent quoted in Collins, *Carol*, 201*n*.

55 Kent quoted in Collins, *Carol*, 201*n*.

56 Qualls, *Secular Pilgrims*, 27.

57 Gladys Storey, *Dickens and Daughter* (London: Frederick Muller, 1939), 120–21.

CHAPTER 4. THE CHILDREN'S HOUR

EPIGRAPHS: Anecdote reported in *A Christmas Carol:* With instructions to teachers, biographical sketch, explanatory notes and critical estimates, ed. A. J. Demarest (Philadelphia: Christopher Sower, 1912), 149; James Whitcomb Riley, "God Bless Us Every One," *Complete Works* (New York: Harper and Brothers, 1916), 2:484; G. K. Chesterton, *Charles Dickens* (London: Methuen, 1906), 70.

1 *The Dickensian* 4 (1908): 32.

2 Quoted in J. M. Patterson, "Charles Dickens and Christmas," *The Dickensian* 10 (1914): 323.

3 Ethel Kidson, "The Dickens Christmas," *The Dickensian* 10 (1914): 328.

4 Introduction to *The Christmas Books* (New York: P. F. Collier, 1911), p. xi.

5 "Dickens and Father Christmas," *Nineteenth Century* 62 (December 1907): 1026.

6 "Mr. Seymour Hicks and 'A Christmas Carol,'" *The Dickensian* 5 (1909): 76.
7 George H. Ford, *Dickens and His Readers: Aspects of Novel Criticism since 1836* (Princeton: Princeton University Press, 1955), 203.
8 *Collected Essays* (New York: Harcourt Brace and World, 1967), 191.
9 *Charles Dickens: A Critical Study* (New York: Dodd, Mead, 1912), 212.
10 "A Christmas Carol: Being a few scattered staves, from a familiar Composition, rearranged for performance, by a Distinguished Musical Amateur, during the Holiday Season, at H-rw-rd-n," *Punch* 89 (23 December 1885): 304–05.
11 E. J. Milliken, "The Spirit of Christmas Present (Passages from a political 'Christmas Carol' of the period, descriptive of a slumbering Statesman's Yuletide Dream)," illustrated by Sir John Tenniel, *Punch* 105 (30 December 1893).
12 "A Christmas Carol; by Charles Dickens and Toby, M. P.," *Punch* 121 (25 December 1901): 451–52.
13 Harold Begbie, "A Political Carol in Two Staves," *Pall Mall Gazette,* 20 and 21 December 1901.
14 *The Critic,* December 1905.
15 London: Free Trade Union, 1909.
16 Charles Whitcombe, "A Free Trade View," *The Dickensian* 5 (1909): 98–99; C. A. Vince, "A Tariff Reform View," ibid., 99–101.
17 Clara M. Kirk and Rudolf Kirk, eds., *Criticism and Fiction* (New York: New York University Press, 1959), 76–87.
18 "Clay," *Dubliners* (Harmondsworth: Penguin, 1957), 97.
19 "Parody as Comment in James Joyce's 'Clay,'" *James Joyce Quarterly* 7 (1970): 75.
21 "A Dickens Party for Children," *Strand Magazine,* January 1911: 776–86.
21 "A Christmas with Dickens," *Ladies' Home Journal,* December 1892: 6.
22 *The Christian Remembrancer* 7 (January 1844): 7.
23 *The Book of Christmas* (Chicago: Cuneo Press, 1951), 52.
24 Introduction to the Everyman edition of *The Christmas Carol* (London: Dent, 1907), xii.
25 Juliet Dusinberre, *Alice to the Lighthouse* (London: Macmillan, 1987), 1.
26 Mark Twain, *Adventures of Huckleberry Finn* (Indianapolis, Ind.: Bobbs-Merrill, 1967), 120.
27 Gissing, *Charles Dickens,* 13–14.
28 Ibid., 212.
29 *The Boss Girl and Other Sketches* (Freeport, N.Y.: Books for Libraries Press, 1971), 7–47.
30 *Complete Works of James Whitcomb Riley* (New York: Harper, 1916), 1:81–85.
31 Peter Revell, *James Whitcomb Riley* (New York: Twayne, 1970), 159*n*.
32 Humphrey Carpenter, *Secret Gardens: A Study of the Golden Age of Children's Literature* (London: George Allen and Unwin, 1985), 86.
33 Ibid., 107.
34 Ibid., 1.
35 U. C. Knoepflmacher, "The Balancing of Child and Adult: An Approach to Victorian Fantasies for Children," NCF 37 (1983): 497–530.
36 Quoted in ibid., 499.

37 Scrooge's exclamation on seeing Dick Wilkins -- "Bless me, yes. There he is. He was very much attached to me, was Dick. Poor Dick! Dear, dear!" – suggests that he, too, like so many of Scrooge's former friends and associates, is dead by the time of the story.
38 Charles Dickens, "My Grandfather at Christmastime," *Ladies' Home Journal*, December 1907.
39 *The Plays of J. M. Barrie*, ed. A. E. Wilson (London: Hodder and Stoughton, 1928), 558. Further citations from *Peter Pan* are parenthetically referenced to this edition.
40 *Dickens and the Invisible World* (Bloomington: Indiana University Press, 1979), 3.
41 *Works of Oscar Wilde* (New York: Walter J. Black, 1927), 526.
42 Forster, *Dickens*, 1:301.
43 Quoted in Carpenter, *Secret Gardens*, 180.
44 Ibid., 180–81.
45 *A Christmas Carol*, edited for school use by Edmund Kemper Broadus (Chicago: Scott, Foresman, 1906), 300.
46 *Dickens the Dramatist* (London: W. H. Allen, 1952), 117.
47 Charles, "Mr. Seymour Hicks," 77.
48 *Cosmopolitan* 32 (December 1901): 165–74.
49 "The Christmas Spirit of Dickens," *The Dickensian* 3 (1907): 333.
50 *Charles Dickens* (London: Methuen, 1906), 130.
51 Introduction to Charles Dickens, *The Holly Tree Inn and A Christmas Tree* (New York: Baker and Taylor, 1907), xi.
52 Gissing, *Charles Dickens*, 36.
53 "A Defence of Skeletons," *The Defendant* (London: Dent, 1914), 48.
54 Quoted in John D. Coates, *Chesterton and the Edwardian Cultural Crisis* (Hull: Hull University Press, 1984), 73.
55 *Tremendous Trifles* (New York: Sheed and Ward, 1955), 64–68.
56 Introduction to the Everyman *Christmas Carol*, vi.
57 "Christmas," in *All Things Considered* (London: Methuen, 1908), 11.
58 *The Daily News*, 22 December 1906.
59 "Christmas and the Aesthetes," in *Heretics* (London: Bodley Head, 1905), 91.
60 Introduction to the Everyman *Christmas Carol*, v.
61 Lynette Hunter, *G. K. Chesterton: Explorations in Allegory* (London: Macmillan, 1979), 49.
62 G. K. Chesterton, *Charles Dickens*, 70.
63 *The Daily News*, 25 December 1909.
64 "A Defence of Penny Dreadfuls," *The Defendant*, 21.
65 Chesterton, *Charles Dickens*, 130–31.

CHAPTER 5. ALWAYS A GOOD MAN OF BUSINESS

EPIGRAPHS: George S. Kaufman and Marc Connelly, *A Christmas Carol: A Play in Three Acts*, *The Bookman*, December 1922: 415–16; Arthur Krock,

"Scrooge and New Deal Ghosts Adorn a Christmas Tale," *The New York Times*, 25 December 1934.

1 *The Benchley Roundup* (New York: Delta, 1962), 36–40. Benchley knew the *Carol* well. In his diary he describes reading the story aloud every Christmas Eve and crying "not at the sad parts, but at the parts that are so glad that they shut off your wind" (quoted in Norris W. Yates, *Robert Benchley* [New York: Twayne, 1968], 64).

2 J. Cuming Walters, "The Fate of Tiny Tim," *The Dickensian* 29 (1933): 72.

3 J. H. McNulty, "Our Carol," *The Dickensian* 34 (1938): 17.

4 Quoted in "Blaming Dickens for Christmas," *Literary Digest* 100 (26 January 1929): 23–34.

5 W. R. Titterton, *The Universe*, 3 December 1937: 24.

6 Introduction to *A Christmas Carol: A Facsimile of the Original Edition* (Boston: Charles E. Lauriat, 1922), ix.

7 "An Epilogue to *A Christmas Carol:* Stave VI. The Last of the Four Spirits," *The Dickensian* 18 (1922): 177–82.

8 *The Daily Worker* [London], 27 December 1932.

9 "*A Christmas Carol* and Economic Man," *The American Scholar* 21 (1952): 93.

10 Quoted in Leslie C. Staples, "When Found," *The Dickensian* 41 (1945): 57.

11 *Charles Dickens: His Life and Work* (New York: Doubleday, Doran, 1934), 111.

12 The fine editions of the thirties included three hand-set editions in 1930, one from W. E. Rudge (Mt. Vernon, N.Y.), one from the Press of the Woolly Whale (New York), and one privately printed for Junius Fishburn by Frederic Warde (Mount Vernon, N.Y.); in 1933, an edition from Judd and Detweiler (Washington, D.C.), with pen drawings by Charles Dunn; and, in 1934, the Limited Editions Club edition from the Marymount Press (Boston), illustrated by Gordon Ross. There was also considerable bibliographic interest in the original editions of the *Carol* during the early thirties. See, for example, E. A. Osborne's "The Variants of *A Christmas Carol*," *The Bookman* 81 (December 1931): 192–94 and *The Facts About "A Christmas Carol"* (London: Bradley Press, 1937).

13 *New Monthly Magazine* 70 (January 1844): 148–49.

14 *A Christmas Carol* (New York: Garden City Publishing, 1938).

15 Quoted in Roy Armes, *A Critical History of the British Cinema* (New York: Oxford University Press, 1978), 80.

16 Ibid., 80.

17 Quoted in Andrew Bergman, *We're in the Money: Depression America and Its Films* (New York: 1971), 30.

18 "When the Movies Really Counted," *Show*, April 1963: 77.

19 "The Dickens Revival at the Bijou: Critical Reassessment, Film Theory, and Popular Culture," *New Orleans Review* 15 (1988): 95.

20 "Scrooge and New Deal Ghosts Adorn a Christmas Tale," *The New York Times*, 25 December 1934: 22.

21 While the British Carol often hearkens back to Victorian England, the American Carol tends to locate itself in the Depression. Two recent television versions, for example, "An American Christmas Carol" (1979) and "John Grin's Christmas" (1986), connect Scroogishness to the Depression. In the American

imagination, the 1930s seem to be the psychic equivalent of the 1840s in the British consciousness.

22 "New-Fashioned Christmas," *Week-end Review*, 5 December 1931: 707–08.

23 Mead, "About the *Christmas Carol* and Dickens in Boston," *Unity* 110 (1932): 234–35; "Christmas with Dickens: An Interview with Lady Dickens," *The Sunday Graphic*, 22 December 1935.

24 Priestley in the *Evening Standard*, 24 December 1931; Pemberton in *Tid-Bits*, December 1931.

25 *The Daily Sketch*, 1 December 1931.

26 "If Dickens Wrote His Carol Now," *The Sunday Times*, 20 December 1931.

27 *Scrooge* (Great Britain: Julius Hagen–Twickenham Productions, 1935), released by Paramount Productions; directed by Henry Edwards; screenplay by H. Fowler Mear. The cast included Seymour Hicks (Scrooge), Donald Calthrop (Bob Cratchit), Robert Cochran (Fred), Mary Glynne (Belle), Athene Seyler (Scrooge's Charwoman), Maurice Evans (A Poor Man), and Philip Frost (Tiny Tim).

28 H. Philip Bolton, *Dickens Dramatized* (Boston: G. K. Hall, 1987), 241, lists the first production of Buckstone's version in 1901 at the Vaudeville Theatre, London, starring Seymour Hicks. The earliest published version of the Buckstone script that I have seen is that published by Samuel French (London and New York) in 1927.

29 Made in 1935, *Scrooge* may have exploited the new technology of the sound track in reducing Marley to voice alone.

30 *The Dickensian* 27 (1931): 83.

31 Seymour Hicks, "Scrooge and the Christmas Joy of Giving," *The Daily Mail*, 22 December 1934.

32 McNulty, "Our Carol."

33 T. H. Elstop objected to such un-Dickensian religiosity in a 1940 version of the *Carol* done on the BBC, arguing that there is no significant textual justification for portraying Scrooge as a churchgoer; see "Scrooge Goes to Church," *Freethinker* 12 January 1941. Similar scenes, however, appear in nearly all film versions of the period.

34 *An American Christmas Carol* is set in the Depression, characterizing Scrooge as a rapacious furniture dealer who repossesses furniture even on Christmas Day. Addressing the different cultural needs of the 1970s, this version presents images of the misery of the Depression which are much stronger than those in any of the film versions of the thirties.

35 Barrymore did the *Carol* on radio every Christmas from 1934 until the mid-fifties, missing only 1936, when his wife died, and 1938.

36 From an undated recording of the radio play (New York: Nostalgia Lane, 1981). By 1944 Barrymore's radio Scrooge had become such a national institution that *Life* ran a picture version of it, the scenes being shot at the MGM studios in Hollywood (*Life* 17 [25 December 1944]: 51–57).

37 *Old Scrooge* (Newark, N.J.: New Jersey Soldiers' Home Print, 1877). The Library of Congress copy of this play is incomplete, so that my account of it is, in part, based on conjecture.

38 *Cosmopolitan* 32 (December 1901): 165–74.

39 Quoted in Charles R. Hearne, *The American Dream in the Great Depression* (Westport, Conn.: Greenwood Press, 1977), 27.

40 Introduction to *A Christmas Carol,* abridged by Mabel Mason Carlton (Boston: John Hancock Insurance Co., 1921).

41 Hearne, *The American Dream,* 27. Horatio Alger himself tried his hand at an early version of the American Carol in "Job Warner's Christmas" (*Harper's New Monthly Magazine,* December 1863). In the story Job Warner, a bank clerk, is denied a raise by his Scrooge-like boss on Christmas Eve. On his way home Warner meets an orphan girl on the street and takes her home with him, using the little money he has to aid her rather than to buy presents for his family. Unbeknownst to Job, his employer has seen his act of kindness and is changed by the sight. He raises Job's salary by $250 and gives Job an extra $200 to care for the orphan. At the end of the story Job reads the biblical Christmas story to his family, giving it new and personal meaning.

This story is closer to the scriptural Carols of the 1870s than to the later American Carols, for although Job centers the story, he is a passive hero whose good fortune is bestowed upon him, not the active figure of the American Carol. The shift in focus to the figure of Cratchit, however, does suggest the shift that becomes essential in the later American versions.

42 *The Greatest Little Book in the World* (Cleveland: Privately printed, 1923), 12.

43 McNulty, "An Epilogue," 181.

44 *A Christmas Carol: The Story of a Sale,* by Charles Dickens, with marginal notes for salesmen [by J. C. Aspley] (Chicago and New York: Dartnell Corp., [1928]).

45 "A Christmas Carol: A Play in Three Acts," with sketches by Herb Roth, *The Bookman,* December 1922: 409–19.

46 Ashley Miller, *Mr. Scrooge: A Dramatic Fantasy after Charles Dickens' "A Christmas Carol,"* with some of the original illustrations by John Lynch [*sic*] (New York: Dodd, Mead, 1928).

47 *A Christmas Carol* (USA: MGM, 1938), produced by Joseph L. Mankiewicz; directed by Edwin L. Marin; screenplay by Hugo Butler. Cast: Reginald Owen (Scrooge), Gene Lockhart (Bob Cratchit), Kathleen Lockhart (Mrs. Cratchit), Terry Kilburn (Tiny Tim), Leo G. Carroll (Marley's Ghost), Ronald Sinclair (Young Scrooge). Lionel Barrymore was originally cast as Scrooge, but he was forced to withdraw from the production. Had he performed the role, the film clearly would have become *the* American Carol, an apt companion piece to Hicks's British Carol.

48 *The Wound and the Bow* (London: Methuen, 1961), 57.

49 Ibid.

50 J. H. McNulty, "Stave VI (An Almost-true Story)," *The Dickensian* 39 (1943): 18.

51 *It's a Wonderful Life* (USA: Liberty Films, 1946), produced and directed by Frank Capra; screenplay by Frances Goodrich, Albert Hackett, Frank Capra, and Jo Swerling, from the story "The Greatest Gift" by Philip Van Doren Stern. The cast included James Stewart (George Bailey), Donna Reed (Mary Bailey), Lionel Barrymore (Mr. Potter), Thomas Mitchell (Uncle Billy), and Henry Travers (Clarence).

52 A year later the story was commercially published as *The Greatest Gift: A Christmas Tale* (Philadelphia: David McKay, 1944).

53 "American Madness," in Richard Glatzer and John Raeburn, eds., *Frank Capra: The Man and his Films* (Ann Arbor: University of Michigan Press, 1975), 181–82.

CHAPTER 6. THE GREENING OF SCROOGE

EPIGRAPHS: Charles Reich, *The Greening of America* (New York: Random House, 1970), 229–30; Philip Slater, *The Pursuit of Loneliness* (Boston: Beacon Press, 1970), 34.

1 *Dickens and Melville in Their Time* (New York: Columbia University Press, 1975), 43.

2 This British-made adaptation aired on ABC-TV on 21 December 1971. It was also "traditional" in using Alastair Sim as the voice for Scrooge. A brief account of its making appeared in *TV Guide*, 18 December 1971: 19–22.

3 Clifford Wigram, London *Times*, 29 December 1969.

4 Caedmon Records, TCS 5001 (1960).

5 *Britain and America: An Interpretation of Their Culture, 1945–75* (New York: New York University Press, 1977), 158–59.

6 *Charles Dickens: A Biographical and Critical Study* (London: A. Dakers, 1950), 245.

7 Potter's role as substitute father to Bailey follows the formula described in the psychological study of postwar movies by Martha Wolfenstein and Nathan Leites, *Movies: A Psychological Study* (Glencoe, Ill.: Free Press, 1950); see especially chapter 2. They note a pattern in American films of a natural father whose ineffectuality allows the hero to assert himself and seek his destiny, and a strong, displaced father-figure who embodies the power missing in the natural father and who acts as antagonist to the hero.

8 *The Nation*, 15 February 1947: 158.

9 "Was Scrooge Right?" *Catholic World* 180 (December 1954): 183–84.

10 *Steppenwolf*, ed. Joseph Mileck (New York: Holt, Rinehart, Winston, 1963), 192.

11 *Charles Dickens: The Progress of a Radical* (New York: International Publishers, 1938), 287.

12 Edgar Johnson, *Charles Dickens: His Tragedy and Triumph* (New York: Simon and Schuster, 1952), 1:485, 489.

13 Snowman, *Britain and America*, 158–59.

14 *The Affluent Society* (Boston: Houghton Mifflin, 1958). See especially chapters 2 and 3.

15 "Traffic," C. F. Harrold and W. D. Templeman, eds., *Victorian Prose* (New York: Oxford University Press, 1938), 996.

16 Ibid.

17 Could Ruskin have read the *Carol* with the same perspective that produced this economic analysis, he might have become the first of its economic revisionist readers. Instead the story's actualization of the principles of affluence

offended his Calvinist religious principles and he criticized it for its lack of spiritual truth. See p. 59 above.

18 Quoted in John Strachey, *The Strangled Cry* (New York: William Sloane, 1962), 212.

19 Quoted in James Bonar, *Malthus and His Work* (New York: Macmillan, 1924), 305–06.

20 Philip Collins, ed., *Dickens: The Critical Heritage* (New York: Barnes and Noble, 1971), 152–53.

21 *The Pursuit of Loneliness*, 103.

22 Monica Dickens, Introduction to *A Christmas Carol: The Original Manuscript* (New York: James H. Heineman, 1967), xi.

23 Don Richard Cox, "Scrooge's Conversion," *PMLA* 90 (1975): 923.

24 *Charles Dickens*, 1:485.

25 Philip McM. Pittman, "*A Christmas Carol:* Review and Assessment," *VIJ* 4 (1975): 25.

26 "Joy, Joy! And Pull out All the Stops! Scrooge," *Writer* 85 (December 1972): 8.

27 W. E. Morris, "The Conversion of Scrooge," *Studies in Short Fiction* 3 (1965): 47.

28 "Dickens' Excremental Vision," *VS* 13 (1970): 339–54.

29 For a full interpretation of the *Carol* as dream narrative, see W. E. Morris's "Conversion of Scrooge."

30 The animated television *Carol* (API Studio, 1969) was adapted by Michael Robinson and directed by Zoran Jangic.

31 *The Dickensian* 65 (1969): 112–13 noted a report in the *Knoxville Journal* quoting the president of Screen Gems. He was providing justification for a new film script of the *Carol* being prepared by Christopher Isherwood.

32 *A Christmas Carol* (Great Britain: Renown Pictures, 1951), released by United Artists; produced by Brian Desmond Hurst; directed by Brian Desmond Hurst; screenplay by Noel Langley. Cast: Alastair Sim (Scrooge), Kathleen Harrison (Mrs. Dilber), Jack Warner (Mr. Jorkins), Michael Hordern (Jacob Marley), Mervyn Johns (Bob Cratchit), Hermione Baddeley (Mrs. Cratchit), Glyn Dearman (Tiny Tim), George Cole (Young Scrooge), Roddy Hughes (Fezziwig).

33 Quoted in Regina Barreca, "The Ghost of an Idea: Freud, Film, and *A Christmas Carol*," an unpublished talk at the Dickens Project, Santa Cruz, Calif., 1985.

34 All citations of Regina Barreca are to the talk cited above and are quoted with permission.

35 *The Pursuit of Loneliness*, 18.

36 Ibid., 25.

37 Ibid.

38 "The Ceremony of Innocence: Charles Dickens' *A Christmas Carol*," *PMLA* 90 (1975): 22.

39 *The Dickens World* (London: Oxford University Press, 1960), 53.

40 *The Moral Art of Dickens* (London: Athlone Press, 1970), chapter 2.

41 "Dickens Time and Again," *DSA* 2 (1972): 163–96.

42 Ibid., 187.
43 Ibid., 196.
44 Gilbert, "The Ceremony of Innocence," 29.
45 Slater, *The Pursuit of Loneliness*, 240.
46 Ibid., 4.
47 *A Christmas Carol*, illustrated by Ronald Searle (Cleveland: World, 1960).
48 *The Greening of America* (New York: Random House, 1970), 4.
49 Ibid., 216.
50 "The Greening of London Town," *Kansas Quarterly* 7, no. 4 (1975): 99–102.
51 *Scrooge* (Great Britain: Cinema Center Films, 1970), released by National General Pictures. Producer: Robert H. Solo; executive producer: Leslie Bricusse; director: Ronald Neame; screenplay: Leslie Bricusse. Cast: Albert Finney (Scrooge), Alec Guinness (Marley), Edith Evans (Christmas Past), Kenneth More (Christmas Present), Laurence Naismith (Fezziwig), David Collings (Bob Cratchit), Richard Beaumont (Tiny Tim).
52 London *Times*, 27 November 1970: 13.
53 Canby, *The New York Times*, 20 November 1970; Hudson, "Cashing in on Christmas," *The Spectator*, 5 December 1970: 736.
54 Hudson, "Cashing in on Christmas," 736; Alex Keneas, *Newsweek* 76 (14 December 1970): 104–05.
55 *The New Yorker* 46 (28 November 1970): 175–76.
56 Elaine Donaldson, "*Scrooge*", adapted from the screenplay by Leslie Bricusse (New York: Cinema Center Films, 1970), 54.
57 Ibid., 127.
58 *Look* 34 (15 December 1970): 26–27.
59 *Mademoiselle* 70 (December 1969): 124, 166, 173–74.
60 *Blackwood's Magazine* 314 (July 1973): 20–27.
61 *The New York Times*, 22 December 1973: 22.
62 Conger, "Joy, Joy!" 8.
63 Letter to C. C. Felton, 2 January 1844, in *Letters*, 4:2.
64 See, for example, Lindsay, *Charles Dickens*, 244; Michael Slater, *Dickens and Women* (London: Dent, 1983), 356–57; and Stone, *Dickens and the Invisible World*, 124–25.
65 Quoted in Lindsay, *Charles Dickens*, 245.

CHAPTER 7. BREAD AND CIRCUSES

EPIGRAPHS: Gregory Moser, artistic director of the Goodman Theater, quoted in E. R. Shipp, "Black Actor Plays Tiny Tim in Chicago 'Christmas Carol,'" *The New York Times*, 24 December 1984; Edwin Meese, speech to the National Press Club, quoted in the *New York Times*, 16 December 1983; Thomas P. "Tip" O'Neill, quoted in the *Washington Post*, 10 December 1983.
1 Hearn (New York: Potter, 1976); Fluck and Law (Harmondsworth: Penguin, 1979); Imsand (Mankato, Minn: Creative Education, 1984); Cole (Woodbury, N.Y.: Barron's, 1985); Hyman (New York: Holiday House, 1983); Foreman

(London: Gollancz, 1983); Hildebrandt (New York: Simon and Schuster, 1983).

2 *A Christmas Carol,* libretto and music by Thea Musgrave. World première performance 7 December 1979 by the Virginia Opera Association, conducted by Peter Mark. The cast included Frederick Burchinal (Scrooge), Jerold Norman (Cratchit), Howard Bender (Fred, young Scrooge), Kathryn Montgomery (Belle, Martha Cratchit), and Carolyne James (Mrs. Cratchit). A recording of the performance is available on MMG 302 (1980). Among the other operatic versions of the *Carol* are *A Christmas Carol,* music and libretto by Gregory Sandow (Bryn Mawr, Penn.: Presser, 1978); *A Christmas Carol,* music by David Gray, libretto by Robert Protherough (London: Novello, 1966); *A Christmas Carol,* music by G. Mallard Kilgore, libretto by Burt A. Kelsey and G. Mallard Kilgore (1960); and *A Christmas Carol,* dramatized by T. Dowall, music composed and arranged by F. W. Wadely (London: Boosey and Hawkes, 1938). Jon Deak's *A Christmas Carol* portrays Scrooge with double bass, bassoon, and bass clarinet. Sheffer describes his libretto as "a kind of pointillist selection of phrases from Dickens," which were sung or spoken by soprano Lucy Shelton in the original performance.

3 *Dickens Dramatized,* 236.

4 "'*Carol* Philosophy, Cheerful Views,'" *Etudes anglaises* 23 (1970): 159.

5 Associated Press wire story, 18 December 1985.

6 "Worst-Case Budget Scenario Should Scare the Dickens out of Us," *The Albuquerque Journal,* 21 January 1986.

7 See Andy Logan, "Around City Hall: God Bless Us, Every One!" *The New Yorker,* 24 December 1984: 68–73.

8 Little's earlier *Scrooge and the Stars,* released early in November 1963 by Capitol Records of Canada, retold the Carol in twenty-two voices. The record was quietly withdrawn a few weeks later, following the assassination of President John F. Kennedy. Kennedy had been cast in the role of the Spirit of Christmas Present, and part of his dialogue ran: "Scrooge, my life upon this globe is brief; it ends tonight. In fact, it ends as fast as you can say your name." See *Current Biography Yearbook* (New York: H. W. Wilson, 1975), 249–50.

9 Wilson, "Dickens: The Two Scrooges," in *The Wound and the Bow* (Boston: Houghton Mifflin, 1941); Schickel, *The Disney Version: The Life, Times, Art and Commerce of Walt Disney* (New York: Simon and Schuster, 1968), 62.

10 "Mickey and Minnie," *The Spectator,* 19 January 1934.

11 Schickel, *The Disney Version,* 58.

12 "Walt Disney's Christmas Carol," *McCall's,* December 1957: 29–36.

13 Quoted in Tom Soter, "Eight Christmas Carols: Scrooge's Victory Tour on Tape," *Video,* December 1984: 177.

14 *Mister Magoo's Christmas Carol* (USA: Henry G. Saperstein Productions, 1962), adapted by Barbara Chain; directed by Abe Levitow. Voices: Jim Backus, Morey Amsterdam, and Jack Cassidy.

15 Schickel, *The Disney Version,* 227.

16 Christmas catalogues in 1984 offered the necktie, decorated with the repeated pattern of "BAH HUMBUG." The *New York Times* (19 December 1985) described the Barney's windows for Christmas 1985; one displayed a mannequin

dressed in a grey flannel suit with a briefcase chained to its wrist and described as "Marley." The "there-never-was-such-a-goose" window showed a roasted goose with a diamond bracelet around its neck.

17 The epithet is Joan Beck's in "Meese Has a Dickens of a Time," *Chicago Tribune,* 19 December 1983.

18 *The Washington Post,* 10 December 1983. For Christmas 1982 President Reagan himself had been cast as Scrooge in *A Bonzo Christmas Carol* (New York, Raft Theater). In spite of some clever touches – Nixon wrapped in tapes as Marley, and Jane Wyman as Christmas Past – the production was faulted by Richard Massa (*The Village Voice,* 28 December 1982) for not focusing its satire on Reagan's social cuts. Perhaps Meese's defense was needed to clarify the social dimensions of the Reagan Carol.

19 *The Washington Post,* 16 December 1983.

20 Gertrude Himmelfarb, *The Idea of Poverty in England in the Early Industrial Age* (New York: Random House, 1983), 463. Similar, though less authoritative, conclusions appeared in several journalistic comments on the controversy at the time.

21 Quoted in Paul Henderson, "Meese Gets the Dickens," *The Washington Post,* 17 December 1983.

22 *The New York Times,* 16 December 1983.

23 "Scrooge's Defense," *The Dickensian* 33 (1937): 35–36.

24 *Defending the Undefendable: The Pimp, Prostitute, Slumlord, Libeler, Moneylender, and Other Scapegoats in the Rogue's Gallery of American Society* (New York: Fleet Press, 1976), 121.

25 "A Kind Word for Ebenezer," *Mensa Bulletin,* December 1981: 18–20.

26 "Dickens Stacks the Deck," *The New York Times,* 24 December 1983.

27 "In Defense of Scrooge: A Second Look at *A Christmas Carol,*" *The New American,* 23 December 1985: 27–31; the article first appeared in the December 1984 *United States Times.*

28 "The Compleat Xmas Story," *Harper's,* December 1985: 63–66.

29 *House and Garden,* December 1980: 88–89.

30 "A Christmas Carol," *The Nation,* 29 December 1984.

31 *Hood's Magazine,* January 1844: 68.

32 "The New Gradgrinds," *Dissent* 31 (1984): 171–81.

33 Thea Musgrave in an interview with Rodney Milnes, "Dickens into Opera," *The Musical Times* 122 (1981): 116.

34 *Chicago Sun-Times,* 16 December 1984.

35 *The New York Times,* 24 December 1984.

36 Ibid.

37 Book by Philip Rose and Peter Udell; directed by Rose; music by Gerry Sherman; lyrics by Udell. The cast included Gregory Hines (Scrooge), John Russell (Cratchit), Tiger Haynes (Marley), Virginia McKinzie (Mrs. Cratchit), and Kevin Babb (Tiny Tim).

38 Guillaume-Margo Productions, 1986; directed by Robert Guillaume; written by Charles Eric Johnson. The cast included Guillaume, Roscoe Lee Browne, Ted Lange, Geoffrey Holder, and Alfonso Robeiro.

39 In describing "Moonlighting" as the first feminist Carol, I also dismiss the

inevitable pornographic adaptation of the seventies, *The Passions of Carol* (1975). In this film the female protagonist, Carol Screwge, the tyrannical editor of a sex magazine, is turned on for Christmas. Although directed by a woman, the film appears, at least in *Variety*'s account of it (19 March 1975: 36), to challenge none of the standard "masculine" assumptions of its hard-core genre.

40 "Moonlighting," 16 December 1986. Directed by Ed Sherin, written by Debra Frank and Carl Sautter. The cast included Cybill Shepherd (Maddie Hayes [Scrooge/George Bailey]), Bruce Willis (David Addison), and Allyce Beasley (Ms. Dipesto [Cratchit]).

41 *A Christmas Carol* (USA: Entertainment Partners, Inc., 1984). Directed by Clive Donner; script by Roger O. Hirson. Cast: George C. Scott (Scrooge), Frank Findlay (Marley), Angela Pleasance (Christmas Past), Edward Woodward (Christmas Present), Michael Carter (Christmas Future), David Warner (Cratchit), Anthony Walters (Tiny Tim), Susannah York (Mrs. Cratchit), Lucy Gutteridge (Belle), Nigel Davenport (Silas), Timothy Bateson (Fezziwig), and Mark Strickson (Young Scrooge).

42 *Scrooged* (USA: Art Linson in association with Mirage Productions, 1988), released by Paramount Pictures; produced and directed by Richard Donner, screenplay by Mitch Glazer and Michael O'Donoghue. Cast: Bill Murray (Frank Cross [Scrooge]), Karen Allen (Claire Phillips [Belle]), John Forsythe (Lewe Hayward [Marley]), Bobcat Goldthwait (Eliot Loudermilk [Cratchit 1]), Alfre Woodard (Grace Cooley [Cratchit 2]), Nicholas Phillips (Calvin Cooley [Tiny Tim], David Johansen (Ghost of Christmas Past), and Carol Kane (Ghost of Christmas Present).

43 Scrooge has also been cast as a media executive in an episode of "WKRP in Cincinnati" and in a comic strip series for "John Darling" in 1984. Among the recognizable figures in the latter version of the story, Edward R. Murrow is cast as the Ghost of Christmas Past instructing Scrooge on journalistic ethics.

44 *The Melancholy Man: A Study of Dickens's Novels* (London: Methuen, 1970), 139.

45 For a discussion of Scrooge and Tiny Tim in terms of the *senex-puer* archetype, see Leslie Fiedler, "Pity and Fear – Images of the Disabled in Literature and the Popular Arts," *Salmagundi* 57 (1982): 70–86.

46 *The Sense of an Ending: Studies in the Theory of Fiction* (New York: Pantheon, 1970), p. xxiii.

47 Quoted in Robert Karl Manoff, "The Week After," *The Nation*, 10 December 1983: 588–89.

A Chronological List of Some Noteworthy Versions of the Carol

*Indicates a version from which illustrations are taken.

*1843 *A Christmas Carol. In Prose. Being a ghost story of Christmas.* With illustrations by John Leech. London: Chapman and Hall.

*1844 "A Christmas Ghost Story." Piracy by Henry Hewitt and Richard Egan Lee. *Peter Parley's Illuminated Library.*

*1844 *A Christmas Carol, or, Past, Present, and Future.* In three staves. Founded on the celebrated work, as performed as the Theatre Royal Adelphi, London. Dramatic adaptation by Edward Stirling. London: William Barth.

1844 *A Christmas Carol; or the Miser's Warning!* Dramatic adaptation by C. Z. Barnett. Royal Surrey Theatre, London, 5 February.

1844 *A Christmas Carol; or, Scrooge the Miser's Dream; or, The Past, Present and Future.* Dramatic adaptation by Charles Webb. Sadler's Wells Theatre, London, 5 February.

1844 *A Christmas Carol.* New York: Harper and Brothers.

1844 *A Christmas Carol.* Illustrations after John Leech. Philadelphia: Carey and Hart.

1846 *A Christmas Carol.* Eleventh edition. London: Bradbury and Evans.

1850 [W. M. Swepstone.] *Christmas Shadows. A Tale of the Times.* A Christmas story derivative of the *Carol.* London: T. C. Newby.

1852 *Christmas Books.* Cheap Edition of the Works of Charles Dickens. London: Chapman and Hall.

1854 *A Christmas Carol.* Dramatic adaptation by F. Fox Cooper. Strand Theatre, London, 11 December.

1861 *Christmas Books.* Illustrated by F. O. C. Darley and John Gilbert. New York: J. G. Gregory.

1863 Horatio Alger, Jr. "Job Warner's Christmas." A story derivative of the *Carol. Harper's New Monthly Magazine* 28:119–24.

*1867 *Christmas Books* and *Sketches by Boz.* Diamond Edition. With original illustrations by S. Eytinge, Jr. Boston: Ticknor and Fields.

1867 *A Christmas Carol.* As condensed by Dickens for his readings. Boston: Ticknor and Fields.

*1869 *A Christmas Carol.* Illustrated by Sol Eytinge, Jr. Boston: Ticknor and Fields.

*1870 *Christmas Eve with the Spirits, or, The Canon's Wanderings through Ways Unknown, with some further tidings of Scrooge and Tiny Tim.* With five illustrations by A. R. Dorrington. London: Bull, Simmons.

1871 *A Christmas Carol.* With instructions to teachers, biographical sketch, explanatory notes and critical estimates by A. J. Demarest. Boston: Houghton.

1874 *A Christmas Carol.* In three staves. Dramatic adaptation by George M. Baker. Boston: Walter H. Baker.

*1876 *Christmas Stories.* American Household Edition. With original illustrations by E. A. Abbey. New York: Harper.

*1877 *A Christmas Carol.* English Household Edition. Illustrated by Frederick Barnard. London: Chapman and Hall.

1877 *"Old Scrooge"; a Christmas Carol in five staves.* Dramatized from Charles Dickens' celebrated story by Charles A. Scott. Newark, N.J.: New Jersey Soldiers' Home Print.

1878 *The Miser.* Pantomime. Fifth Avenue Theatre, New York.

1882 *A Christmas Carol.* Edited for school and home use by Albert F. Blaisdell. New York: Clark and Maynard.

*1885 "A Christmas Carol. Being a few scattered staves from a familiar composition, rearranged for performance by a distinguished musical amateur, during the Holiday Season, at H-rw-rd-n." With four illustrations by Harry Furniss. *Punch,* 23 December: 304–05.

1887 *A Christmas Carol.* Illustrated by I. M. Gaugengigl and T. V. Chominski. Boston: S. E. Cassino.

1890 *A Christmas Carol.* A facsimile reproduction of the author's original manuscript. With an introduction by F. G. Kitton. New York: Brentano's; London: Elliot Stock.

1892 *A Christmas Carol.* With twenty-seven illustrations by Charles Green. *Pears' Christmas Annual.*

1893 "Dickens up to Date. A Christmas Carol in two Staves." Illustrated. *Funny Folks,* 23 December: 26–27.

*1893 E. J. Milliken. "The Spirit of Christmas Present (Passages from a political 'Christmas Carol' of the period, descriptive of a slumbering Statesman's Yuletide Dream)." Illustrated by Sir John Tenniel. *Punch,* 30 December: 306–07.

1896 "Jobkin's Christmas Eve." Illustrated parody. *Scraps,* Christmas number.

1898 Saul Smiff. *A Modern Christmas Carol.* London: Greening and Co.

1899 *A Christmas Carol.* With numerous original illustrations by George T. Tobin. New York: Frederick A. Stokes.

1899 *Christmas Books and Stories.* Illustrated Temple Edition. London: Dent.

*1900 *A Christmas Carol.* Illustrated by Frederick Simpson Coburn. New York and London: G. P. Putnam's Sons.

1901 *Scrooge.* One-act dramatic adaptation by J. C. Buckstone. Vaudeville Theatre, London, 3 October.

1901 *Scrooge, or, Marley's Ghost.* Silent film. Produced by R. W. Paul; directed by W. R. Booth (Great Britain).

1901 [Harold Begbie.] "A Political Carol in Two Staves. Stave 1. – Krooge and Morley. Stave 2. – The Three Spirits." *The Pall Mall Gazette,* 20 and 21 December.

1901 "A Christmas Carol. By Charles Dickens and Toby, M. P." *Punch,* 25 December: 451–52.

1901 W. Pett Ridge. "New Christmas Carol." *Cosmopolitan* 32:165–74.

1902 *A Christmas Carol.* Illustrated by Bertha B. Davidson. New York and Boston: Caldwell.

1902 *A Christmas Carol.* Decorations by Samuel Warner. East Aurora, N.Y.: The Roycroft Shop.

*1905 *A Christmas Carol.* Illustrated by C. E. Brock. London: Dent; New York: Dutton.

*1905 *A Christmas Carol* and *The Cricket on the Hearth.* Illustrated by George Alfred Williams. New York: Baker and Taylor.

1905 *A Christmas Carol.* Embellished with eight plates from drawings by Charles Pears. London: Library Press.

1905 "The Awakening of Scrooge." Sound recording by Bransby Williams. British Edison.

1905 "Scrooge's Christmas Morning." Sound recording by Albert Whelan. Gramophone Co.

1905 F. A. "The Final Stave of 'A Christmas Carol.' (With profound apologies to the Genius of Charles Dickens). Stave Five." *Punch,* 20 December: 437–38.

1905 "Old Scrooge on the Day After." *The Critic,* December.

1905 *A Christmas Carol* and *The Cricket on the Hearth.* Edited and with an introduction and notes for the common school by James M. Sawin, with the collaboration of Ida M. Thomas. New York: Macmillan.

1906 *A Christmas Carol.* Edited for school use by Edmund Kemper Broadus. Chicago: Foresman.

1906 "Final Stave of *A Christmas Carol* with Apologies to Dickens." *Living Age* 248:124–27.

1907 *A Christmas Carol.* Rewritten for young readers by Margaret Waters. Illustrated by Hugo von Hofsten. Chicago: Brewer, Barse, and Co.

1907 *A Christmas Carol.* Illustrated by John Leech and Fred Barnard. Introduction by Sir William P. Treloar. Published in aid of Lord Treloar's Home for Crippled Children. London: Chapman and Hall.

1908 *A Christmas Carol.* Silent film. Essanay (USA).

1909 *A Message from the Forties, being a Story of Protection adapted from "The Christmas Carol" of Charles Dickens.* Dramatic adaptation by Mrs. Alfred Mond. London: Free Trade Union.

1909 G. K. Chesterton. "The Modern Scrooge." London *Daily News,* 25 December.

*1910 *Christmas Books.* Illustrated by Harry Furniss. Dickens Library Edition. London: Educational Book Co.

1910 *A Christmas Carol.* Silent film. Directed by Ashley Miller. Thomas A. Edison (USA).

1910 *The Regeneration of Old Scrooge.* A dramatic adaptation by Sara Elizabeth Edwards. Kansas City, Mo., 2 July.

1910 *A Christmas Carol.* Dramatic adaptation by Fanny Amanda Comstock. Bridgewater, Mass., 29 November.

1910 J. H. "Scrooge Up to Date." *The Clerk,* January.

1910 Fred M. White. "A Modern Scrooge." *Winnipeg Telegraph,* 17 December.

*1911 *A Christmas Carol.* With illustrations by A. C. Michael. New York: Hodder and Stoughton.

1911 *A Christmas Carol.* With a facsimile of the signed preface from the original manuscript. Illustrations by E. H. Stanton. London: Robert Scott.

1912 *A Christmas Carol.* Edited by Katherine Gill West. Illustrations by Milo K. Winter. Chicago: Rand, McNally.

1912 *Scrooge.* Dramatic adaptation by Tom Terriss. London, 3 February.

1912 "Scrooge before the Dream," "Scrooge's Dream," and "Scrooge's Awakening." Sound recording by Bransby Williams. Columbia Records.

1912 *A Christmas Carol.* Introduction and notes by A. J. Demarest. Philadelphia: Christopher Sower.

1912 "Bob Cratchit's Speech: Supposed to be delivered after the events depicted in 'A Christmas Carol." From an unknown American newspaper, 12 December. Reprinted in the *Dickensian* 13 (1917): 313–14.

1913 *A Christmas Carol.* Illustrated by Carle Michel Boog. Boston: L. C. Page.

1913 *A Christmas Carol.* Illustrated by Spencer Baird Nichols. New York: F. A. Stokes.

1913 *Scrooge.* Silent film. Zenith Films (Great Britain).

*1914 *A Christmas Carol.* Illustrated by A. I. Keller. Philadelphia: David McKay; London and Edinburgh: W. and R. Chambers.

1914 *A Christmas Carol.* Illustrated by Honor C. Appleton. London: Simpkin, Marshall, Hamilton, Kent.

1914 *A Christmas Carol.* Silent film. Produced, directed, and written by Harold Shaw. London Film Company (Great Britain).

*1915 *A Christmas Carol.* Illustrated by Arthur Rackham. London: Heinemann; Philadelphia: Lippincott.

1915 *A Christmas Carol* and *The King of the Golden River* (John Ruskin). For use in public and high schools. With annotations by O. J. Stevenson. Toronto: Copp, Clark.

1915 *A Christmas Carol.* Pictured by John R. Neill. Chicago: Reilly and Britton.

1915 *A Christmas Carol.* Dramatic adaptation by Lucile Blackburn Berry. Lebanon, Ohio: March Brothers.

1915 Seymour Hicks. "The Christmas Carol of 1915." *Weekly Dispatch,* 26 December.

*1916 *A Christmas Carol.* Designed by Alan Tabor, with a frontispiece by Monro S. Orr. London: George G. Harrap.

1916 *A Christmas Carol.* With pictures by Gordon Robinson. London: Charles H. Kelly.

1916 *The Right to Be Happy.* Silent film. Directed by Rupert Julian; screenplay by E. J. Clawson. Bluebird Photoplays (USA).

1916 *A Christmas Carol.* Dramatic version by Russell Thorndike. Old Vic, London, December.

1917 *The Three Spirits.* Dramatic adaptation by Captain F. Charley Fowler. London: Office of the Dickensian.

1920 *A Christmas Carol.* Illustrated by Harold Copping. London: R. T. S.

1920 "A Christmas Carol Revised to December 1920." *Red Tape,* December.

1921 *A Christmas Carol.* Abridged by Mabel Mason Carlton. Boston: John Hancock Mutual Life Insurance Co.

*1921 Robert Benchley. "Christmas Afternoon: Done in the Manner, if not the Spirit, of Dickens." In *Of All Things.* Illustrated by Gluyas Williams. New York: Holt.

1921 Alex Rowley. *A Christmas Carol.* Suite for piano in two parts. London: Swan and Co.

1922 *A Christmas Carol.* Introduction and notes by Carol L. Bernhardt. Chicago: Loyola University Press.

*1922 George S. Kaufman and Marc Connelly. "A Christmas Carol." Play in three acts, with sketches by Herb Roth. *The Bookman,* December: 409–19.

1922 *Scrooge.* Silent film. Directed by George Wynn; starring H. V. Esmond (Great Britain).

1922 J. H. McNulty. "An Epilogue to *A Christmas Carol:* Stave VI. The Last of the Four Spirits." *The Dickensian* 18:177–82.

1923 *A Christmas Carol.* Illustrated by Francis D. Bedford. New York: Macmillan.

1923 *Scrooge.* Silent film. Directed by D. Edwin Greenwood; starring Russell Thorndike (Great Britain).

1924 *A Christmas Carol.* Illustrated in color from special drawings by Ethel F. Everett. New York: Crowell.

1925 *A Christmas Carol.* Designed by Richard W. Ellis. Muncie, Ind.: Currier Press/Ball Brothers.

1926 J. H. McNulty. "Twenty Years After: A Christmas Carol of To-Morrow." *The Dickensian* 22:52–56.

1927 *A Christmas Carol.* With fifty illustrations by Helen Nyce. Cover design by Frances Brundage. Akron and New York: Saalfield.

1927 *Scrooge.* Dramatic adaptation by J. C. Buckstone. London and New York: Samuel French.

1928 *"A Christmas Carol": The Story of a Sale.* With marginal notes for salesmen [by J. C. Aspley]. Chicago and New York: Dartnell Corp.

1928 *Mr. Scrooge.* A dramatic fantasy by Ashley Miller, with some of the original illustrations by John Lynch [*sic*]. New York: Dodd, Mead.

1928 *Scrooge.* Black-and-white sound film. Directed by Hugh Cloise; script by

Bransby Williams; starring Bransby Williams. British Sound Film Productions.

1929 *A Christmas Carol.* Dramatic production by J. T. Grein. People's Theatre, London, December.

1930 *A Christmas Carol.* For the friends of William Edwin Rudge. Mount Vernon, N.Y.: W. E. Rudge.

1930 *A Christmas Carol.* Decorations by W. A. Dwiggins. New York: Press of the Woolly Whale.

1930 *A Christmas Carol.* Designed by Frederic Warde. Mount Vernon, N.Y.: Privately printed for Junius Fishburn.

1930 *A Christmas Carol.* Illustrated by Gilbert Wilkinson. With a foreword by Sir John Martin-Harvey. London: Oldhams Press.

1930 *A Christmas Carol.* Marionette play. Pittsburgh, Pa., 15 December.

1931 *A Christmas Carol.* With notes by N. Howard Aich. Illustrated by Matilda Breuer. Chicago: Hall and McCreary.

1932 *A Christmas Carol.* Illustrations by Louis Koster. New York: Cheshire House.

1932 "Scrooges of To-day." *John Bull,* 24 December.

1932 "Mr. Scrooge – 1932." London *Daily Worker,* 27 December.

1933 *A Christmas Carol.* With pen drawings by Charles Dunn. Washington, D.C.: Judd and Detweiler.

1934 *A Christmas Carol.* With lithographs by Jack Heard. Van Nuys, Calif.: Scholastic Press.

*1934 *A Christmas Carol.* With illustrations by Gordon Ross and introduction by Stephen Leacock. Boston: Limited Editions Club/Marymount Press.

1934 *Christmas Tales by Charles Dickens.* Illustrated in color by H. M. Brock. New York: Dodd, Mead.

1934 *A Christmas Carol.* First performance of Lionel Barrymore's annual radio version.

*1935 *Scrooge.* Black-and-white sound film. Directed by Henry Edwards; screenplay by H. Fowler Mear; starring Seymour Hicks. Julius Hagan–Twickenham Productions (Great Britain).

1935 Ralph Vaughan Williams and Adolph Bolm. *On Christmas Night.* Folk dance ballet. Cecil Sharp House, London, 29 December.

1936 *A Christmas Carol.* Musical play in three acts. Book and lyrics by Sarah Grames Clark; music by Bryceson Treharne. Cincinnati: Wills Music Co.

1936 *A Christmas Carol.* Abridged by Edward L. Thorndike. Illustrated by Dorothy Bayley. New York: D. Appleton-Century.

1936 *A Christmas Carol.* Radio drama by Philip Wade. BBC.

1936 *A Christmas Carol.* Dramatic adaptation by Gilmore Brown. Pasadena, Calif., Playhouse.

1937 J. H. McNulty. "Scrooge's Defense." *The Dickensian* 34:35–36.

1937 *A Christmas Carol.* New York: Privately printed by the Plantin Press.

1938 *A Christmas Carol.* Illustrated by Corydon Bell. Cleveland, Ohio: Privately printed at the Roger Williams Co.

*1938 *A Christmas Carol.* Illustrated by Everett Shinn. Introduction by Lionel Barrymore. Philadelphia: John C. Winston.

1938 *A Christmas Carol.* Dramatized by T. Dowall. Music composed and arranged by F. W. Wadeley. London: Boosey and Hawkes; New York: Boosey, Hawkes, and Belwin.

1938 *A Christmas Carol.* A Christmas story in one act (nine staves) adapted by Cora Wilson Greenwood. New York and London: Samuel French.

*1938 *A Christmas Carol.* Black-and-white film. Produced by Joseph L. Mankiewicz; directed by Edwin L. Marin; script by Hugo Butler; starring Reginald Owen. Metro-Goldwyn-Mayer (USA).

1939 Charles Dickens. *Five Christmas Novels.* Illustrated by Reginald Birch. New York: Heritage Press.

1939 *A Christmas Carol.* Illustrated by Donald Gregg. Cleveland, Ohio: Bonnar-Vawter Fanform Co.

1939 *A Christmas Carol.* Illustrated by William Mark Young. New York: Grosset and Dunlap.

1939 *A Christmas Carol.* Illustrated by Julian Brazelton. New York: Pocket Books.

1939 *A Christmas Carol.* Illustrated by Erwin L. Hess and F. D. Lohman. Racine, Wis.: Whitman Publishing.

1940 *A Christmas Carol.* Illustrated by Philip Reed. Chicago: Monastery Hill Press for Holiday House.

1941 Gilbert Frankau. "A New Christmas Carol." *Strand Magazine*, December.

1942 *A Christmas Carol.* Dramatic adaptation by Ursula Bloom. Regency Players, Theatre Royal, Leicester.

1942 *A Christmas Carol.* Radio drama. Produced by John Burrell; written by Max Kester. BBC.

1943 *A Christmas Carol.* Illustrated by Fritz Kredel. Mount Vernon, N.Y.: Peter Pauper Press.

1943 *A Christmas Carol.* Dramatized and abridged by Harold G. Sliker. Drawings by Marion E. Caps. Evanston, Ill.: Row, Peterson.

1943 J. H. McNulty. "Stave VI (An almost-true story)." *The Dickensian* 39:17–20.

1944 *A Christmas Carol.* Illustrated by Emil Weiss. London: P. R. Gawthorne.

1944 *A Christmas Carol.* Illustrated by Hans E. Schwarz. Birmingham: City of Birmingham School of Printing.

1944 J. H. McNulty. "The Carol after Edgar Allan Poe." *The Dickensian* 40:14.

1946 Charles Dickens. *Christmas Stories.* Illustrated by Howard Simon. Introduction by May Lamberton Becker. Cleveland, Ohio: World.

1946 *A Christmas Carol.* Illustrated by Tom Kerr. London: Golden Galley Press.

1946 *A Christmas Carol.* Television play. Adapted by Bransby Williams. BBC.

*1946 *It's a Wonderful Life.* Black-and-white film. Directed by Frank Capra. Liberty Films (USA).

1946 *A Christmas Carol.* Harmondsworth: Penguin.

1947 *A Christmas Carol.* Black-and-white film. Written and directed by Manuel Tamayo (Spain).

1947 Benjamin Britten. *Men of Goodwill: Variations on "A Christmas Carol" for Orchestra.* London: Faber; New York: Schirmer.

1947 J. H. McNulty. "The Last of the Spirits." *The Dickensian* 43:9–12.

1948 Hilda Butler Farr. *Dickens' Christmas Carol in Verse*. New York: William Frederick Press.

1948 *A Christmas Carol*. Television production on "Philco Goodyear Playhouse" (USA), December.

1949 *A Christmas Carol*. A play in three parts dramatized by Kenelm Foss. London: Samuel French.

1949 *A Christmas Carol*. Adapted as a play in three acts by Shaun Sutton. London: Samuel French.

1949 *A Christmas Carol*. Sound recording by Ronald Colman. Decca.

1950 *A Christmas Carol*. Illustrated by Ruth McCrea. Mount Vernon, N.Y.: Peter Pauper Press.

1950 *A Christmas Carol*. Illustrated by Robert Ball. New York: Macmillan.

1950 *A Christmas Carol*. Philadelphia: Privately printed for Samuel A. Dalton.

1950 *A Christmas Carol*. Initials by Malletto Dean. San Francisco: Printed by the Grabhorn Press for Ransohoffs.

1950 *A Christmas Carol*. Teleplay. Script by Eric Fawcett from the play by Dominic Roche. BBC, 25 and 27 December.

1951 *A Christmas Parable*. Play in three acts by Harold H. S. Jackson. London: Epworth Press.

*1951 *Scrooge*. Black-and-white film. Produced and directed by Brian Desmond Hurst; script by Noel Langley; starring Alastair Sim. Renown Pictures (Great Britain).

1951 *A Christmas Carol*. Illustrated with stills from the Renown Pictures film. London and Melbourne: Ward Lock.

1951 *A Christmas Carol*. Television adaptation by D. Swift, starring Ralph Richardson. NBC (USA).

1951 *A Christmas Carol*. Radio version starring Alec Guinness. WQXR, New York.

1951 *Lefty Gallagher's Christmas Carol*. Radio play starring Alan Ladd on "Hollywood Theater" (NBC).

1951 *Scrooge*. Ballet devised by Alan Carter; music by W. Hill Bower. Empire Cinema, London.

1954 *A Christmas Carol*. Illustrated by John Leech. Washington, D.C.: Privately printed for the National Geographic Society. An edition annotated by Alexander Melville Bell and Alexander Bell for reading to their children.

1954 *The Little Carol*. Being *A Christmas Carol* in prose by Charles Dickens, abridged and edited by Philo Calhoun for reading aloud at Christmas time. Waterville, Maine: Colby College Press.

1954 *A Christmas Carol*. Television adaptation by Maxwell Anderson. Music by Bernard Herrmann; starring Frederick March. "TV Shower of Stars" (CBS).

1955 *A Christmas Carol*. Illustrated by Donald McKay. Mount Vernon, NY: Peter Pauper Press.

1955 Charles Dickens. *Christmas Stories*. Illustrated by Walter Seaton. Garden City, N.Y.: Junior Deluxe Editions.

1955 *The Man Who Fled from Christmas.* Radio play. WNYC, New York.

1955 *A Christmas Carol.* Operetta in two acts. Music and lyrics by Virginia Hageman; dialogue by Eleanor Jones. Bryn Mawr, Pa.: Theodore Presser.

1956 *A Christmas Carol.* Sound recording by Frank Pettingell. New Rochelle, N.Y.: Spoken Arts.

1956 *The Stingiest Man in Town.* Television musical. Music by Fred Spielman; lyrics and book by Jamie Torre; starring Basil Rathbone. "The Alcoa Hour" (USA).

1957 *A Christmas Carol.* Sound recording by Eleanor Roosevelt. New York: Spoken Word.

1957 "Walt Disney's Christmas Carol." *McCall's* 85 (December): 29–36.

1957 Wilfred Sheed. "Modern Christmas Carol." *Catholic World* 186 (December): 186–92.

1958 *A Christmas Carol.* Illustrated by Maraja. New York: Grosset and Dunlap; London: W. H. Allen.

1958 *A Christmas Carol.* Sound recording by Shibban McKenna. Dramatized by Dominick Roche. Vanguard.

1958 *A Christmas Carol.* Free adaptation by Joan Littlewood. Produced at the Theatre Royal, Stratford, 16 December.

1959 *A Christmas Carol.* Illustrated by Charles Rapp. Milwaukee, Wis.: Ideals Publishing.

1959 *A Christmas Carol.* Film narrated by Vincent Price. Paramount Pictures (USA).

1960 *A Christmas Carol.* Sound recording. Directed by Howard Sackler; narrated by Paul Scofield; starring Ralph Richardson. Caedmon.

1960 *A Christmas Carol.* Sound recording by Basil Rathbone and the Murray Singers. Harmony.

1960 *A Christmas Carol.* Opera. Music by G. Mallard Kilgore; libretto by Burt A. Kelsey and G. Mallard Kilgore.

1960 *A Christmas Carol.* Musical play. Adapted by Don Nichol and Peter Hart. London: Dash Music.

1960 *A Christmas Carol.* Black-and-white film. Directed by Robert Hartford-Davis. Alpha (Great Britain).

*1960 *A Christmas Carol.* Illustrated by Ronald Searle. London: Perpetua Books; Cleveland, Ohio: World.

1961 *A Christmas Carol.* Illustrated by Charles Wilton. Boston: Nimrod Press.

1961 *A Christmas Carol.* Dramatic version by Robert Vance. Chicago: Coach House Press.

1962 *A Christmas Carol.* Illustrated by Charles Beck. New York: Scholastic Book Services.

1962 *Mister Magoo's Christmas Carol.* Animated film. Score by Jule Styne and Bob Merril; starring Jim Backus. UPA Pictures (USA).

1962 *A Christmas Carol.* Film version by Desmond Davis with the cooperation of the Dickensian Society, London. Narrated by Frederic March; starring Basil Rathbone. Coronet International Films (USA).

1963 *A Christmas Carol.* Illustrated by John Groth. Afterword by Clifton Fadiman. New York: Macmillan.

1963 *A Christmas Carol.* Television musical adaptation by Edwin Coleman, starring Stephen Manton, Forrester Pike, and Trevor Anthony. BBC.

1963 *Mr. Scrooge.* Musical. Book by Richard Morris and Ted Wood; music by Dolores Claman; lyrics by Richard Morris, Dolores Claman, and Ted Wood. N.p.: Dramatic Publishing Company.

1963 "Rich Little's Christmas Carol." *Scrooge and the Stars.* Recorded parody. Capitol Records (Canada).

1964 William Iverson. "The Christmas Carol Caper." *Playboy* 11 (December): 122–26ff.

1965 *A Christmas Carol.* Radio drama. Produced and written by Charles Lefeaux. BBC, 26 May and 25 December.

1966 *A Christmas Carol.* With special study aids by Henry E. Vittum. New York: Bantam Books.

1966 David Gray. *A Christmas Carol.* Opera in two acts. Libretto by Robert Protherough. London: Novello.

1967 "A Christmas Carol." Smothers Brothers television parody, starring Tom Smothers as Scrooge and Jack Benny as Cratchit. CBS (USA).

1968 *A Christmas Carol.* Musical play. Book by Christopher Bedlow; adaptation and lyrics by James Wood; music by Malcolm Shapcott. London: Evans Plays.

1969 *A Christmas Carol.* Illustrated by Charles Mozley. New York: F. Watts.

1969 *A Christmas Carol.* Animated film. Adapted by Michael Robinson; directed by Zoran Jangic. Air Programs International (Australia).

1969 "The Ghost and Christmas Past." Television parody on "The Ghost and Mrs. Muir." ABC (USA).

1969 Thomas Meehan. "Christmas Carol." *Mademoiselle* 70 (December): 124ff.

1970 *A Christmas Carol.* Television production. Directed by John Salway; illustrated by John Worseley; read by Paul Honeyman. Anglia Television (Great Britain).

*1970 *Scrooge.* Color musical film. Produced by Robert H. Solo; directed by Ronald Neame; script by Leslie Bricusse; starring Albert Finney. Cinema Center Films (Great Britain).

*1970 Elaine Donaldson. "*Scrooge*". Adapted from the screenplay by Leslie Bricusse. New York: Cinema Center Films.

1971 *The Christmas Books.* Introduction and notes by Michael Slater. Harmondsworth: Penguin.

1971 *A Christmas Carol: The Public Reading Version.* A facsimile of Dickens' prompt-copy. Introduction and notes by Philip Collins. New York Public Library.

1971 "A Christmas Carol." Television animated cartoon. Drawn by Richard Williams; narrated by Michael Redgrave; starring Alastair Sim. ABC (USA).

1973 *A Christmas Carol.* Dramatic adaptation by Guy R. Williams. London: Macmillan.

1973 "A Christmas Carol." Mime version by Marcel Marceau. BBC Television, 27 December.

1973 Marion M. Markham. "What Really Happened to Scrooge?" *Blackwood's Magazine* 314 (July): 20–27.
1973 Russell Baker. "The Ghost of Christmas Endless." *The New York Times*, 22 December: 22.
1974 *A Christmas Carol.* Dramatized by Michael Hardwick. London: Davis-Poynter.
1975 *The Passions of Carol.* Pornographic film adaptation by Amanda Barton. Ambar Production (USA).
1976 *A Charles Dickens Christmas.* With illustrations by Warren Chappell. New York: Oxford University Press.
1976 Michael Patrick Hearn. *The Annotated Christmas Carol.* New York: Clarkson N. Potter.
1976 *A Christmas Carol.* Illustrated by Wolfgang Lederer. Nevada City, Calif.: Harold Berliner.
1976 *A Christmas Carol.* Dramatic adaptation by Dennis Powers. American Conservatory Theater, San Francisco, 7 December.
1977 *A Christmas Carol.* Sound recording by Roy Doltrice. Decca.
1977 *A Christmas Carol.* Dramatic adaptation by Barbara Field. Guthrie Theater, Minneapolis.
1978 *A Christmas Carol.* Illustrated by Synette Hemmant. Kingswood, Surrey: World's Work.
1978 *A Christmas Carol.* Dramatic adaptation by Israel Horovitz. New York: Dramatists Play Service.
1978 *A Christmas Carol.* Dramatic adaptation by Doris Baizley. Center Theatre, Los Angeles, 22 December.
1978 *A Christmas Carol.* Classics Comics. Text by Doug Moench; illustrations by diverse artists. New York: Marvel Comics Group.
1978 *A Christmas Carol.* Opera. Music and libretto by Gregory Sandow. Bryn Mawr, Pa.: Theodore Presser.
1979 *A Christmas Carol.* Illustrated by puppets created by Peter Fluck and Roger Law. Photographed by John Lawrence Jones. New York: St. Martin's.
1979 *A Christmas Carol.* Dramatic adaptation by Charles Ludlam. Ridiculous Theatrical Company, New York.
1979 *A Christmas Carol.* Teleplay by Elaine Morgan, produced by Jonathan Powell; starring Michael Hordern. BBC, 25 December.
1979 *A Christmas Carol.* Opera. Music and libretto by Thea Musgrave. Virginia Opera Association, Norfolk, 7 December.
1979 *Comin' Uptown.* Musical. Book by Philip Rose and Peter Udell; music by Gerry Sherman. Winter Garden Theater. New York, December.
1980 *The Dickens Christmas Carol Show.* Adapted by Arthur Scholey, with music by Norman Beedie. New Orleans: Anchorage Press.
1980 *A Christmas Carol.* Sound recording. Directed and abridged by Ward Botsford; read by Tom Conti. Caedmon Records.
1981 *A Christmas Carol.* Dramatic adaptation by Darwin Reid Payne. Carbondale: Southern Illinois University Press.

1981 Alexander Frater. "A Down Under Christmas Carol." *Punch* 218 (2 December): 982–83.

1982 John Q. Simmons and Joel Perry. *A Bonzo Christmas Carol: A Mutation of the Dickens Classic.* Raft Theater, New York.

1983 *A Christmas Carol.* Illustrated by Michael Foreman. New York: Dial Books/Dutton.

1983 *A Christmas Carol.* Illustrated by Greg Hildebrandt. New York: Simon and Schuster.

1983 *Mickey's Christmas Carol.* Animated film. Walt Disney Productions (USA).

1983 Kevin Curran. "A Reggae Christmas Carol." *The National Lampoon,* December: 36, 56, 58.

1984 *A Christmas Carol.* Illustrated by Marcel Imsand. Mankato, Minn.: Creative Education.

1984 *A Christmas Carol.* Illustrated by John Worsley. New York: Gallery Books.

1984 *"A Christmas Carol" Christmas Book.* An International Business Machines Corp. Book. Boston: Little, Brown.

1984 *A Christmas Carol.* Dramatic adaptation by Gregory Moser and Larry Sloane. Goodman Theater, Chicago.

1984 *A Christmas Carol.* Television film. Directed by Clive Donner; script by Roger O. Hirson; starring George C. Scott. Entertainment Partners (USA).

1985 *A Christmas Carol.* Illustrated by Michael Cole. Woodbury, N.Y.: Barron's.

1985 Tony Kisch. "A Christmas Carol in Harlem." *The National Lampoon,* December: 16–23.

1985 Andrew Angus Dalrymple. *God Bless Us Every One! Being an Imagined Sequel to "A Christmas Carol."* New York: St. Martin's.

1986 *A Christmas Carol.* Abridged and illustrated by Mercer Mayer. New York: Macmillan.

1986 "John Grin's Christmas." Television adaptation. Directed by Robert Guillaume; script by Charles Eric Johnson. Guillaume-Margo Productions (USA).

1986 "It's a Wonderful Job." Television parody on "Moonlighting," 16 December. Directed by Ed Sherin; script by Debra Frank and Carl Sautter.

1987 *A Christmas Carol.* Dramatic adaptation by David Richard Jones. New Mexico Repertory Theater, Albuquerque.

1988 *A Christmas Carol.* Illustrated by Lisbeth Zwerger. Salzburg, Austria: Neugebauer Press; Saxonville, Mass.: Picture Book Studio.

1988 *Scrooged.* Color film. Produced and directed by Richard Donner; script by Mitch Glazer and Michael O'Donoghue; starring Bill Murray. Mirage Productions/Paramount Pictures (USA).

Index

Page number in **boldface** refer to illustrations.